Tennis: Its History, People and Events

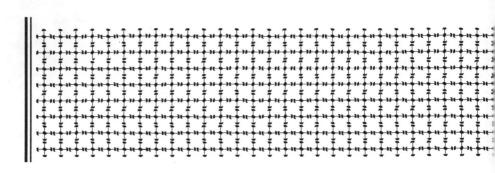

Styles of the Greats by Julius D. Heldman

PRENTICE-HALL, INC.,

TENNIS

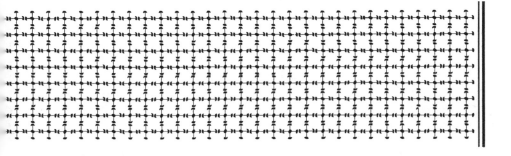

ITS HISTORY, PEOPLE AND EVENTS

By Will Grimsley

ENGLEWOOD CLIFFS, NEW JERSEY

Also by Will Grimsley
GOLF: Its History, People and Events
FOOTBALL: The Greatest Moments in the Southwest Conference

Tennis: Its History, People and Events by Will Grimsley
    Copyright © 1971 by Will Grimsley
    All rights reserved. No part of this book may be reproduced in
    any form or by any means, except for the inclusion of brief
    quotations in a review, without permission in writing from the
    publisher.
    ISBN 0–13–903377–7
    Library of Congress Catalog Card Number: 76–144006
    Printed in the United States of America T
    Prentice-Hall International, Inc., London
    Prentice-Hall of Australia, Pty. Ltd., Sydney
    Prentice-Hall of Canada, Ltd., Toronto
    Prentice-Hall of India Private Ltd., New Delhi
    Prentice-Hall of Japan, Inc., Tokyo

Foreword

Since first seeing Will Grimsley's exhaustive book, *Golf: Its History, People and Events,* I had hoped someone might undertake a similar project involving tennis. Now I am pleased to find that Grimsley has done this himself, and tennis is certain to be better off for it.

Tennis is a game rich in tradition, personalities, exciting events and even controversy. To attempt to reach back and try to capture all—or at least most of this—and put it inside the covers of a single book is a monumental endeavor. I must congratulate Grimsley on his enterprise and his bravery.

This must be the most comprehensive and ambitious volume written on the sport. Library shelves are loaded with excellent books dealing with every phase of the game but I know of none that has tried to explore the broad reaches from the first primitive bats and balls right up to open competition, with all that has happened between.

I have known Grimsley for years, as have other tennis players whose exploits he has followed from Wimbledon to Melbourne and Madras to Paris. For most of the last two decades he has been a sort of ex-officio member of the Davis Cup teams traveling to Australia. He has lived or seen firsthand much of the drama of which he writes.

As a world-girdling writer for The Associated Press, Grimsley has written graphically on many sports, ranging from the Olympic Games to World Cup golf matches, and has done probing stories behind the Iron Curtain. But he seems to write with the greatest warmth and vividness when he writes of tennis, a sport he apparently loves.

This massive book, which also includes an interesting and knowledgeable study of the styles of the great by Julius Heldman, is an example. It is written in Grimsley's easy, flowing style. It moves. And it doesn't miss much.

William F. (Bill) Talbert

Preface

I recall the first tennis racket I ever owned. It was ordered from Sears Roebuck and it cost all of eight dollars. It was overly embellished and loosely strung with cheap gut, but every night I slipped it inside its canvas cover, tightened the clamps on the press and stuck it away where it would be safe. It was like some rare gem.

As in the case of Jack Kramer and undoubtedly legions of others down through the years I was ashamed to carry it on a streetcar or walk with it the few blocks to South Park in Nashville, Tennessee, where people queued up to play on the single hard clay court. A player of talent and stamina could remain on the court until he was beaten.

One of my greatest thrills as a schoolboy was seeing Big Bill Tilden, who visited the school to promote his pro tour. To me, there always has been a fascination about the game although in later years it had trouble capturing the people's fancy. I liked to play it, although I never advanced beyond the club stage. I enjoyed watching and covering it. Thus researching and writing about it proved more pleasure than work.

However, completion of this book would not have been possible had not hundreds of others before me felt a similar interest, delved into its exciting history and put their findings on paper. There is no way of properly expressing my debt of gratitude to all those historians, biographers and journalists whose brains I picked— through their published works—to get this project completed.

Malcolm D. Whitman's *Tennis Origins and Mysteries*, Parke Cummings' lively *American Tennis* and the U.S. Lawn Tennis Association's *Fifty Years of Lawn Tennis in the United States* were particularly helpful in exploring the historical background and development of the game.

Rich background and a graphic insight to the personalities, successes and failures of the early giants were provided by E.C. Potter, Jr., in his *Kings of the Court* and Norah Gordon Cleather in *Wimbledon Story*. Bill Talbert's *Tennis Observed* brought every American champion, his style and disposition, right into the living room, and C.M. Jones, editor of Britain's *Lawn Tennis* magazine, did the same for the great Wimbledon titleholders. Frank G. Menke's *Encyclopedia of Sports* was always handy to fill in needed holes.

Judith Davenport of the Physical Education Department of the University of Illinois and later Ohio State University did a magnificent job in researching the open controversy while Jack Kramer took time out personally to describe operations of the pro tour.

Gladys Heldman's *World Tennis* magazine was a treasure of information and art, and we even had to borrow her husband, Julius. Articles from such magazines as *Sport, Sports Illustrated* and *The Saturday Evening Post* were invaluable. On top of these there were the great personal stories and biographies of such stars as Big Bill Tilden, Fred Perry, Don Budge, Pancho Gonzales, Althea Gibson and Rod Laver.

I am particularly indebted to Alice Valentine of the U.S. Lawn Tennis Association offices in New York for her kindness and patience in permitting use of the USLTA library. Special thanks go also to Alistair Martin, USLTA president; the man he succeeded, Bob Kelleher; Bob Malaga, executive director; Ed Baker, former executive secretary; Harold Zimman, publisher of the *USLTA Tennis Year Book;* Arthur Woodard of *Sport;* Bud Collins of the Boston *Globe,* and Allison Danzig, long time tennis writer of *The New York Times* and a man who has written a tennis library himself.

This book I consider a part of us all.

Will Grimsley

CONTENTS

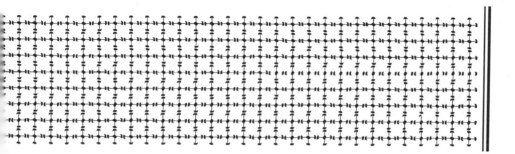

Foreword by William F. Talbert

Preface

ONE

ONE

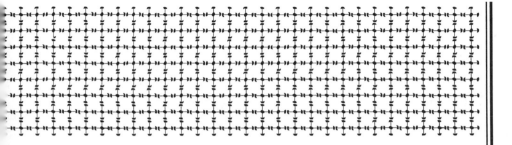

How It Began — With a Hand, a Wall and a Ball

Tennis probably dates back to prehistoric time. Presumably a caveman one day fashioned a round object from, let's say, the fruit of a gum tree and amused himself by throwing it against a tree, rolling it down a hill or belting it with a stick. His neighbors joined him in the fun. Some hit the object along the ground with various-shaped sticks: a primitive version of hockey, croquet and polo. Others preferred to knock it through the air like Neanderthal baseball, cricket and golf enthusiasts. Still others flung their rude missile against a wall or back and forth among themselves. At first they used bare hands and when calluses resulted, they wrapped their palms in lion hide. Eventually they carved small paddles to strike the ball and refined this implement with a mesh of catgut. Tennis was far from being as we know it today but it was on its way.

Modern tennis, initially associated with the aristocracy, was slow to reach the masses. Even as late as the 1930's it was regarded as a "sissy" pastime to be shunned by red-blooded athletes, and young men were reluctant to be seen on the street carrying a racket. Archaic customs prolonged this effeminate image. Tennis was played largely at exclusive clubs restricted to persons of more than modest means. Players were required to wear white attire—an inflexible rule at Wimbledon and Forest Hills until 1968 when the American Davis Cup team broke tradition by donning yellow shirts. Spectators were prohibited from "whooping it up" as they might in less proper sports, and there were snickers at use of the word "love" to signify no-score.

The game finally started to lose its starchiness after World War II. Gardnar Mulloy, an international tennis star for a quarter century, was the most militant spokesman in a campaign to rid the sport of its stuffed-shirt customs. In Britain the Wimbledon fathers succeeded in eliminating barriers preventing professionals from competing with amateurs. By mid-century the men had exchanged their long flannel trousers for shorts that revealed their thick masculine calves while the ladies had traded in their ankle-length dresses and multiple slips for ballerina skirts that bounced up on every serve to display sexy lace or embroidered panties.

Tennis showed the sporting public it was no sissy sport but one which put a premium on speed, endurance and basic athletic skills.

The game grew in popularity. It offered a quick means of exercise, since a single hour did the work of a full day on the golf course. Equipment wasn't overly expensive and facilities became readily available as public courts, indoor and outdoor, for rich and poor alike, sprang up. By the late 1960's tennis players in the United States numbered nine million, exceeding golfers by a million. Some fifty million played in other countries while in Australia the sport was almost a religion.

The game had changed in other ways too. Grass surface courts were superseded by turf surfaces of various types. Concrete and hard courts provided a quick bounce for the ball and scientists developed plastic materials that promised to make all natural surfaces obsolete. Tennis had come a long way from its primitive beginnings when our playful caveman first batted his makeshift ball over an earthen net.

Lawn tennis, as the sport is formally known, was invented in 1873 by Major Walter Clopton Wingfield, a British Army officer who was seeking to liven up a lawn party. It was actually a variation of a game called court or royal tennis, played almost exclusively by royalty and titled gentry.

A scholar of sorts, Wingfield had done some research on the sport and believed he had proof it dated back to ancient Greece. Homer, in *The Odyssey*, for instance, tells how white-armed Princess Nausicaa, playing a game with her handmaidens, knocked the ball into the river. Horace, describing his journey from Rome to Brundisium in the *Fifth Satire*, relates that during one stop Maecenas "goes to play at Tennis while he and Virgil sleep." On the other hand, though Grecian vase art shows a sport played with a ball and a curved stick, it resembles hockey more than tennis.

Nevertheless, right or wrong, Wingfield was sufficiently convinced of his theory to dub his own version of the game "Sphairistike," a Greek word meaning "to play."

Attempts have also been made to trace tennis back to ancient civilizations of the Near and Far East. Antiquarius, an English chronicler, wrote that the Greeks acquired the game from the Persians or Egyptians as far back as the fifth century, B.C., and it found its way into France as a result of the Saracen invasion. During the fourth century, A.D., the Persians had a game called "tchigan" which was played in an enclosed space with rackets four feet long and which resembled "chicane," an ancient sport in Languedoc.

Most tennis historians cut through these vague conjectures and pick up the game in thirteenth century France. Here it was known as "jeu de paume" or "a game played with the palm." The indoor version was called "jeu de courte paume," meaning short game, while the long game was "jeu de longue paume." As the name suggests, the ball was struck with the palm, a gambit which the French borrowed from the Irish sport of handball.

The balls were made of soft cloth sewn into a hard, round shape. The first "nets" were wooden obstacles or mounds of dirt. Participants played each other or hit the ball against a wall. In time, instead of using bare hands, they substituted gloves or crude bats. Nearly a century after its introduction in France the sport reached England where Edward III (1327–1377) ordered a court built in his palace and encouraged his subjects to take up the game.

The general feeling is that the word "tennis" evolved from

the French "ten-ez," meaning "to play." It has been suggested that the earliest players began a contest with the shout "ten-ez," an equivalent of the golfing expression "play away." The word "tenililudium," translated as "play of tennis," is said to have a Latin derivative. The Greek "phennis," meaning the same thing, has appeared in some scholars' works. Others have related the name to the German "tanz," referring to the bounding motion of the ball. An Italian account written before 1370 tells how an ecclesiastic played ball with some newly arrived cavaliers, and the author adds that this incident "was the beginning in these parts of playing at tenes." The first known use of the word in the English language was around 1400 in a message to Henry IV and has been quoted two ways: "Of the tennes to winne or lose a chace" or "Off the tenetz to winne or lese a chace."

More intriguing, though less believable, is the contention that the game's name originally derived from an Egyptian city, Tennis, said to have sunk into the sea in 1226. Tennis was renowned for its fabrics and the tennis ball was, in early days, made from cloth. A somewhat far-fetched connection has been drawn between the two facts, a theory which brings to mind the old English poem:

My mistress is a Tennis-Ball
Composed of cotton fine.

In the beginning "jeu de paume" was the game of priests, then kings, one of whom, Louis X, caught a chill and died after a feverish match at Vincennes. It was first played on monastery courtyards and was responsible for at least one bishop neglecting his duties. In 1245 the Archbishop of Rouen prohibited his priests from playing. For the same reason Louis IX outlawed the sport. But this and succeeding edicts were virtually ignored. One of the oldest known courts was described in a sales notice for the Hotel de Nesle in 1308; Benvenuto Cellini was supposed to have played here. Walled-in courts began to appear in France in 1368 and the people began to bet on matches. By 1600 there were two thousand courts throughout the country, indoor and outdoor.

Tennis came of age not without growing pains. In England it was prohibited in 1388 along with other games because the people were failing to practice archery. Parisians were hit with a similar ordinance in 1397 because they were neglecting their families and jobs. Holland outlawed the sport in 1401 and 1413. There was one grisly episode when James I of Scotland was assassinated while attempting to escape through a castle vault which he himself had ordered walled up to keep from losing tennis balls. In 1447 there was a controversy between the Bishop and the Mayor of Exeter: The Bishop complained his glass windows were endangered because the Mayor allowed youngsters to play tennis in the cloisters and the Mayor counter-charged that the Bishop's officers were bootleggers. Court records show that in 1508 four men were arrested for "keeping tennys-playes."

As the game grew in popularity England and France engaged in international matches but these shortly degenerated into gambling fests. The players, holding high opinions of their abilities, often wagered heavily on the outcome, placing the stakes at the net before hitting the first ball. The situation became so intolerable that France banned public tennis exhibitions in the seventeenth century. Many abandoned outdoor courts became overgrown with weeds while locks were put on the public indoor courts. Moving inside the sport once again became the province of the rich.

From this sequence of events emerged court tennis, referred to wryly by commoners as royal tennis. Confined largely to the uppercrust, court tennis was a complex indoor sport involving penthouses, grilles and walls which few men could play or score. The stage was set for Major Wingfield to contribute his own crucial innovation to the game.

Wingfield, a handsome man with beard, sideburns and a flowing mustache, came from one of England's most distinguished families. In 1860, at age twenty-seven he was put in charge of a cavalry force in the China campaign. He became a major in the Montgomery Yeomanry Cavalry and later a member of the elite Honorable Corps of Gentlemen-at-Arms, the bodyguard of the sovereign at all public and state occasions.

Although a military figure, he was also a country gentleman and a sportsman who excelled at popular games of the day—court tennis, racquets, badminton and cricket. He frequently confided to friends his idea for an outdoor sport that would be a variation of court tennis, which was played by batting balls against a wall and picking them up on the rebound. One December afternoon in 1873 he held a lawn party at Nantclwyd and at that time he unveiled what he called "The Major's Game—Sphairistike or Lawn Tennis."

The major marked out a court on the lawn. The court had an hourglass figure, narrower at the net than at the base lines. The balls were uncovered hollow rubber. The net was about four feet high in the center and five feet at each of the two posts. The posts were fragile, held by guy ropes with small flags on top of each. The rackets were similar to those used in court tennis, spoon-shaped with long handles. Scoring was the same as in racquets: A one-two-three system with fifteen points needed to win a game. Scoring by "fifteens," although in existence apparently as early as the twelfth century, was not adopted for lawn tennis until 1877.

Wingfield acknowledged he had incorporated the features of other racket games into his new invention. Though its primary source was court tennis, it contained characteristics of racquets, a slum game until it was taken up in the early 1800's at Eton and Harrow. It was also obviously influenced by badminton which had originated in India and was played on an outdoor court with small rackets and winged "birds."

The makeup of the court and the net were borrowed from badminton, the equipment came from court tennis.

The major's friends were so delighted with the game that they asked him how they might obtain rackets and balls and set up courts of their own. Wingfield applied for a patent in 1874 and began marketing the game, complete with rackets, balls and a set of twelve rules. The commercial venture failed but Wingfield earned his place in history as the father of lawn tennis, although not without some dispute.

One historian wrote: "The game had several fathers . . . and three mothers—tennis, rackets and badminton."

ONE

2

A Lady Brings the Game to America

In the winter of 1874 Miss Mary Ewing Outerbridge, member of a socially-prominent family living on Staten Island, New York, embarked on her traditional holiday to Bermuda. There she expected to enjoy the usual pastimes—swimming, sunning on the beaches, croquet and evenings of dining and dancing with the visiting swains.

Instead, Miss Outerbridge found a new attraction. In a grassy corner of the cricket field, some British army officers had laid down chalk lines, stretched a net and were spending delightful afternoons batting a ball back and forth across the barrier with spoon-shaped implements strung with catgut. These officers had been guests at the lawn party thrown by Major Wingfield at which lawn tennis had been introduced, and when time came to sail to the New World, they brought along some rackets and balls.

Miss Outerbridge was entranced. She stood for hours, watching the officers in white pants and jackets play this strange game. Perhaps one of the officers, noting the lady's interest, may have called over to her, "Would you like to try your hand, miss?" Whereupon she might have taken the strange-looking bat and given the ball a ladylike whack over the net. In any event she was bitten by the tennis bug.

When Miss Outerbridge returned to the United States in late March, she had a parcel that attracted the attention and suspicion of customs inspectors. It contained tennis rackets, balls and a net. The paraphernalia was promptly confiscated.

Miss Outerbridge immediately contacted her brother A. Emilius Outerbridge who was prominent in shipping circles, and after the usual red tape the equipment was cleared duty-free.

The weather in New York delayed the debut of the game until warm spring weather arrived.

The sports-minded Outerbridge family belonged to the Staten Island Cricket and Baseball Club of which Emilius, a noted cricketer, was a director. Another brother, Eugenius, who later would serve on the executive committee of the U.S. Lawn Tennis Association, was secretary of the club.

Through the influence of her brothers, Miss Outerbridge was given permission to lay out a court on the edge of the cricket field. The court bore little resemblance to those in use today. It was shaped like an hourglass, twenty-four feet wide at the net and thirty feet wide at the base line. Miss Outerbridge probably didn't follow too precisely an early specification that the service lines should be twenty-six feet from the net which would have made the service area deeper than the area between the service line and the back line.

Wearing a dress down to her high button shoes, perhaps a tightly-drawn corset and half a dozen slips, Miss Outerbridge began to play the new game with her brothers and friends. She thus became the "mother" of American tennis. Her right to the title, however, was later disputed by a group of New England men who claimed they had introduced the sport to these shores.

At first Miss Outerbridge had difficulty finding partners. Most of her girl friends considered it unladylike to go bounding after a ball. The men were also reluctant. Tennis, after all, was sponsored by a female, and there seemed something "sissy" about skipping across the grass and delicately stroking the ball. Moreover, they resented the word "love" in scoring.

The Outerbridge men, perhaps in deference to their sister, shrugged off such inhibitions and played the game at an accelerated pace. They found it far more demanding than cricket and with their support it soon became a popular recreation of the Staten Island social set. Meanwhile, tennis was also taking root in New England which was to give the sport its greatest early impetus. The region even boasted that it was the birthplace of the game. This claim was made several years later in an article written by Dr. James Dwight who said:

The first set of lawn tennis in New England—indeed, I fancy, in the country—was played at Mr. William Appleton's place at Nahant. In the summer of 1875 a set of sphairistike or lawn tennis, was brought out from England, where the game was just coming into fashion.
Mr. F.R. Sears, the elder brother of the champion, and I put up the net and tried the game. . . . That is the first tennis that I know of that was played in New England, and for two years we played incessantly. At the end of our second summer, in August, 1876, we held our first tournament.

Sears' younger brother Richard, who in time won the first seven national tennis championships, supported Dwight's contention. But the calendar didn't.

If Miss Outerbridge visited Bermuda in the first months of 1874, then it must be assumed that she set up her court that year. This would have meant she was hitting tennis balls in the United States a year ahead of the New Englanders.

According to Dwight, a second lawn tennis set was brought over from England in 1876 by a Mr. W.W. Sherman. In the next few years courts, mostly private, were bobbing up in various places on the East Coast. Dwight tells of playing matches in Newport at the Powels', Boits', Parans', Stevens' and Bennetts'.

The movement was not restricted to the Atlantic Seaboard. William H. Young of Santa Monica, California, returned from a trip to England in 1879 and established a crude court on the site where the Santa Monica Municipal Pier now stands.

It was inevitable that devotees of the new sport would not confine themselves to friendly pat-ball games. Clubs, tournaments and ultimately organizations began to develop.

A tournament was organized at Nahant in the late summer of 1875. There were fifteen competitors. Racquets scoring—similar to that in table tennis—was used. A larger tournament was held the following year.

It was the posh Newport Casino in Newport, Rhode Island that was destined to become the home of the national championships from their inception in 1881 until they moved to Forest Hills, New York, in 1915. The Casino was born as a result of a wealthy publisher's pique. Newport was the stuffy social capital of the nation where tycoons built multi-million dollar mansions and Presidents and princes rubbed elbows with the very rich. One of the city's most revered establishments was the Reading Room, a frame structure facing Bellevue Avenue. It was a club given more to socializing than to actual reading. "The young men who throng the corridors or fill the windows are the smartest in town," wrote Mrs. John King Van Rensselaer in 1905.

One day in 1879 a former British cavalry officer named Captain Candy, acting on sudden impulse, rode a horse up Bellevue, into the front door of the Reading Room, through a narrow hall and into the club bar where well-tailored members looked up in astonishment. Then, without so much as a salute, the Englishman wheeled his mount and galloped out into the street.

Officials of the Reading Room were livid. They promptly revoked Candy's membership card.

It so happened the captain had come by his card through a close and influential friend, James Gordon Bennett, Jr., flamboyant publisher of the New York *Herald*. Bennett was a leader of Newport society. Hearing of the action against Candy, he sought immediate reversal from the Board of Governors and, when they refused to budge, he retaliated by purchasing a $60,000 cottage a quarter mile up the avenue from the Reading Room. It was called Stone Villa and his original plans—they grew increasingly grandiose—were to convert it into a rival club.

He moved into the Villa as his own summer residence. Shortly afterward he purchased 126,000 square feet of land across the street. Then he formed a joint stock company, offering shares at $500 each. Wealthy friends responded in large numbers. He commissioned the firm of McKim, Mead and White to draw up plans for a club.

From the drawing boards came an elaborate complex including three buildings for bowling, billiards, restaurant, court-tennis, theater, reading room and bachelor quarters. Space was provided for shops adjacent to the main building, a three-story brick structure with fish-scale shingles.

It was possible—as it still is—to step through the paneled entryway off Bellevue and suddenly come upon a sylvan view of tennis courts, trees, shrubs and pathways. There was the Horseshoe Piazza and a yellow-faced clock on a tower which looked like the helmet of a London bobby but which actually was patterned after one in the Loire Valley of France.

This was the Newport Casino, an ambitious undertaking said to cost $200,000. It opened with a lavish party on July 28, 1880.

The Casino soon became the social center of Newport.

Ultimately tennis turned into the leading sport. The Casino's poorest patron, it is said, was the creator, James Gordon Bennett, Jr.

Bennett played tennis, though not well, but friends said he seldom crossed the street to see how the enterprise was going, and he never once played a game on the grass courts. Later he moved to France and rarely visited his old summer stamping grounds.

He was happy. He had avenged the insult to his friend and provided the site for the first national tennis tournament.

ONE

3

Evolution of the Equipment —
From Bare Hands to Gleaming Steel

If Major Wingfield and Miss Outerbridge were to see a lawn tennis match today they would undoubtedly blink in astonishment.

The fuzz-faced ball whizzes across the net with such speed that it is almost impossible to follow. Instead of spoon-shaped, loosely strung bats, players flash rackets made of glistening steel or aluminum, precision-tuned like a rare violin. Equipment has come a long way since the game's swaddling days.

The first balls were made of strips of cloth rolled together and stitched with thread. Later, as in the case of golf balls, they were made of leather stuffed tightly with feathers and light fabrics. In the days of the Crusaders, the French were said to have come upon a city named Tennis, now extinct, where the best fabric was manufactured. The city was on an island in the Delta of the Nile, called "Tanis" by the Greeks, "Tinnis" by the Arabs, "Tennis" by the English.

The first name given to the ball was "esteuf" or "etoffe," French for stuff or fabric. In 1480 an ordinance was passed in France by Louis XI prohibiting the use of inferior materials. Shakespeare made reference to tennis balls stuffed with human hair.

Even with the introduction of rubber, tennis balls for years remained primitive. They either were too heavy, giving the player a feeling of hitting rocks, or too light, bald and fast with no wind resistance.

In the early 1870's a British sportsman, John Heathcote, developed the predecessor of today's ball. He and his wife designed a pattern of two strips of flannel. These strips were applied to the uncovered sphere and sewn tightly.

When a modern player purchases a hermetically-sealed can of tennis balls, opens the can with a key and hears the hiss of escaping air, he has little conception of the workmanship that has gone into their manufacture.

A.G. Spalding and Bros. Inc. in Chicopee, Massachusetts, is the major producer of tennis balls. From the East Indies the company imports crude rubber which is processed into cylindrical slugs of solid red rubber measuring one inch thick and one and one-fourth inches long. Every slug is placed in a press where it is molded into a shell forming half a ball center. Each of these hemispheres has a lip, or a flash, around the entire edge where it is joined with another hemisphere to make the whole center. The lip is removed by cutting machines, operated by women, and the edges are buffed and coated with cement.

In preparing the shells for vulcanizing craftsmen inject 18 pounds of air pressure into every ball. Then follows a period of curing. The surface of the balls are roughed up, coated with another cover of cement and then sent from a washer to a gauging bin where each is measured for conformance.

Meanwhile, other workers are cutting out covers from huge rolls of synthetic fibers and wool. Nylon and Dacron are used for strength and durability, wool for fluffiness. These covers are applied by hand and spooled down by a technician holding the ball against a spinning wheel. The process firms up all cemented edges. The balls are sent through a steamer to bring out fluffiness and are then moved by a conveyer belt through a line of inspectors. The finished product must meet rigid specifications.

The net is also the result of a long period of development. Originally, tennis was played over dirt or wooden barriers. Later a single cord was stretched across the court. Historians of the nineteenth century described nets that were five feet high at the posts and dipped to four feet in the middle; flags were attached to the slim posts and the net was constantly slipping and needing adjustment.

The racket and its use have undergone an equally exotic coming of age.

Around the twelfth century, players of "jeu de paume" grew concerned about the calluses on their palms from hitting the ball with their bare hands, so they started wearing gloves. A hundred years later they switched to thong bindings. By the fourteenth century the "battoir," a long-headed bat with a leather-bound grip, had appeared. Battoirs eventually assumed the shape of a table tennis paddle; the heads were hollowed out and given a striking surface first of parchment, then of strings.

No one knows exactly how the word "racket" came into use. The Arabs had a word, "rahat," meaning the "palm of the hand." Conceivably, racket could have emerged from that. The Germans have a verb, "racken," meaning "to stretch" and there's a Latin word, "reticulum," which means "net-covered instrument."

Regardless, we know that gut-strung instruments were used in games as far back as the twelfth century. In chicane, a cross between polo, lacrosse and tennis, horsemen chased a ball and tried to hit it with a long-handled stick with a small, gut-strung head. If horses were scarce chicane was played on foot and from such beginnings may have sprung lacrosse, perhaps croquet and field hockey.

The first mention of strings in a tennis battoir was made

by Scaino da Salo, an Italian priest who wrote a comprehensive book on the subject in 1555. Apparently the first
rackets were triangular with a square top. Variations followed: round, oblong and spoon-shaped. Court tennis players were said to prefer the last for the greater spin it imparted. Scaino and others attributed the popularity of the
spoon-head to its usefulness in scooping balls out of corners
—a function certain to have been appreciated by those
sporting monks playing the game in their monastery courtyards.

The first rackets were strung diagonally. Later horizontal
and perpendicular stringing was adopted although the diag-
onal method remained popular in Europe for many years.

Since the Middle Ages rackets have been strung with a
tough, resilient material—catgut. Actually cats have nothing
to do with it. The material comes from the intestines of
sheep but has been misnamed ever since it was used to
string harps and lyres and to bind wounds in ancient Greece
and Rome. Centuries ago there was a small violin—a "kit"
—whose strings were called "kit-gut." The affinity between
"kit" and "cat" resulted in the misconception. It's doubtful
the tennis player recognizes the lowly sheep's sacrifice when
he shells out for the best set of strings. He ought to. They
are very expensive, the heart of the racket.

The finest strings come from what is known as the split gut
from the smooth side of the intestine. This is a narrow strip
about twenty feet long. It takes twenty-five of these twisted
together like cable to make the string. Some fifty sheep must
surrender their lives to string one racket.

There are cheaper rackets which are strung with nylon.
These are durable, moisture-proof and adequate for average
and even better-class players. However, most world class
players stick with gut because of its resiliency.

From the 1760's until the 1880's rackets were sturdily
built with a handle of medium length, lopsided in shape and
designed to pick up and slice low balls. Such a weapon was

used by O.E. Woodhouse when he won the first major tournament in the United States at Staten Island in 1880.

As the game progressed, acquiring smashes and powerful ground strokes, the Woodhouse racket was found to be inadequate. A more symmetrical type was adopted and when R.D. Sears won the U.S. title in 1881 he used a 16-ounce bat with a face rounded at the top and narrowing almost to a point at the junction with the handle.

The heads of the old rackets consisted of a single piece of wood. They were inclined to warp and often would split at the throat. With the development of improved glues, manufacturers turned to making laminated rackets. A lamination is a separate piece of wood, rawhide or plastic. In the case of the tennis racket, there are usually from three to eleven strips of ash and maple—ash for strength and flexibility, maple for balance and beauty. The more laminations, the less susceptibility to warping and cracking.

Unlike golf, tennis has no rigid specifications concerning rackets and balls. Improvements have evolved through tradition but the basic ideas have remained.

The modern racket is 27 inches long (one inch shorter for junior models) with grips ranging from 4⅝ inches to 5 inches and weigh from 12 to 13 ounces for children and women to 14 ounces and over for men. Jack Kramer used a very heavy racket; Rod Laver, with wristy shots, an extremely light one.

All rackets have hollow handles and the balance is changed by removing the grip and drilling out the butt end, removing or inserting a section of lead-impregnated rubber or lead-weighted dowel. The balance point is located halfway from the top to the bottom of the racket. A racket with a light head is supposed to help the player who goes to the net. A heavy head is said more suited to the baseline player.

The most revolutionary change in racket construction came in the middle 1960's and the innovator was a millionaire Frenchman named Rene Lacoste, a member of the "Four Musketeers" who held the Davis Cup from 1927 through 1932, and a former Wimbledon and twice United States champion.

After ending his tennis career Lacoste turned to aeronautics and became one of France's leading air age manufacturers; he also marketed a popular sport shirt with a crocodile emblem. But his interest in tennis never waned. For years he insisted wooden rackets were as outmoded as were hickory-shafted clubs in golf. He felt tubular steel was the answer.

"No matter how intricately or how well manufactured, no two wood frame rackets are alike," he said. "There is a different feel or balance. With steel it is possible to make rackets that conform to the minutest specification."

His words fell on deaf ears. Tennis always had been reluctant to change.

Lacoste developed a steel racket and showed it around. The novelty drew polite examination and some praise. Nobody had the nerve to buy it—the idea was simply too revolutionary.

Finally the Wilson Sporting Goods Company, with principal offices in Chicago, took the gamble and bought the privilege to experiment with Lacoste's theory. The Wilson "steelie," a gleaming weapon called the T 2000, made its formal debut in 1967.

Billie Jean King of Long Beach, California, used the steel racket in sweeping the Wimbledon and U.S. Women's titles. Clark Graebner and Eugene Scott, a pair of Americans whose tournament records had been unimposing, were the last American survivors in the men's division of the United States Championships at Forest Hills, both using steel rackets. Scott, unseeded, went to the semifinals where he lost to the ultimate winner, John Newcombe of Australia. Graebner, serving and playing powerfully, upset Roy Emerson and Jan Leschly to reach the final.

"It's the steel racket—it has improved my game twenty-five percent," said Graebner. Scott and Mrs. King, not overlooking the commercial value to the company they represented, echoed Graebner's sentiments. There was such a rush for steel rackets that the manufacturer was unable to keep them in stock although, with the best strings, the price was much more than that of the best wood frame racket. The going rate was between $50 and $60.

The racket was made of tubular steel, with a circular head and an open throat where two pieces of steel extended down to the normal taped wooden handle. There was a departure from the traditional stringing. Instead of holes for the locking in of each individual string there was a unique suspension system with the strings attached to a spiral wrap.

"A resiliency you've never had—equalization of string tension for greater overall power," the advertisements trumpeted. The suspension system, however, had a drawback. Few people knew how to string the racket and the price for doing so was double the usual rate. Moreover "patching"—putting in a single string or more at a time— was virtually impossible. Nevertheless the public was smitten and manufacturers hastened to jump on the bandwagon.

Another Illinois producer, the Sterling Automotive Manufacturing Company of Elk Grove Village, came out with its own version of the steel racket—"The Lively One"—offering a reinforced throat with a special crossbar and conventional stringing.

Spalding, long a pioneer in golf and tennis equipment, met the challenge with an aluminum racket dubbed "The Smasher." The pitch went: "Faster, easier to control. You get more power with the same swing. 'The Smasher' has a sensitive, easy-to-control touch for the critical drop, lob and placement shots. Its unique aluminum frame keeps the ball on the racket face a fraction of a second longer." An aging Pancho Gonzales, enlisted in "The Smasher's" behalf, claimed it enabled him to pull off shots with less effort.

As the game moved into the 1970's, the two top professional players, Rod Laver and Tony Roche, abandoned wood frames for a gold-embossed aluminum racket made by the Chemold Corporation of Long Island, New York. Arthur Ashe, Jr., made a deal with the Head Ski Company for a big-throated gray metal racket that looked like a rug-beater.

There were experiments with fiber glass and similar materials. One well-known manufacturer came up with "The Composite," a racket boasting the playing qualities of wood, the flexibility of fiber glass and the strength of steel.

Meanwhile, playing surfaces continued to vary according to national and regional preferences. Originally the surface used by Major Wingfield and later by Miss Outerbridge had been grass. Hence the name lawn tennis. But this feature was not to remain constant.

Only England, the United States and Australia were able or of a mind to maintain grass courts which had to be cultivated as tenderly as a golf green. Because these countries dominated the Davis Cup, grass became the traditional surface for the tournament. It was also used in three of the four major national championships. The exception was France which played on the red clay Roland Garros courts outside Paris. In the first sixty-eight years of Cup competition only six Challenge Rounds were held on anything but grass. These were the five years France successfully defended the title (1928–32) plus the 1964 matches in Cleveland, Ohio, on a composition surface.

Despite demands that a uniform surface be adopted for the major international tournaments tennis remained a lawn game to its conservative directors. Clay was the only surface common to all countries but was considered too slow. Most of Australia and much of England stuck with grass. So did well-to-do Easterners in the United States, while middle-class Americans generally settled for clay and the West Coast turned out a slew of champions from lightning-fast hard courts made of asphalt, concrete or a combination of the two.

The rest of the world was largely committed to clay, although Scandinavian countries, because of the severe cold, got most of their practice on hardwood indoor courts. Spain, Italy, France, Belgium, even Russia developed players on clay, then sent them, like lambs to a slaughterhouse, against the stars of England, Australia and the United States who were accustomed to the quick put-away enabled by grass.

Nevertheless, as tennis moved into the 1970's behind new, young and aggressive leadership eager to discard stuffy traditions, the adoption of a uniform surface seemed a possibility. Plastic and rubber manufacturers were producing surfaces which had all the qualities of grass yet provided a uniform bounce and stable playing conditions. They could be made available to any country wishing to stretch them over a hardwood floor, an ice rink or a turf stadium. The pros used such composition surfaces in many of their events, so it was just a matter of getting the amateur fathers to see the light.

ONE	*Evolution of the Scoring —*
4	*A New Englander Challenges the Ages*

Of all the stodgy traditions to which tennis has stubbornly clung none is as vexing as the scoring system. Handed down through the ages and justified by no logical reason, it allows matches to drag on interminably and has thus cut into the game's popularity. In desperation the professionals adopted their own streamlined substitute—the "pro set"—and a bouncy little New Englander, James Van Alen of Newport, Rhode Island, overseer of the National Lawn Tennis Hall of Fame and Museum, waged a spirited, if never fully successful, campaign to replace the outmoded method.

He called his plan the Van Alen Simplified Scoring System or VASSS. Points were scored just as in table tennis—one, two, three and so on—with 31 comprising a set. The deuce and advantage points—knotty aspects of the old way—were eliminated to ensure against overlong matches. Indeed, under VASSS the longest match lasted less than an hour.

Van Alen found supporters, particularly among the pros. Several tournaments, all unofficial, tried his system, and the U.S. Lawn Tennis Association published it in its *1968 Guide*.

Nevertheless, tennis fathers stuck with the method first used by monks and kings during the Middle Ages. That method is highly confusing to a person unfamiliar with the sport. Here's how it goes:

A player wins a point. He isn't "one." He is "fifteen." If he wins a second point he is "thirty" and a third he is not "forty-five" but "forty." Why the third point should be worth five less than the first or second never has been explained. A player who wins four points wins a game but only if he's two points ahead of his opponent. If not they continue playing until one of them is two points ahead. This brings us to two other scoring terms, "deuce," meaning the players are tied, or "advantage," meaning the person holding it needs only one more point to clinch the game.

No one knows how "fifteen" became the basic scoring unit but there is historical evidence that it has been used almost since the game began. A ballad composed by Charles d'Orleans while he was imprisoned in Wingfield Castle in 1435 refers to "quarante cinq" or "forty-five" in comparing life to a tennis game. An account of a match in 1505 tells how King Philip of Spain gave the Marquis of Dorset a "handicap of XV."

Scaino da Salo relates that fifteen points were given for each winning stroke, making the score go 15, 30, 45 and finally 60, although the last figure has never shown up in the records. He refers to "a due," meaning two strokes are needed to win. This is thought to be the antecedent of the term, "deuce." The word, "advantage," also was used to signify that a player was one point away from game.

Scaino had no clear-cut explanation for the complex scoring. He wrote ambiguously of three types of game—the simple game, in which both players scored; the double game, in which one player won with four straight points, and the triple game, in which a player after losing the first three points rallies to win five points in a row.

Scaino speculated that tennis scoring evolved from the triple game, the winning of which was considered an outstanding feat. Seeking a figure that would be a combination of three and five, early architects of the sport naturally came up with fifteen, he said. Later scholars disputed this theory, though most agreed with the Italian that the third point was watered down from forty-five to forty for no other reason than that it was easier to call.

Investigating the "fifteen" puzzle in 1579 a French scholar and librarian Jean Gosselin wrote, "I have been unable to find a man who could give me a reason for it." He made two guesses. Being a student of astrology he suggested that the basic score was derived from a sextant, a sixth part of a circle composed of sixty degrees. Or it may have been taken from the geometric figure Clima, sixty feet square, four times fifteen.

Later explanations were more plausible if no more verifiable. One theory was that the decision had been arrived at by consulting tower clocks; they tolled every fifteen minutes and four quarters made the hour. Another pointed to gambling on early matches as the source; in France during the Middle Ages the monetary unit was composed of sixty sous with four coins worth fifteen cents each.

Mystery also shrouds the use of the word "love" to signify no-score. It may be an outgrowth of the French word "l'oeuf," meaning egg. Perhaps the French were influenced by the English cricket habit of calling a zero a "duck egg," later softening the expression into "love." The Scots also have a word "luff" which means zero, and the Americans, of course, commonly use the term "goose egg." Then too, according to another theory, "love" itself has long been a synonym for "nothing" as is indicated by such expressions as "neither for love nor money," "play for love" and "labor of love." In the 1700's shopkeepers put signs in their windows: "See for love, buy for money."

One thing is sure, however: The expression didn't help tennis overcome its long-time reputation as an effeminate sport. Back in 1414 French ambassadors cast aspersions on the masculinity of Henry V by offering to send him "little balls to play with" and "soft cushions to rest on" until he should become a man. Shakespeare and *Punch*, the British humor magazine, derided tennis as a game for the soft and weak. In 1878 the Harvard *Crimson* expressed alarm over the growth of lawn tennis clubs on campus and said, "The game is well enough for lazy and weak men, but men who have rowed or taken part in nobler sport should blush to be seen playing lawn tennis."

Gardnar Mulloy, one of America's leading players for a quarter of a century, insisted the word "love" was a detriment to the popularity of the game, as were rules that players should dress in white and that the gallery maintain strict silence during play. He campaigned for elimination of these traditions but gained little ground.

Give the professionals and doughty Mr. Van Alen their way, and such questions will be academic, for they would replace the ancient scoring system with a simpler one based on first grade arithmetic. The pros began to experiment with a new system during the 1940's when overlong matches caused the pro tour to decline in popularity.

The answer was "the pro set," introduced by Jack March, promoter for the World Professional Championship in Cleveland, Ohio. Under this system the first player to win eight games took the match. Thus instead of being on the court for three hours, as was often the case in a best three-out-of-five set match, players were finished in thirty or forty brisk minutes. Naturally, such streamlined scoring appealed to TV sponsors.

The television dollar was also a chief talking point in Van Alen's campaign in behalf of his own system. Under VASSS the 31-point set could be played in thirty minutes, rarely varying more than a couple minutes either way. Scoring, with a winning stroke representing a single point, was simple enough for a child to understand. The serve changed hands every five points and each five-point sequence was called a "hand." Sides always changed on the odd hand, at five, fifteen and twenty-five.

The winner of a set had to lead by two points or go into what was called a "tie-break." Thus if the score was tied 30–30 it was necessary to play nine more points. The player winning five of the tie-break points became the victor.

In case of a tie-break, players spun rackets for service. The winner of the spin had the choice of serving first (1, 2, 5, 6) or second (3, 4, 7, 8, 9). If he chose second, he had the advantage of serving five times to four for his opponent.

Van Alen proposed that a match consist of either two 31-point sets or four sets, with a nine-point tie-break in case the sets were split. An alternative was a best-of-three or best-of-five set match. In either case, there was a definite time limit.

The New Englander toured the world, espousing the merits of his plan. He lobbied at conventions of the U.S. Lawn Tennis Association and the International Lawn Tennis Federation. He carried his drive to newspapers and magazines. He preached a sermon of doom for tennis as a spectator sport unless it could throw off its old-fashioned robes and go modern.

Van Alen argued that the bottom frequently fell out of major championships with elimination of the brightest stars in the early rounds. He proposed a round robin formula designed to give every player more exposure and create added gate appeal.

Under the Van Alen system, a field of sixty-four players

was divided into eight flights of eight players each. Each competitor played one VASSS 31-point set against each of the other seven in his group.

The eight winners qualified for a second round robin in which the four top players entered the semifinals. The semifinalists played two sets—one against three and two against four. The survivors then clashed to determine the top four places.

Van Alen listed seven advantages to his formula:

1. Every player assured of seven one-set matches against seven different opponents. The old plan eliminated 50 percent of the field in the first round.

2. Elimination of the marathon set and match. All matches start and end on time.

3. The gallery sees every match played as advertised, not an hour or more later.

4. No player suffers the injustice of a second round defeat because of an exhaustive first round match.

5. Television can be programmed to the minute.

6. One hundred percent instead of ten percent of the TV audience understands the terminology.

7. The center court gallery is assured of seeing top players throughout the tournament.

In 1969, after promoting several VASSS tournaments which he subsidized, Van Alen achieved a major breakthrough. The United States Lawn Tennis Association adopted a motion to give Van Alen's tie-break an exposure on an experimental basis in some tournaments.

Van Alen was able, through twelve years of persistent lobbying which cost him a small fortune, to bring tennis authorities to acceptance of his theory that the game—as in football, baseball and golf—must have a terminal point.

He got them to try one of his modified sudden-death systems for the tie-break.

The system was used by the professionals in a dramatic winner-take-all match between Rod Laver and Pancho Gonzales at Madison Square Garden, and some 16,000 spectators found it fascinating.

It was incorporated in the World Cup Matches of 1971 at Boston, a tournament conceived by sports writer Bud Collins of the Boston *Globe,* and in the indoor professional championships at Philadelphia, conducted by Ed and Marilyn Fernberger.

The pros had mixed feelings. The spectators loved it. The International Lawn Tennis Federation, slow to change, found the departure from tradition repugnant and slapped the wrists of the tournament promoters and the U.S. Lawn Tennis Association. Penalties were assessed.

The experience ignited a spark in the minds of American tennis progressives, one of the foremost of whom was Alastair B. Martin, president of the USLTA. With some prodding from Joseph Cullman, the cigarette tycoon who served as tournament chairman, and Bill Talbert, the ex-Davis Cup captain who took over as director, Martin went before the international body and asked permission to use the tie-break system on an experimental basis in the 1970 U.S. Open Championships at Forest Hills. The ILTF had little alternative except to agree.

Wimbledon followed suit in 1971 with a 12-point tie break, more conservative than that used at Forest Hills. It was the most revolutionary move in the game since Major Wingfield's lawn party in 1873.

The tie-break was a resounding success. Fans flocked into the big concrete horseshoe at West Side Tennis Club by the thousands, breaking all attendance records, and buzzed with excitement over the innovation.

The nine-point sudden-death tie-break was used in the

Open Championships. There are variations but this was the method chosen by Martin, Cullman and Talbert for their great adventure.

Under the system, when the score of a set reaches 6–6, the competitors play a best five-of-nine point series for the set, which then would be recorded as 7–6. No set could go beyond 13 games. There would not be the necessity of a two-game spread in order to win the set.

The plan called for alternating services in this fashion: The player whose service was coming up would serve the first two points, the first from the forehand and the second from the backhand side of the court. Then the serve would pass to his opponent, who would proceed to serve twice in the same fashion. The original server got the next two serves, with the final three serves passing to his opponent.

Some players complained it was unfair that one player should get only four services while the other should get five. Proponents of the nine-point sudden death argued that this advantage was balanced by the fact that the first server was able to serve four of the first six times and thus, if points followed service the original server would have a 4–2 lead going into the last three points, needing only one good shot to win the tie-break.

"I like the twelve-point plan better," said Arthur Ashe, who lost two tie-break sets to John Newcombe in the quarter-finals of the tournament. "As far as I am concerned, I never lost those two sets. They are still going on."

Newcombe, although winner, agreed.

"It's a lousy way to win a match," he said. "I served first so I led 4–2 with Ashe having the last three serves. It's like being down 0–40. Arthur had three match points on him, and he didn't deserve them because he hadn't lost a service."

However, both agreed that the tie-break infused new interest in the game and should be continued in some form or another.

"If the fans like it and it helps us get tennis on the big television networks, then we all should be for it," said Newcombe. "That's where our money comes from."

Both Ashe and Ken Rosewall, who won the 1970 U.S. Open 14 years after he had taken the championship on the same center court, told of the tension created by the tie-break.

"It's really eerie out there," said Ashe. "There's not a sound. You can't hear people breathing."

"It's nerve-wracking," said Rosewall.

Pancho Gonzales, still a tournament threat at 40-plus, said he believed the tie-break worked to the detriment rather than the benefit of the older players.

"In the tie-break you have to be alert and sharp on every point," Pancho said. "It's tough on the old guys. They like to pace themselves. I think the twelve-point plan is better. Each one has the same number of services. You must be two points ahead to win."

However, it was the sudden-death aspect of the nine-point break that fascinated the fans. In several matches, the outcome hung on a single service. There were cases of simultaneous match point.

Ecstatic that he had achieved even this mild breakthrough, Van Alen announced that he would continue his campaign until his entire VASSS system became the law of the tennis land.

"This is only a part of VASSS," he insisted after the successful trial in the U.S. Open. "We must get rid of that silly scoring—fifteen, love and deuce—and count one, two, three, four.

"After that, I intend to change the name. This is not tennis, as it was played originally. It is not lawn tennis, because we have few lawns any more. It's played on synthetic surfaces. So we must find another name."

TWO

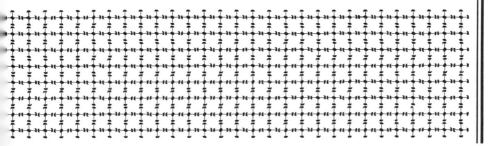

Dick Sears and the Early Pioneers

When Dr. James Dwight and Fred Sears set up a net at Nahant, Massachusetts, in the summer of 1875 and started playing a new game called "Sphairistike," or lawn tennis, which had been brought over from England, one spectator was an eleven-year-old boy who followed every shot with wonder.

His name was Richard D. Sears, Fred's younger brother, destined to become the first men's single champion of the United States and to hold the title for seven straight years.

The informal match—played in the rain with both men wearing boots and raincoats—was held on the estate of Dwight's uncle, William Appleton. Dwight, who later served as president of the U.S. Lawn Tennis Association for twenty-one years and became known as the "Father of American Tennis," contended that this was the first tennis match played in the United States, a claim disputed by some historians who believe the game was brought here by Mary Ewing Outerbridge of Staten Island.

Dwight was a slight, athletically-inclined man who loved tennis but never became a truly great player. He was frequently beaten by his friends and by his chief pupil, Dick Sears.

Dwight and Fred Sears played regularly. Often the doctor would call young Richard onto the court and let him practice swinging a racket at the heavy rubber balls. Richard was delighted and played at every opportunity.

Dwight once took him on a trip to England where the youngster became acquainted with the great English players, William Renshaw and Herbert Lawford. Renshaw gave him a racket, a prized possession which Sears took home, polished, restrung and used in winning eight of his various championships. Lawford taught him a stroke—the "Lawford," a sweeping drive with considerable top-spin.

Sears was nineteen when the first U.S. Championship was held at Newport in 1881. By modern standards he was an unlikely-looking athlete. He had steel-rimmed spectacles, a rakish mustache and wore long white flannels, a striped blazer, a cap and a striped necktie. If any of his opponents thought him peculiar—and they probably didn't since mustaches and blazers were the style—they had little to laugh about by the tournament's end.

With a 16-ounce racket the youthful New Englander slashed his way to the final where he crushed W.E. Glyn 6–0, 6–3, 6–2.

He owed his success to an aggressive game that was rather revolutionary for the period. Not content with remaining in the backcourt and patting the ball back and forth he moved to the forecourt and hit the ball before it touched the ground. Planting himself in the middle of the court, because the net was one foot lower there than at the posts, he used his marvelous reflexes to become America's first volleyer.

"All I had to do was tap the balls as they came over, first to one side and then the other, running my opponent all over the court," he explained.

Sears entered the doubles with Dwight, who had passed up the singles, and they were eliminated by the ultimate champions, Clarence Clark and Fred Taylor, whose strategy was to play one man at the net and one in back court. It wasn't long before such a technique was discredited by tacticians who found the most efficient way for doubles was to keep the two players side by side.

Sears went on to win seven national singles crowns in a row, losing only three sets during the entire period. His sweep was aided by the introduction of the "challenge system" in 1884 which permitted the defending champion to wait on the sidelines until his opponent could be determined from an all-comers eliminations.

That was the year he dropped his first set in the championships. After taking the opening set from Howard Taylor without loss of a game Sears apparently eased up because of overconfidence and lost the second 1–6. He took the final two, 6–0, 6–2.

The champion had his hardest match in 1886 when he lost the first set to Livingston Beekman. The latter borrowed a page from Sears' book and met attack with attack. He played an aggressive game, frequently moving into the forecourt. Sears, troubled with cramps in his hands, finally won 4–6, 6–1, 6–3, 6–4.

Meanwhile, Sears and Dwight had improved their doubles combination well enough to capture that event the second year, 1882, and win it five of the next six years. In 1885, when the doctor was unavailable, Sears teamed successfully with J.S. Clark, thus chalking up six straight doubles triumphs to go with his seven singles victories.

In these championships the nets were made of very light material, secured in the center by a steel rod. In the first tournament, some players served underhand but by the second year most men found it more effective to strike every ball overhand.

Winners in both singles and doubles were presented medals instead of loving cups.

Sears won his final championship in 1887, beating Henry W. Slocum, Jr., 6–1, 6–3, 6–2. Then, bothered by a neck ailment, he retired undefeated, the first of America's multiple champions.

Sears was succeeded by Slocum, a wiry player with handle-bar mustache and slicked-down brilliantined hair. His policy was to avoid mistakes. He kept the ball in play until his opponent erred or until he had an opportunity to put a shot away, a strategy good enough to rout Howard

Taylor in the 1888 final 6–4, 6–1, 6–0 and to win in four sets from Q.A. Shaw in 1889. The latter tournament had its first foreign entry, E.G. Meers of Britain, beaten in the semifinals.

Oliver S. Campbell, a Columbia student utilizing a net-rushing attack, deposed the cautious Slocum in 1890, holding the title three years. Campbell did not defend in 1893 and was succeeded by Robert D. Wrenn, a Harvard student who lettered in football, hockey and baseball.

Wrenn was a powerful left-hander who scampered all over the court, using a wide variety of shots. He stunned Fred Hovey in the 1893 final and proceeded to win the title four out of five years, a string broken in 1895 by his old rival, Hovey, who changed to a retrieving, back court game for the occasion.

Malcolm Whitman, a tall, slender man credited with originating the reverse serve in which the ball bounces away from the receiver, took over in 1898 while Bob Wrenn and Bill Larned were helping fight the Spanish-American War. Whitman defeated Dwight Davis in the final and held the title the next two years.

Larned, one of the great early champions, returned from the war and grabbed the first of his seven championships in 1901. A Cornell graduate who rode with Teddy Roosevelt's "Rough Riders," he was ranked Number One for eight years, Number Two five years and Number Three four years. Over a period of twenty years, he was ranked in the nation's Top Ten nineteen times.

J. Parmley Paret, a contemporary, said of him: "There is little doubt that William A. Larned was the most consistently brilliant player this country had turned out before Tilden's skill ripened."

Larned was a go-for-broke player. He played a daring, ever attacking game, refusing to compromise for safety. Although his forehand was sound, even deadly at times, his backhand was his most potent stroke. Like Don Budge and Rod Laver who came along years later, he could whistle a shot down the line or cross-court it, leaving his opponent gaping at the net.

A stocky man with the shoulders and wrists of a blacksmith, Larned successfully defended his title in 1902, beating Reggie Doherty of England in the final. The following year, however, he lost to the Englishman's younger brother Laurie. Holcombe Ward, Beale Wright and William J. Clothier all won the championship before Larned could regain it in 1907 to begin a final string of four straight championships.

Maurice McLoughlin came off the public park courts of California to win the crown in 1912, 1913, and Geneva-born R. Norris Williams held sway from 1914 through 1916, ending the pre-World War Era.

McLoughlin, a redhead who became known as the California Comet, is credited with introducing the so-called "Big Game," which became a popular phrase half a century later when Don Budge, Jack Kramer and Pancho Gonzales were at their destructive best.

The early pioneers had included men who went to the net and attacked, but until the rise of McLoughlin, tennis was a comparatively slow-paced, social pastime. McLoughlin was constantly on the move, hammering away at every ball. He was superbly conditioned. He had speed, dash and power and he kept all these attributes at full blast while on the court.

Dick Williams, tall, good-looking with a full head of curly hair, was similar. He hit the ball with tremendous pace, always going for the corners and the lines. Like Ellsworth Vines, who came along about fifteen years later, he was at times erratic. When he was on top of his game, cutting the lines, he was almost unbeatable. On an off day, with his timing slightly off-key, he could be beaten by a second-rater.

Williams learned the game as a youngster by batting a

ball against a brick wall in his native Switzerland. He won his first tournament at twelve, moved to the United States and developed into one of the country's top Davis Cup players and champions.

One of Williams' early rivals was Little Bill Johnston, who is another story.

TWO
——
2

Little Bill Johnston and the Transition Years

William M. (Little Bill) Johnston was such a thin, frail figure—five feet, eight-and-one-half inches tall, 120 pounds with a lady-like four-and-one-half shoe size—that he invited pity until he drew back and hit a forehand. The ball came off his racket like a bullet and traveled with such speed and spin that a man might be driven to distraction trying to return it.

It was a devastating stroke—the deadliest weapon in the orthodox arsenal of a mite-sized man who won national championships in 1915 and 1919 and gave Big Bill Tilden some of his toughest battles.

Johnston was born in 1895 in San Francisco. He grew up around Golden Gate Park where as a youngster he hung around the public parks watching untrained players belt away at the ball awkwardly. He wasn't quite twelve when he decided to try the game himself.

"I picked up my California forehand drive probably as the result of playing on hard cement courts where the bound is high," he explained once. "It was practically necessary to stand and meet the ball on the rise, and the California (or Western) grip, with the face of the racket turned toward the ground, seemed to meet the rising ball more directly."

In the Western, as contrasted to the Eastern or Continental "shake hands" grip in which the racket appears to be an extension of a finger, the hand is behind the racket. Johnston hit the ball with a full sweep and a curving follow-through imparting tremendous spin.

In winning the 1915 U.S. title, Johnston defeated Dick Williams in the semifinals and Maurice McLoughlin in the final. Against Williams he concentrated on dulling the Swiss star's net-charging attack by hitting the ball at his feet. In the final, McLoughlin almost blew Johnston off the court in the first set but Little Bill settled down to win the next three sets.

"My theory was to play everything possible to his backhand and get to the net," Johnston said. "In the fourth and final set, he made less errors than I did but I made thirty-two placements to his twenty and won 10–8."

In the 1916 final Williams avenged the defeat, rallying from two sets to one deficit to take the last two. World War I interrupted the championships the following year, Williams entering the Army, Johnston the Navy. In 1918 Lindley Murray won the title by crushing William (Big Bill) Tilden in three sets.

Tilden, however, was destined to be the great tennis player of the 1920's and with Little Bill at his peak and Big Bill on the way up, the stage was set for a dramatic rivalry. Johnston-Tilden duels soon became routine and the fans looked forward to them.

Returning to competition in 1919, Johnston immediately found himself face-to-face with the towering stoop-shouldered Tilden. He beat him in the clay court championships but lost to him at Newport and in the East-West matches. Then came the National at Forest Hills. Thrown into opposite brackets, the two swept to the final where Johnston won 6–4, 6–4, 6–3.

"I went to the net a great deal, sending most of my shots down the middle of the court and using the center theory in getting in," Johnston said later. "I exploited his weak backhand and I never lost a service."

Tilden, because of his victory at Newport, had been favored in the match but the crowd was solidly behind the diminutive Johnston.

"It took Little Bill to show up that big stiff," chortled one spectator within earshot of Tilden.

In 1920 Johnston and Williams went to Europe for the Inter-Zone Davis Cup campaign and preliminary tournaments leading to Wimbledon. Johnston won at Queens but at Wimbledon he lost to J.C. Parke while Tilden went on to take the championship, beating Zenzo Shimizu in the final round. The two rivals joined in recapturing the Davis Cup from the aging Norman Brookes and his Australasians at Auckland, New Zealand, at the end of the year.

But, according to E.C. Potter, Jr., a well-known tennis historian of the day, the relative curve of the two rivals was diverging. Tilden's line was going up, Johnston's down.

In the 1920 final at Forest Hills Tilden beat Johnston in five sets. The following year, when the championships shifted to the Germantown Cricket Club in Philadelphia, the two met in an earlier round and again the edge went to Big Bill, who went on to take the title.

One of the great matches of all time was played in the 1923 final at Germantown, Tilden rallying from two sets down for the championship.

Johnston avenged the setback shortly afterwards in one of his few latter-day triumphs over his tall rival, but an umpire's error took some of the taste out of the victory.

The two were playing in the East-West matches at Forest Hills. A large crowd had come out to see the renewal of their bitter rivalry. With the score one set each Johnston led 7–6 in the third and had Tilden down 0–40 on service.

Tilden served. The linesman called "Fault." There was another service and a rally ensued.

"I called a (double) fault," the linesman said.

"Let's play a let," said Johnston. But Tilden had already

stalked to the dressing room for the ten-minute intermission.

When the players were at last brought back they found two women playing an exhibition. After strong protests by both men, the match was resumed.

Johnston won the set. In the fifth, the temperamental, petulant Tilden merely went through the motions of making shots. Johnston ran it out 6–0. But he felt his victory had been tainted.

The little Californian went overseas in 1923, winning at both Paris and Wimbledon. At Wimbledon he defeated Vincent Richards in a terrific match and downed Francis T. Hunter, another compatriot, in the final.

But the strain was beginning to tell on him. He looked gaunt and tired. He did not move with his old zip. In the Davis Cup matches against the Australasians at Forest Hills, he lost to Jim Anderson, missing shots that he had always made easily.

Tilden-Johnston duels for the U.S. crown were a regular attraction but Big Bill was now the master. He won the title in 1923, losing only nine games. In 1924 he scored another straight set victory. In 1925 Johnston mustered all his strength and tenacity for a heroic stand but again Tilden emerged the winner in five sets.

Meanwhile, the pair continued shouldering the Davis Cup load through 1927 when Little Bill's health failed. Stricken with a respiratory ailment he died in the prime of life. Nevertheless his plunky stand at the top of world tennis had given little men all over new hope.

TWO — Big Bill Tilden —
3 — Champion and Shakespearean Actor

All the world was a stage to William Tatem Tilden II, the frustrated Shakespearean actor who took his thespian proclivities to the tennis court and became the greatest player in the world. Unable to attain success on the stage, although he tried to the end, he wound up delighting millions of sports fans.

Big Bill was undisputed king of tennis in the Roaring Twenties, the mad, flapper, easy-money era known as the Golden Age of Sports. He shared headlines with such giants as heavyweight champion Jack Dempsey, grand slam golfer Bobby Jones, baseball's Babe Ruth and the great thoroughbred, Man o' War.

Tilden was equal to the occasion. A gangling, lantern-jawed man with broad, sloping shoulders and a fluid, almost ballet-like grace, he swept over the courts of the world with an air of majesty. There was an electric quality about him that captivated audiences. He took a game that was restricted largely to the snobbish country club set and converted it into a booming public spectacle. No one did more to propel tennis to the forefront.

Tilden did it partly with his thundering cannon-ball service, his powerful drives off both backhand and forehand and his rare faculty of tearing an opponent to pieces with a clever mixture of shots and pace. He was always exciting. He was never predictable and more important was never dull.

Tilden was a tall man, towering over six feet. He walked with long, quick strides. On the court he moved effortlessly from side to side and appeared to have an endless reach. He had a habit of often taking a short, mincing step before hitting the ball. It became a trademark.

An even greater trademark was his incessant feuding with both top officials and lowly linesmen. "I must own to a special dislike for amateur sports officials in general," he once said. He resented their efforts to curtail his writing activities. Once he was suspended for violating rules by receiving money for an article describing a match in which he had played.

Tilden was not given to tantrums as were some later

stars. He never screamed at himself as did Dennis Ralston. He never threw a racket or, as in the case of Pancho Gonzales, never stalked into the gallery to challenge a heckler. But his temperamental outbursts, if less violent, were more outlandish.

In one match, berated by the crowd, Big Bill strode to the net, picked up his gear and without a word departed, defaulting. Once, as a pro, he staged a sit-down strike on the court until some spectators were removed from tree-tops approximately a quarter mile away.

When a linesman called a close shot against him, Big Bill would stop abruptly, put his hands on his hips and give the offender a withering stare. His reaction was the same if he thought the official had made a bad call in his favor. Inevitably he would respond by throwing the next point to his opponent. The crowd always applauded wildly, as Big Bill knew it would.

With his game under control Tilden liked to stage dramas. Facing a green competitor in the early rounds, he would drop the first two sets. This would generate an electric charge of excitement and the word would spread: "Hey, Big Bill is down!" People would flock to the court's edge to witness the upset whereupon Tilden, finally turning on the steam, would run out the match. He did this so frequently that seasoned observers ceased to get alarmed; they believed he fell behind on purpose just to give the gallery a thrill. Big Bill denied this but remained a showman to the end. His career was as tempestuous off the court as well as on, for late in life he served two sentences in jail on morals convictions.

Tilden learned tennis at an early age but his game matured late. He was unable to win an American championship until he was twenty-seven. Once under way, there was no stopping him. He won the National Clay Court title seven times, six in a row, also the National Indoor and the Hard Court. He captured the National Doubles five times with three different partners and the National Mixed Doubles on four occasions.

He was the first American to win the Wimbledon men's singles, capturing his first of three crowns in 1920. That same year he began his string of six straight U.S. Championships and in 1929 at age thirty-six he came back to win his seventh. Next year, gaining his third Wimbledon, he said farewell to amateur tennis, then ruled professional ranks until a younger Ellsworth Vines beat him in 1934.

When the Associated Press conducted a poll of sports broadcasters and writers to choose the outstanding athletes of the first half of the twentieth century, Tilden was an overwhelming choice as the top tennis player.

A greater honor came in 1969 when an international panel of tennis writers named Big Bill THE GREATEST PLAYER OF ALL TIME.

In the years following Tilden's hey-day, the game underwent drastic change. The all-court technique, of which Big Bill was the master, became passé. Power took over. Soon big time tennis was strictly a serve and volley game with few top players developing ground strokes to the fullest and concentrating on the kind of strategy that made Tilden great. "Go for broke" became the motto of the day. The idea was to end every point with one big stroke —if not the service, then the first volley. Rallies were rare, all-court tacticians even rarer.

Yet Tilden's various books of instruction remained a bible for not only the neophyte but the tournament player as well. Big Bill was a prolific writer who poured out an unbelievable quantity of literature—fact and fiction—on tennis. One of his finest books, *Match Play and the Spin on the Ball*, was revived in 1969 and hailed by reviewers.

Tennis is not simply "attack and attack," he said but a perfect blend of both offense and defense. As to whether a perfect baseliner could defeat a perfect volleyer, Tilden first explained that no such players existed but if they did the decision would go to the baseliner.

"The baseliner would pass the volleyer every point," he argued. "You cannot volley the service."

Although a strong driver off both backhand and forehand, Tilden never relied on sheer power to blow an opponent off the court. He utilized a lot of spin shots, slicing and chopping the ball to break the rhythm of his adversary.

Spin, he said, had three purposes: to gain control, to force an opponent to err, to change pace.

"Never allow a player to play the game he prefers if you can possibly force him to play any other," Big Bill advised. "Never give a player a shot he likes to play." This is sound tennis strategy whether it be 1877, the year of Colonel Wingfield, or 1970, the year of Arthur Ashe.

William Tatem Tilden II was born February 10, 1893, in Germantown, Pennsylvania, a suburb of Philadelphia. His father was a prominent wool merchant, a Union League president. His mother was an accomplished violinist.

As a youngster, Bill did not play in the municipal parks and had a private tutor until his junior year in high school. The family belonged to the exclusive Germantown Cricket Club. Summers were spent in the Catskills where young Tilden met such stage luminaries as Julia Marlowe and Maude Adams. It may have been here that his affinity for the theater was born.

Bill had a racket thrust in his hand almost as soon as he was big enough to stand. His brother Herbert, seven years his senior, was a good player and got him started. Bill won a tournament for boys 15 years old and under when he was just eight, but gave no sign of being a tennis prodigy. His interest in the game, at best, was casual and, although strong and fast, he was ungainly.

In 1913, at age twenty, he caught the eye of Mary K. Browne, the U.S. women's singles champion, and she suggested they pair for the National mixed doubles. Surprisingly, they won the event two years in a row. Still, no one paid much attention to the youth from Germantown. Miss Browne, after all, was the top U.S. women's player and they said she carried her young partner.

Tilden's name did not appear in the national ranking until 1915 when he was placed in Class 6. He played in his first National Championship in 1916, losing to an 18-year-old named Harold Throckmorton. That year his name was included in the "second ten." In 1917 he ranked Number Two behind William M. (Little Bill) Johnston, destined to be his chief rival. Finally in 1920 Big Bill was placed Number One, a spot he held for ten years until he was ousted by Johnny Doeg in 1930.

When World War I broke out Tilden tried to get into the service but failed to pass the physical examination for regular army duty because of flat feet. He entered the Medical Corps and served in Pittsburgh. After the war he enrolled at the University of Pennsylvania. He played on the varsity team but failed to impress anyone as a future champion.

People began to take note of him in the 1918 Nationals when the tournament was resumed after the World War I suspension. The gaunt, long-legged young man from Philadelphia battled his way into the final round where he lost in straight sets to a California left-hander, R. Lindley Murray, who had won the substitute Patriotic Tournament the year before. He also won the men's doubles with a chubby, 15-year-old boy named Vincent Richards.

Tilden possessed more power than fans had ever seen. When he delivered a flat service, the ball steamed across the net. He covered the court with long, easy strides and seemed almost able to return shots that were beyond his reach. Yet he was still an unfinished player and his backhand was particularly weak.

Little Bill Johnston concentrated on this flaw when he defeated the Philadelphian decisively for the 1919 championship. Tilden, proud and vain, brooded on the debacle. That winter he went into hibernation at a friend's home in Providence, Rhode Island, and there he worked on his backhand.

By the time the 1920 season dawned he was ready for all comers. The big test came at Wimbledon, the symbol of the world championship. Tilden had been chosen an alternate on the Davis Cup squad which listed Johnston and Norris Williams as the top singles players. This gave him an opportunity to campaign in England and particularly to play on the famed center court on Worple Street.

Johnston and Williams were unceremoniously eliminated in the earlier rounds. Tilden found himself facing Japan's Zenzo Shimizu for the right to meet Australia's Gerald Patterson, the defending champion, in the challenge round.

Against Shimizu, Tilden took a bad spill and reactivated an old cartilage injury in his left knee. He pulled out the match, playing virtually on one foot, and described the occasion later as "an afternoon of acute physical and mental suffering."

As he prepared to meet Patterson he doubted whether he would be able to last the match. Would his knee hold up? But after dropping the first set Big Bill discovered the Australian's Achilles heel—a tentative, unsure backhand. Pounding away at this weakness he became the first American to capture the Wimbledon crown.

Inspiration did it, Tilden said years afterward.

"I remembered it was July 3," he recalled, "and we had a famous holiday to celebrate tomorrow in the United States. It seemed to me an omen of good luck. In my pocket was a four-leaf clover that had grown under Abraham Lincoln's chair in his garden. It had been presented to me by Samuel Hardy's sister-in-law, Mrs. Ben Lathrop.

How could an American throw down Abraham Lincoln and Uncle Sam on the same day, the day before Independence Day?"

Tilden returned to the United States to win the American title for the first of seven times, avenging his loss twelve months before to Little Bill Johnston. It was one of the most dramatic matches in the annals of the game, marked by a plane crash a few blocks from the stadium at the height of the action.

The season was climaxed when Tilden, and Johnston invaded Auckland, New Zealand, and wrested back the Davis Cup with a stinging 5–0 rout of Australia's Norman Brookes and Gerald Patterson. Tilden stayed long enough to win the New Zealand championship.

The victory signaled the beginning of a seven-year U.S. reign in Cup competition, ended only by the aging of Big Bill's legs and reflexes and by the emergence of France's "Four Musketeers." During this period Tilden won thirteen of his fourteen Davis Cup singles matches and shared in three doubles triumphs. He compiled this record despite a series of illnesses and freak accidents.

In 1921, for instance, he was taken seriously ill while playing in the French Championships. At the tournament's finish he entered a London hospital where he remained until the day before Wimbledon. Still extremely weak he met B.I.C. Norton in the challenge round and dropped the first two sets 2–6, 1–6. Then, with Norton leading 5–4 in the fifth set and 40–30, Big Bill hit a drive that he thought went out. As he hurried to the net to shake hands, however, he saw the ball land on the line. Norton, thinking his opponent was charging the net, rushed his shot and batted it out. After that his game went to pieces and Tilden rallied to win.

In 1922 Big Bill's career was almost brought to an abrupt close when, playing an exhibition in Bridgeton, New Jersey, he ran into a wire fence at the back of the court and gashed the middle finger of his racket hand. Blood poisoning developed and doctors feared they would have to amputate his arm. The one alternative—a risky gamble—was to amputate only the tip of the infected finger. Accepting the risk, Tilden recovered and although many thought his tennis days were over, he went on to other victories.

That same year, in the final of the U.S. Championship, Tilden played what he considered his greatest match against arch rival Little Bill Johnston. The individual trophy could be retired by anyone winning it three times and both men had already won it twice. Interest among fans was high and the gallery was sharply divided. Down two sets to one and behind 30–40 in the fourth game, Big Bill hit a lucky lob with a lunging volley that turned the tide. The eager and determined Johnston suddenly saw his game collapse as Tilden ran out six games in a row and took the final set 6–4.

The Davis Cup Challenge Round against France in 1925 produced two exciting matches. Tilden—again the victim of illness—was stricken with incipient ptomaine poisoning and it appeared he might have to withdraw. Since such a move would have proved disastrous under the rigid Davis Cup Code, he stayed.

In the first match Jean Borotra won two sets and led 6–5 in the fourth before Big Bill pulled it out. On the last day Rene Lacoste swept through the first two sets and led 4-0 in the third. At 5–3 in the third he had four match points. Only a series of fantastic breaks and heavy doses of aromatic spirits of ammonia enabled Tilden to turn the tables.

Lacoste had his revenge the following year, defeating Big Bill in the Davis Cup. With the score one set each and Tilden leading 6–5 and 40–30 he lunged for a drop shot and his left knee buckled. Lacoste won the match, although not easily, and then in the U.S. Championships the hobbling Tilden lost to France's Henri Cochet, thus ending the tall

Philadelphian's six-year reign as national titleholder.

Tilden was now thirty-four years old and had a game knee. He was still capable of playing great tennis but victories came fewer and farther between. He admitted he had grown accustomed to hearing a different ending to the traditional court refrain.

"Instead of 'Game . . . Set . . . Match . . . Tilden!' " he said, "it's 'Game . . . Set . . . Match . . . Lacoste . . . Cochet . . . Or Somebody Else!' "

Throughout these years Big Bill never despaired of becoming a great actor. He tried his hand at everything from Shakespeare to productions called *Dracula* and *They Got What They Wanted*. He played the title role in Booth Tarkington's *Clarence* and in 1942 appeared in his own drama *The Nice Harmons*.

He pursued a literary career with equal vigor. A prolific writer, he wrote fiction and plays; many of his stories had a tennis background but none was successful. His factual books on the sport were better received and have proved more durable. Some of these are *Match Play and the Spin on the Ball, The Art of Lawn Tennis, Mixed Doubles* and *The Common Sense of Tennis.*

It was his writing that had him suspended from amateur tennis which almost caused an international incident. After the 1928 Wimbledon tournament Tilden wrote a series of articles for which he was paid, and as a result he was promptly banned by the U.S. Lawn Tennis Association.

But, when the American Davis Cup team invaded France for the Challenge Round, a clamor went up for a rematch of Tilden and Rene Lacoste, who had beaten Big Bill the year before. The French appealed to U.S. Ambassador Herrick, who interceded with the State Department to have Tilden reinstated. The USLTA succumbed to the pressure. Although the Americans failed to recapture the cup, Tilden defeated Lacoste, playing one of his greatest matches.

Aging and slowing, Tilden nevertheless managed on occasion to muster his game for brilliant performances. He defeated Francis X. Hunter for the American championship—his seventh—in 1929. He scored singles victories over Jean Borotra in the Davis Cup Challenge Rounds of 1929 and 1930. And in the latter year—at age thirty-seven—he won another Wimbledon, beating Texan Wilmer Allison in the final. It was one of the most remarkable sports feats of all time.

In 1931 Tilden turned pro and put a show on the road. As the main attraction on stage, playing under floodlights and dictating his own script, he was in seventh heaven. From Madison Square Garden to the big indoor arenas of the Pacific Coast, with one-night stands enroute, he would give the audience a demonstration of his tennis prowess and throw in some informal theatrics for good measure. Moreover he dominated the pro game as he had the amateur, defeating such players as Karel Kozeluh of Czechoslovakia, Hans Nusslein and Roman Najuch of Germany, Henri Cochet and Marin Plaa of France and America's Vinnie Richards, Bruce Barnes, Emmett Pare, Lester Stoefen and George Lott.

The gaunt, graying court hero of the twenties finally came to the end of the winning road when Ellsworth Vines turned professional and defeated him in their cross-country, head-to-head tour, 47 matches to 26.

"My tennis days are over," Tilden wrote in his reluctant valedictory. "The aged net star, that Patriarch of United States tennis, bids official farewell to international play.

"However, that rising youngster, William T. Tilden 2nd, the individual himself, in person not a picture, will still in leisure moments miss his passing shots, volleys and smashes with even greater regularity than usual. I hope to be able to play for years in exhibitions, at schools and colleges or in the public parks where I can feel that I am aiding in the development of future champions."

Tilden did just that. He remained active in California as

Skirts dropping almost to the ankles, long-sleeved blouses, ties and bandanas were the style of the World War I era. Left, Marie Wagner, Mrs. C. V. Hitchins and Molla Bjurstedt strike up a pose at the West Side Tennis Club in Forest Hills, N. Y. Right, a group of ladies assemble at the Seventh

Paul Thompson

Regiment Armory in New York for
some indoor tennis. They are
(front row, left to right)
Emily Weaver, Nora Schmidts, Edith
Beard and Helen McLean;
(back row, left to right) Clare
Cassel, Marie Wagner and Elizabeth
Moore.

When Eleanor Goss Lanning (above) was playing tennis in the 1920's, rackets were of one-piece construction. Horace W. Hall, Harvard Forestry School wood technologist (upper left) was inventor of the laminated racket in which small strips of wood were cross-branded and glued together. He is shown with some of his frames. Technicians (upper right) begin the process with nine sheets of thin wood. From the cutting rooms, the laminated frames go to the inflated sanding drums (center right) where the rough edges are smoothed down and hand-sanded. After passing inspection, the rackets are sprayed with lacquer and put on the special revolving drying wheel (lower). The finished product is almost like a fine violin.

Edwin Levick

Two of the world's best players during the early days of the twentieth century were Gerald Patterson (left), a talented Australian, and Dwight F. Davis (right), donor of the Davis Cup. The picture of Davis was taken twenty-two years after he donated the Davis Cup and played in the first international match in 1900.

Edwin Levick

Signal Corps

Edwin Levick

Major George L. Wren (left), shown in uniform, was one of America's champions in the pre-World War I era. Dr. James Dwight (right), dapper in his stiff collar and straw hat, contended that he played in the first game of tennis on America's shores. He served for many years as president of the U.S. Lawn Tennis Association.

R. S. Oliver (left) was the president
of the U.S. Lawn Tennis Association
in 1881. Hazel Hotchkiss (right),
one of America's greatest champions,
and later, as Mrs. Hazel Wightman,
donor of the Wightman Cup for
women, is shown with Dorothy Green
in 1910.

Edwin Levick

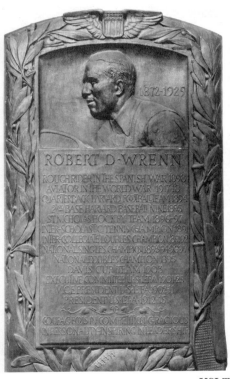

USLTA

USLTA

Molla Bjurstedt Mallory, dour and
intent in hitting a backhand in a
1915 match, was one of America's
pioneer women champions. Two of
the leading men players, Robert
D. Wrenn and William A. Larned,
distinguished themselves as members
of Teddy Roosevelt's Rough Riders
in the Spanish American War. These
two plaques were erected in their
honor.

A rakish cap, mustache and flowing
bow tie were trademarks of the
pioneer tennis star, as shown in this
picture of J. S. Clark (extreme left)
made in 1891. By the time Little Bill
Johnston and Big Bill Tilden
came along, the styles had
become more relaxed. Johnston,
in the next picture, receives
congratulations from Japan's Ichiya

USLTA

Wide World Photos

Kumagae at the West Side Tennis
Club in Forest Hills in 1921. In
the picture second from the right,
Johnston (left) and Tilden wave
good-bye while embarking on an
overseas trip in 1919. Two decades
later, Tilden (left) still appears trim
as he greets Britain's Fred Perry
before a pro tennis match at
Forest Hills.

Borotra was a Basque—later to be internationally acclaimed as "The Bounding Basque"—who learned the game with his two brothers, Fred and Edouard, in the province of Pelote. From the beginning, playing in obscure tournaments in the Basses-Pyrenees, he was a gallery favorite. He had little form. He grunted when he served. His ground strokes were unorthodox. But he was an intense battler. He scrambled over the court in pursuit of every ball. He spun, he leapt and he lunged. In a day when attacking tennis was rare, he scampered to the net at every opportunity, planted himself there and volleyed wildly but effectively.

Cochet, three years younger, was cut from another bolt of cloth. Whereas Borotra was a country boy from the outlying provinces, Cochet was city-born and city-bred. He grew up in Lyons, famed for its silk, his home a lob shot from Lyons' best indoor courts.

Young Cochet virtually lived on the premises. He spent his afternoons serving as ball boy for the older players. When the courts were free, he would pick up a heavy racket and play with his sister and friends. His love of the game was ensured when he saw Australia's Tony Wilding and an Austrian named Salm play an exhibition in Lyons before the war.

Cochet was thirteen when the war broke out. The indoor court became a garage for army trucks. But when peace was restored, the youngster took up the game with new enthusiasm. Undersized but stocky and tough, he usually found himself playing bigger, stronger and older men. The experience was good. He was lightning-quick and he began taking the ball on the rise and going to the net. He became so adept at this maneuver that in later years he planted himself in "No Man's Land," just inside the service line, where he turned the half-volley into an offensive weapon.

In 1920 he entered a tournament at Aix-les-Bains, winning five of six events. Shortly afterwards, he won the championship of Lyons. Now the big time in Paris lay ahead and he set out for the covered court tournament where he was to play his first match with Borotra, later a teammate in numerous Davis Cup campaigns.

Cochet won the match easily. Borotra took stock of himself and decided that if he were to become a world-class player he must improve his ground strokes. In succeeding months he worked diligently on his game. While he never developed a classic style, he got to a point where he could bang both forehands and backhands down the line and go to the net behind a forcing shot. The next time he met Cochet he carried the match to five sets but lost. Cochet appeared to have his number.

The fourth member of France's great tennis quartet emerged in 1922. His name was Jean Rene Lacoste. He was six years younger than Borotra and three years younger than Cochet.

Lacoste was the son of a wealthy automobile magnate in Paris. Rene was fifteen when his father took him to London where he saw a tennis court for the first time. The youngster begged his father to let him buy a racket and take up the game. The father demurred. He wanted his son to eventually take over his automobile business and felt tennis might lead him to frivolous pursuits.

Finally, Rene's persistence won out and his father acceded to his request—with conditions.

"All right," Papa Lacoste is reported to have said. "If you play tennis, you must be the best. I will give you five years. If at the end of that time, you have not attained this goal, then you will give up the game and apply yourself to the business."

Rene agreed. He began taking weekly lessons from a professional named Darsonval. It was an uphill fight. Lacoste, unlike Cochet and Borotra, had not been exposed to the sport as a child and he lacked the natural talent of his contemporaries. A thin, dark youngster with a long nose, he was quiet and stayed to himself. But he had strong assets: He was ambitious, determined and an indefatigable worker who practiced endlessly. He charted his own progress and kept a notebook on the strengths and weaknesses of his opponents. There may have been greater players than Rene Lacoste but it's doubtful that tennis ever produced a smarter one.

Lacoste's progress was slow. In 1920 and 1921, he was beaten by subordinate players. This only drove him to greater effort. He made his international debut at a tournament in Brussels, beating Roper Barrett but losing shortly afterwards. Finding his ground strokes inadequate, he worked on his volleying.

Meanwhile, Cochet and Borotra had moved into the forefront of French tennis, supplanting the aging Gobert and Decugis, and Brugnon had resigned himself to picking up silverware as a doubles player.

The "Four Musketeers"—Brugnon, Borotra, Cochet and Lacoste—were chosen as members of the Davis Cup team in 1924, and that signaled the beginning of a nine-year French dynasty during which they won ten French singles championships, six consecutive Wimbledons and three U.S. titles, not to mention innumerable conquests in doubles and mixed doubles.

Borotra, with his aggressive, primitive style, was the pacesetter, capturing the first of his two French titles in 1924. At Wimbledon, though he banged into a chair while going wide for a shot, he refused to stop and went on to win the final over teammate Lacoste. Wearing a rakish beret, he played with a gusto that staid Britons had rarely seen. But they loved him and christened him "The Bounding Basque"—a nickname he never lost.

Cochet, out of the army, was set up in a profitable sporting goods business. Borotra worked as an engineer. Lacoste, from a wealthy family, was free to practice as much as needed, cutting the gap between him and fellow Musketeers.

Their individual rivalry was keen. Lacoste turned the tables on Borotra at Wimbledon in 1925 but the Basque came back to win in 1926. Cochet had his hour on the famed center court in 1927, beating Borotra in the final. Lacoste won in 1928, defeating Cochet, who proceeded to turn the tables in 1929, ousting Borotra in the final round.

Cochet won five French titles compared with three for Lacoste and two for Borotra. Lacoste captured the U.S. singles crown in 1926 and 1927 and Cochet won at Forest Hills in 1928. Borotra never won at Forest Hills but he crossed the Atlantic to win four U.S. indoor championships.

Twice the Frenchmen fought their way to the Davis Cup Challenge Round—in 1925 and 1926—only to be repelled by Tilden, Johnston and the doubles team of R. Norris Williams and Vincent Richards. They had been favored to win in 1926 but, being clay court specialists, they found the grass surface at the Germantown Cricket Club in Philadelphia difficult to handle.

One ominous note was struck for the Americans. In the fifth match, with the French already down four games, the wily Lacoste, following his notebook, scored an upset over Tilden 4–6, 6–4, 8–6, 8–6. "There it goes," commented Big Bill prophetically, striding off the court with his shoulders hunched in disappointment. It was his first Davis Cup defeat and a portent of things to come. The United States was to lose the cup to France the following year and not see it for ten years.

In 1927 at Germantown, Lacoste again beat Tilden and also added Johnston's scalp. Cochet, after bowing to Big Bill, crushed Little Bill for a 3–2 French victory and the cup made its first trip to France where the Musketeers, defending on the red-clay Roland Garros courts, held it for six years.

While Lacoste, Cochet and Borotra battled among themselves for tournament honors, they also found pleasure in picking on the great Tilden, who was reaching the end of a brilliant career. In 1926 Big Bill lost to all three in America and in 1927 he succumbed to Cochet at Wimbledon and dropped three important matches to Lacoste.

The Wimbledon match was historic. Tilden, playing superbly, led two sets to none and 5–1 in the third, moving within two points of victory on service. Then the match took a sudden and bizarre turn. Cochet fought back to break Big Bill's cannonball service and before Tilden could recover the Frenchman had run off seventeen straight points.

Shaken, Big Bill tried desperately to regain control but Cochet's confidence was brimming. Though Tilden led in both the fourth and fifth sets, the Frenchman won and in the final against Borotra, although he dropped the first two sets and four times had match points against him, he also emerged victorious.

In addition to his 1927 Davis Cup victory Lacoste beat Tilden in both the French and American championships.

In the French final at St. Cloud, Tilden, having defeated Cochet in the semifinals, grabbed a two to one set lead over Lacoste when the latter suffered leg cramps in the third set. Lacoste, treated at intermission, won the fourth set to level the match, setting a dramatic climax. The last set went twenty games with the temperamental Tilden showing displeasure over repeated foot-fault calls. In the seventeenth game Big Bill reached match point and served what appeared to be a clinching ace. But the ball was called out and Tilden, upset, lost three games in a row.

At Forest Hills, Lacoste, en route to the championship, defeated both Johnston and Tilden.

Tilden always regarded Lacoste as the most formidable of his rivals.

"Lacoste has no one shot that is a gift of the gods like Richards' volley, Johnston's drive or Patterson's overhead," he once said. "But at the same time one sees no weakness in Lacoste's game, no hole that can be pounded.

"Lacoste set out to solve my game following our first

meeting. How successfully he did so is clearly shown when in 1927 against as good tennis as I have ever played he defeated me in Paris for the French championship, at Germantown in the Davis Cup and at Forest Hills for the United States Championship.

"Many people watching Lacoste on a tennis court think of him as a drab, uninteresting and almost morose person, so restrained and unemotional is his style. In the perfection of his stroking, he is a machine . . . but, more than that, he is a charming, cultured gentleman."

But the Four Musketeers could not be expected to go on winning forever. In 1933 Fred Perry and Bunny Austin of Britain took the Davis Cup from them, thus signaling an end to their impressive six -year reign.

TWO
5
Ellsworth Vines — Greatest for a Day

When old-timers gather in locker rooms during major championships to debate the prowess of tennis' greats the name of H. Ellsworth Vines always crops up.

There are those who contend that the tall, tousle-haired product of California's public courts could—on a given day—beat any player who ever lived. Big Bill Tilden's brilliant record over many years and against a wide variety of opponents certainly gives him claim to being the greatest, although some lean to Don Budge who never lost a significant match during a two-year stretch. Other names cited are Fred Perry, the classic Briton, and later such court wizards as Jack Kramer, Pancho Gonzales and Rod Laver.

But no matter whom they put at the top the experts generally agree that Vines, when playing at his peak, was invincible. If he's never classed among the all-time greats it's simply because he wasn't around long enough.

Vines flashed across the tennis sky and then was gone. He

was national champion almost before authorities knew how to spell his name. He never stuck around long enough to play on a winning Davis Cup team. Instead he turned pro at his peak and a few years later quit tennis. He took up golf to become a top player and teacher. He was good enough to reach the semifinals of the Professional Golfers Association championship.

"Nobody ever hit a tennis ball harder than H. Ellsworth Vines, Jr.," wrote William Talbert, long-time player, a Davis Cup captain and author. "Nobody ever played tennis with less margin of error. Vines had a cannonball serve that had very little of the spin which other players needed for control. On all his shots he tried to clear the net by inches or smash the ball as close as possible to the lines.

"When he was hitting the small targets which he gave himself, Vines was as invincible as any player has ever been. When he was missing them, he could lose to almost anyone."

According to Talbert, only Gonzales approached the destructive power of Vines' hard, flat serve. While Vines lacked the all-around virtuosity of Tilden and the net-charging aggressiveness of Kramer, he could drill sledge-hammer shots past his opponents from the back court.

Vines was born in 1912 in Los Angeles. Like other West Coast greats who preceded him, Little Bill Johnston and Maurice McLaughlin, he learned his tennis on the park courts. He had little professional tutoring. The main ingredients of his game, besides sheer power, were dedication and desire.

In 1929, at age seventeen, he and Keith Gledhill won the national junior doubles title. Gledhill was believed to be the stronger player but Vines let it be known that his ambition had no bounds. He was determined, he told friends, to win the national championship at Forest Hills and recapture the Davis Cup.

American tennis had fallen into the doldrums. The aging Tilden was unable to retain his U.S. men's title in 1930 and left-handed Johnny Doeg beat Francis T. Hunter in the final.

In 1931, when the United States picked a Davis Cup team to play an inter-zone match against the British, Ellsworth Vines was ignored. The American squad consisted of Sidney B. Wood, Jr., Frank Shields, George Lott and John Van Ryn. The Yanks lost to the Britons, who went on to bow to the Musketeers of France.

Returning home for the grass court circuit leading to the nationals, the Davis Cuppers found they had to contend with the lean young man from California who hit a ball with the force of a rocket and played as if his life were at stake.

Now nineteen, hardly known, Vines suddenly emerged as the sensation of the summer tour. With the Davis Cup stars in Europe he had won at Seabright and Longwood in Boston. At Newport, he encountered the world's best players, assembling after the Cup campaign. There he defeated Frank Shields and England's Fred Perry in successive rounds. Then came the nationals at Forest Hills.

On the basis of his spectacular season, Vines was seeded first but Perry headed the foreign list and strong competition was expected from such players as Shields, Wood, Doeg and Lott.

Vines bulled his way into the semifinals, losing only one set, and there, rallying from two sets down, he scored an impressive victory over Perry. In the final he took on Lott, a strong, polished player. But the Californian made up for his mistakes by the boldness with which he pulled off winners whenever he fell behind and won 7–9, 6–3, 9–7, 7–5.

Next year the U.S. Lawn Tennis Association did not dare leave Vines off its Davis Cup team. By this time, hopes of a tennis revival had sprung up in the United States and many were predicting young Vines was destined to be another Tilden. Vines, along with Shields, Allison, Van Ryn and Wood, went to Europe to prepare for Wimbledon and the inter-zone Davis Cup matches.

Wood was the defending champion at Wimbledon. Henri Cochet, who had just won his fifth French crown, and the ebullient Borotra represented France while Perry and Bunny Austin played for England. Vines and Austin swept into the final, the American yielding only thirteen games in his quarter-final and semifinal matches. It was no contest. He crushed the Englishman with the loss of only six games.

The British hailed Vines as the new wonder boy, successor to Tilden, Cochet and Lacoste. It seemed inevitable he would carry his nation into the Davis Cup Challenge Round, then wrest the trophy from France. But the prophets failed to reckon with the Californian's inconsistency and the determination of the Musketeers.

In the inter-zone matches the Americans faced a strong German team with a formidable player named Gottfried von Cramm, born of nobility in the town of Nettlingen and coached by the famed Roman Najuch. The United States barely squeezed through. Vines won both his singles matches while Frank Shields, playing in the other individual spot, lost twice, leaving the decision to the doubles where the champion team of Wilmer Allison and John Van Ryn finally struck the winning blow.

Now came France. Allison, a rugged Texan with a strong volley and attacking game, was substituted for Shields. Still, the competition looked keen. Jean Borotra, who had quit his team in a pique over newspaper criticism, was persuaded to return, and the French elected to use him and Cochet in singles and Cochet and Jacques Brugnon in doubles.

From the start the Americans were demoralized when Vines succumbed to Borotra in the opening duel. The Bounding Basque, calling upon hidden resources, played one of his greatest matches. Running, scooting, attacking incessantly, he won in four sets while his teammate Cochet duplicated the feat against Allison. The French were up 2–0.

Allison and Van Ryn succeeded in taking the doubles

but the U.S. cause remained shaky. Both Allison and Vines had to win their final singles against a pair of inspired Frenchmen. Although Allison had played two tough matches in a row, he put up a stirring fight against Borotra, gaining a 5–3 lead in the fifth set with one match point. Serving what appeared to be a double fault at match point, Borotra went to the net to shake hands only to be ordered back by the umpire because the lineman had failed to make a call. Thus reprieved the Frenchman went on to pull out the match.

In the meaningless fifth match Vines, discouraged, played lackadaisically against Cochet who won the first two sets easily as his opponent merely went through the motions. Then Vines had a change of heart and he began blasting away at the ball. Unnerved by this sudden surge Cochet saw his game fall apart and Vines ran out the victory. It was the Frenchman's first Davis Cup defeat in six years.

Cochet had a chance for revenge in the U.S. final at Forest Hills. But Vines was at his peak and needed only fifty-nine minutes to crush the great French star, 6–4, 6–4, 6–4, for his second straight American title.

Despite his failure to win back the Davis Cup, Vines was the undisputed Number One tennis player in the world. Pro promoters waved handsome contracts, endeavoring to entice him into a world tour with Big Bill Tilden.

Vines made a mistake: He decided to play one more year, 1933, before turning pro. Perhaps he was overanxious to end on a high note or perhaps his erratic tendency took hold. Whatever, he had a disappointing season.

In the final at Wimbledon he lost a big match—one of the classics—to Australia's Jack Crawford. In the Davis Cup inter-zones he dropped both his singles matches to Perry and Austin. Playing Perry, just as he was preparing to serve with match point against him, he twisted his ankle and fainted. The final ignominy came in the U.S. Nationals when Bryan (Bitsy) Grant, the pint-sized retriever from

Atlanta, crushed him in a fourth round match 6–3, 6–3, 6–3.

Nevertheless, Vines' appeal as a professional was apparently untarnished. Signing a lucrative contract, he joined Tilden on a highly successful tour. The opening match at Madison Square Garden drew 14,637 spectators with receipts totaling $30,125. The two played seventy-two cities, grossing $243,000, and Vines, winning 47 matches to Tilden's 26, collected $52,000.

In 1938 Vines held his world pro championship by beating Perry in a cross-country series, 49 matches to 35. In 1939, Don Budge took charge, defeating Vines in a close series, 21–18.

Shortly afterwards Vines stored his rackets away and took up golf, becoming a successful teaching professional who held top jobs at country clubs in California and Long Island. In 1961 he gained the semifinals in the PGA championship at Oakmont Country Club outside Pittsburgh but lost to Walter Burkemo who was in turn beaten for the title by Sam Snead.

Win or lose, golf became his main passion. The former American champ, who had swept through the tennis world like a whirlwind, never swung another racket and never cared to. Said H. Ellsworth Vines: "There is nothing in tennis to compare with the pressure of looking at a four-foot putt."

TWO
6

Fred Perry — The British Master

There was a majestic air about Britain's Frederick J. Perry. As tall, dark and handsome as the proverbial Hollywood movie star he had strong, regular features and neatly-combed, raven-black hair. He could also hit a tennis ball and as a result it was Perry who, during the 1930's, gave England a brilliant, if short-lived taste of tennis glory.

A.W. Gore had been Britain's last men's singles champion at Wimbledon who had won his final of three titles in 1909. Ten years had elapsed since England had taken the doubles and as for the Davis Cup, symbol of world court supremacy, the last time Britain had held it was 1912. Hence the cradle of the lob and drop-shot was more than ready when Perry came out of the London suburbs and with a companion, Henry W. (Bunny) Austin, raised his country to the pinnacle of the sport.

Starting in 1933 Perry's reign lasted four years. The swashbuckling Briton won three straight Wimbledons and as many U.S. titles, not to mention Australian and French crowns. With Austin's help he loosened France's six-year grip on the Davis Cup and kept the silver trophy on British soil with three successful defenses.

For the next thirty-five years, Britain never came close to winning the cup, failing even to gain the Challenge Round. Nor was the champagne toast raised to a British champion at Wimbledon, although Jaroslav Drobny, a Czech defector who once called London home, won the tournament in 1954.

Perry fit the mold of a great champion. Opponents called him egotistical but friends maintained he was just supremely self-confident. Moving with long, easy strides he gave the same impression of aloofness that had characterized Big Bill Tilden. He intensified the image by smoking a pipe and rarely engaging in locker room gab sessions.

Compared with the game's immortal stylists and power players, the Englishman could not be rated as a classic stroke-maker. His shot production was average but he had a devastating forehand, backed up by a boldness that few contemporaries possessed.

Perry's forehand, which he hit with a Continental grip that left the face of his racket open, required strong wrist action. His wrists were like steel bands and he developed the stroke into an accurate and explosive weapon. He also moved with speed and grace and such great hitters as Tilden and Vines found it almost impossible to put a ball beyond his long reach.

Perry was born in 1909 in Stockport, Lancashire, the son of an artisan. While he was still in school, his family moved to the London suburb of Ealing to be near Parliament, since Perry's father had been elected as a Labor member.

Although Ealing was a tennis center with numerous public and private courts Perry was not exposed to the game until his late teens. Instead, he played table tennis, competing in tournaments and winning several trophies. He was going on nineteen when he seriously picked up his first racket. Compared with the paddles he was accustomed to, the racket was like a telephone pole. But he took to the sport immediately; it was, after all, table tennis on an enlarged scale.

The game came easy to him and before the first year was out he won the 1928 Middlesex junior doubles crown. When he brought the trophy home, his father was delighted.

"Son," he said, "if you want to play this game, you must be the best. We will have to get you some lessons."

Perry got the best coaching and progressed rapidly. Strong and athletic, he had natural talent and his table tennis experience had developed his speed and reflexes. He retained his whip-like wrist stroke, although this violated the fundamental rules of a classic swing.

Within two years Perry was one of the best players in England. In his first Wimbledon appearance, in 1930, he reached the round of sixteen. Selected on a team that toured South America, he won the Argentine championship in Buenos Aires.

Meanwhile, fans were getting excited about another player, Bunny Austin. Austin began learning tennis when he was six, coached by his father. While at Repton, he won the public schools championship four straight years. He captured the junior crown in 1922 and the Middlesex and South of England championships in 1927. A student at Cambridge he captained the varsity in 1928.

Austin seemed to have all the ingredients to lead Britain out of the tennis wilderness. Though rather short and thin he possessed a beautiful style and was well-grounded. He was the nation's top player when Fred Perry, trying out for the Davis Cup team in 1931, carried him to five hard sets. England was placing its hopes on the pair.

It would be another two years before they would really begin to fulfill their promise. In the 1931 French Championships Austin, troubled most his life with leg cramps, defaulted because of a twisted ankle while Perry lost to Italy's Giorgio Di Stefani. At Wimbledon, after having one match point, Austin succumbed to America's Frank Shields in the quarter-finals. Another Yank, Sidney Wood, eliminated Perry in the semifinals.

The two fared somewhat better in the Inter-zone Davis Cup matches between Britain and the United States. Big Bill Tilden had turned professional and Ellsworth Vines had been overlooked by U.S. selectors.

In the opening singles the Americans got off to a 2–0 lead when Austin and Perry bowed respectively to Wood and Shields. But the Britons won the doubles and then, with Perry toppling an over-confident Wood while Austin trimmed Shields, they managed to squeeze out the match.

In the Challenge Round, France's Henri Cochet was invincible as he smashed both Austin and Perry and teamed with Jacques Brugnon for the important doubles victory— virtually a one-man sweep.

In 1932, Perry was again beaten at Wimbledon while Austin was smothered in the final by Vines. That year the British Davis Cup team failed to even make the Challenge Round.

Tennis greatness did not dawn for Perry and the British Empire until 1933. That year he won the first of his three American championships by beating Australia's Jack Crawford, the Wimbledon titleholder, in five sets. It was also the year he and Austin finally overtook the fading Frenchmen in the Davis Cup, winning 3–2. Perry was magnificent in beating Cochet 8–10, 6–4, 8–6, 3–6, 6–1 and newcomer Andre Merlin 4–6, 8–6, 6–2, 7–5. The other point came on an Austin triumph over Merlin and a four-year British reign was launched.

Perry repeated as American champ in 1934, winning a five-set duel from Wilmer Allison, and captured his third title two years later, this time outlasting Don Budge in a five-set marathon with the final set going eighteen games. He began his Wimbledon string in 1934, beating Crawford, and his victim in the 1935 and 1936 finals was Germany's Baron Gottfried von Cramm.

Turning professional Perry made his debut against Vines at Madison Square Garden in the winter of 1937. The tour grossed $412,181 and Vines won 32 of the 61 matches. Next year, with a gross of $175,000, Vines again had the edge, 49–35. In 1939 Perry and Budge made a tour, the latter winning about three-fourths of the games.

Returning to England with a comfortable bankroll, Perry, among other things, became tennis correspondent for a London daily. Years later, still fit and tanned, his hair white and his lips clamped on a pipe stem, he roamed the courts at Wimbledon, Forest Hills and Stade Roland Garros, writing about the game he had once dominated for Britain's brief reign.

TWO
7
Don Budge — The Redoubtable Redhead

In the late 1930's a redhaired comet streaked out of the West to set the tennis world ablaze. His name was Don Budge and he is considered by many to be foremost among the all-time greats.

As a youngster Budge was slow to take up tennis, preferring other sports. He won his basketball letter in high school and played football with neighborhood teams. His big passion was baseball and he scarcely touched a tennis racket until he was fifteen. His brother Lloyd, four years older, loved the game and kept trying to lure his sibling onto the courts. Don would hit a few balls, then stroll off to the baseball diamond or hockey field.

One June night in 1930 the older brother began needling the younger at family dinner. The California State Boys' Tennis Tournament was starting in a week or so and if Don had any gumption, said Lloyd, he would go out and win it. Everyone laughed except Don.

The following day he began to practice in secret. Day after day he worked on his game until the tournament opened. Playing in corduroy pants he swept to the final and, wearing a pair of white ducks furnished by Lloyd, he whipped his opponent 6–0, 6–4. He had won the first tournament he ever entered and, in the process, caught the tennis bug.

Budge was a court artisan without flaw. Most tennis greats compensate for certain weaknesses by concentrating on their particular strengths. Budge mastered every stroke and became the complete player.

He hit a serve like a cannon-shot and possessed a powerful forehand. He covered the court with grace and ease. He never had to compromise his attack or rush the net because of weakness in ground strokes. Sound off both wings from the back court, he could move confidently to the net when he pleased, ending the point with a formidable volley or smash. His temper was smooth and he accepted controversial line calls graciously. His powers of concentration were remarkable and he had the ability to forget past errors and apply himself to the point at hand.

But it was the Budge backhand that was his deadliest weapon. He picked it up as a boy using his brother's heavy rackets. In baseball Don threw righthanded and batted lefthanded. Consequently he started his tennis backhand with a two-fisted baseball grip. The left merely steadied and guided the swing until it was underway. The result was a ferocious, whip-like action—similar to that of an uncoiling spring—which unleashed a mighty shot from almost any position. Budge could deliver these bolts from the wrong side down the line or cross-court for clean winners.

His appearance on the scene ended a ten-year U.S. Davis Cup drought. He went on to score an unprecedented sweep of international amateur championships and to rule professional ranks until World War II. In 1937 he won the Wimbledon and United States trophies. In 1938 he repeated these triumphs and added the French and Australian crowns in a "Grand Slam" that escaped such predecessors as Little Bill Johnston, Big Bill Tilden, Ellsworth Vines and such later stars as Jack Kramer, Pancho Gonzalez, Frank Sedgman and Lew Hoad. Not for twenty-four years would a player duplicate the feat: and it was another redhead, Rod Laver of Australia.

The Budge family was of modest means but they had athletic ability to spare. Don's father played soccer with the Glasgow Rangers in his native Scotland. During a practice match he was seriously injured and subsequently contracted pneumonia. When bronchitis developed he was advised to seek a warmer climate if he wanted to live. So the Scotsman moved to Oakland, California, where he met and married a pretty Irish colleen who in time bore him two competitive sons.

Once tennis had become Don's consuming passion other laurels began to fall to him. In 1932 he won the Pacific Coast junior championship and in 1933, beating Charlie Hunt who had crushed his hopes in two previous finals, he took the California State junior crown. That same year, the stringy, gawky-looking lad of eighteen also entered the State senior tournament and won. To do this he had to defeat such players as Edward Chandler, holder of the national intercollegiate title, and Bobby Riggs, later to become one of his arch rivals on the professional and amateur trail.

By this time the red-haired youngster had begun to attract attention and the Northern California Tennis Association decided to enter him in the Junior Championships at Culver, Indiana. There he captured his first national title, beating Gene Mako of Los Angeles in the final. Becoming fast friends, the pair later teamed to win two national doubles crowns and help regain the Davis Cup.

Mako, a good-looking, blond youngster with a breezy manner, played a big role in loosening up Budge's personality. Free and easy, even a bit prankish among friends, Don was inclined to be bashful in public. He would often cross the street to keep from running into a girl, and he had a fear of saying or doing the wrong thing. After a few months with the extrovert Mako, he lost most of his inhibitions.

Budge was pretty much of a double novice when he teamed with Mako in 1933 for the National Clay Court Championships and his partner quickly warned him: "I don't care what you do, Don. Just don't miss the ball." In the beginning Mako was the team general and Budge always credited him with a major share of their success. But after Budge grew to championship stature it was Mako who was usually blamed by press and public for any setbacks they suffered.

Budge was nineteen when he first went East in 1934 to play the grass court circuit. En route, he stopped off in Chicago for the National Clay Court event where he defeated Frankie Parker in the semifinals and lost to Bryan (Bitsy) Grant, Atlanta's "Mighty Atom," in the final. This, however, was on a heavy, slow surface where the retriever, Bitsy, was at his best.

The California redhead didn't exactly set the world on fire with his first appearance in the stuffy, fashionable East, where the sport had its American birth. He was far from the dynamic player he would become.

Fretting with an unsure forehand, he lost at Seabright in the second round to Henry Prusoff of Seattle; and at Longwood to Berkeley Bell 6–1, 6–0, 6–0. He fared little better at Rye and Newport. In the Nationals at Forest Hills, he avenged his clay court loss to Bitsy Grant but failed to make much of an impression—except on one observer.

Walter Pate, who would one day be Budge's Davis Cup captain and tutor, was on the sidelines. "That boy has the makings of a future champion," Pate told companions. "His forehand needs a little work, but he's the fellow we need to win back the Davis Cup."

When Pate was asked to serve as Davis Cup captain he accepted only on condition that the U.S. Lawn Tennis Association throw out all the old players who had been losing to France for the past several years and let him start with a new team. "I had my eye on Budge," he said later. "I knew he'd be ready in a couple of years."

In 1935, Pate invited Budge to join the squad in Mexico. The gaunt, long-limbed Californian had already attempted to correct his faulty forehand.

He had first learned to hit the ball with the eastern grip, known as the "shake hands" grip. It was used by Tilden, Vinnie Richards and most other leading players of the period. However, when Berkeley Bell, George Lott and Gregory Mangin came to the West Coast with their western grips, Budge was impressed by their top-spin power and he changed.

In the western, first popularized by Little Bill Johnston, the palm of the hand grips the back of the racket from behind as if picking it off the floor. It is effective for high-bounding balls on asphalt surfaces but not as good for low bouncers on soft turf.

Sidney Wood was among the players who urged Budge to return to the eastern grip. Tom Stow, coach of the University of California and pro at the Claremont Country Club, spent an entire winter experimenting with various forehand grips for Don. It took Pate to clinch it. At Mexico he instructed him to use the flat eastern grip. This time the change was permanent but Budge never really mastered the stroke until 1937.

The year 1935 marked Budge's emergence as an international player although he was barely twenty years old and his game had not fully matured. At Philadelphia in a preliminary Davis Cup round against Australia Budge was matched with Jack Crawford, the world's Number Two ranking amateur behind England's Fred Perry.

He stunned everyone by winning the first two sets easily, then fell victim to a common error—particularly among the uninitiated. He relaxed and, before he knew it, found himself on the defensive. Crawford tied the score at two sets each and moved ahead in the fifth and decisive set 5–3 and 30–15 on service. A double-fault by the Australian and two good returns by Budge enabled the Californian to take the set 13–11 and with it the match. The marathon, played in 105-degree heat, lasted four hours and ten minutes.

"As soon as that final point was won I developed leg cramps," Don admitted afterward. "I would have been forced to default. As I hobbled off the court, I heard a murmur from the crowd. I looked around. Crawford had passed out cold."

The victory meant an overseas trip for the U.S. Davis Cuppers, who were to play at Wimbledon before meeting Germany in the Inter-Zone final and, if victorious, the British in the Challenge Round.

The trip gave rise to various anecdotes about Budge, such as the way he and his buddy Mako almost missed the boat. Team members and officials awaited them nervously on the ocean liner's deck. Just as the gangplank was going up the waywards rushed aboard, bare-headed and in shirt sleeves, explaining that they had simply been doing some last-minute shopping.

Then there was the time, just before reaching England, that Budge was awakened by a knock on his door. "Pardon me, sir," said a ship official. "May I see your visa?"

Sleepy and confused, Budge rubbed his eyes. "You mean my visor," he corrected. "What in blazes do you want to see that for?"

"I've been in this business twenty years," sniffed the official, "and I know how to pronounce 'visa.'"

Budge, still shaking off the cobwebs, was nonplussed. "I don't care how long you've been in the business," said he. "I've been wearing eyeshades for years and from where I come we call them visors."

Two other stories, one perhaps apocryphal, are told about Budge to indicate his relaxed and ingenuous attitude. On the night before the team faced Germany he was walking down the hotel corridor at 3 A.M. Noticing a light still on in the room of senior squad member Wilmer Allison, he knocked on the door.

"I never sleep before a big match," Allison lamented. "I guess you're restless too."

"Restless?" said Budge. "No, I'm getting a drink of water. I'll sleep four more hours before breakfast."

English sports writers reported that Budge, appearing on the center court at Wimbledon for the first time, waved his racket at the Queen in her royal box and that, much to the gallery's amusement, Her Majesty waved back. The tale became legend despite Budge's attempts to discredit it. "I may have been green," he insisted, "but not that green."

This first overseas campaign was at once disappointing and successful. In the Inter-Zone Budge scored singles victories over German aces Henner Henkel and Gottfried von Cramm. At Wimbledon, though he upset Britain's Bunny Austin, he succumbed to Austin and Fred Perry in the Challenge Round. Teammate Allison also lost both his singles and England won 5–0. On the profit side of the ledger, however, Budge had a chance to study the great Perry in action. Impressed by the Englishman's ability to move quickly to the net behind a forcing shot, he made a mental note of the tactic and thus strengthened his own game.

Budge got off to a bad start in 1936, losing again to the relentless Bitsy Grant. But he recovered to whip Jack Crawford and Andrian Quist of Australia in the Davis Cup matches at Germantown, Pennsylvania and he scored triumphs over such players as Bunny Austin, Bobby Riggs and Frank Parker. In the two major championships in which he played—Wimbledon and the U.S. Nationals—he was cut down by Perry. In the semifinals at Wimbledon the English stylist eliminated him in four sets while in the final at Forest Hills he won in five despite the fact that Budge led 5–3 in the fifth set. The Californian's reversal was unexpected since he was only 21, sinewy and strong. There appeared no reason why—even attacking the net as aggressively as he did— he should not be able to stand up under a normal five set match.

The reason came out later. Budge and Gene Mako, who spent their leisure hours listening to records, playing cards and drinking rich malted milks, had suffered stomachaches two days before the final. The malts were apparently to blame.

Still, during that season, Perry was the only player to beat Budge on grass and the redhead reaped a measure of vengeance later that summer by defeating the dark-haired Briton on cement in the Pacific Southwest tournament. Shortly afterwards Perry turned professional, leaving Budge and Germany's Von Cramm to fight it out for the top amateur position.

If there were any doubts about who would emerge the best they were quickly banished in 1937. Coming into his own, Budge swept through his early Davis Cup tests without losing a match. He smashed Japan's Jiro Yamagishi 6–2, 6–2, 6–4. He won from Australia's Crawford and John Bromwich. He beat Parker and Von Cramm for his first Wimbledon championship. Then, in the fifth and deciding game of the Inter-Zone final at Wimbledon, he climaxed his European campaign with a dramatic victory over Von Cramm. Many rate it the greatest Davis Cup match ever played.

"War talk was everywhere," Budge recalled. "Hitler was doing everything he could to stir up Germany. The atmosphere was filled with tension although Von Cramm was a known anti-Nazi and remained one of the finest gentlemen and most popular players on the circuit.

"The two teams had split the first four matches, so the series hinged on our final singles match. I remember just before we took the court, Von Cramm was called to the telephone. It was a long distance call from Hitler himself exhorting Von Cramm to win for the Fatherland. Gottfried came out pale and serious and played as if his life depended on every point."

The German won the first two sets. Budge won the next two but fell behind 1–4 in the fifth. At this point he decided to take desperate measures. Attacking Von Cramm's service and going to the net behind it, he got the matching break in the seventh game, making the score 3–4, and held to tie it at 4–4.

The score went to 5–5 and then 6–6. In the thirteenth game, Budge achieved another break and five times had match point on his own service, only to have the German fight back to make the game score deuce.

"The crowd was so quiet I am sure they could hear us breathing," Budge said afterward.

On the sixth match point there was a prolonged rally. Von Cramm set up a lob. Budge raced back and returned it. Von Cramm then hit a forehand cross-court. Budge tore after the ball, got his racket on it and took a desperate swing, sprawling to the court. It was a placement—game, set, match and Davis Cup series.

The final score was 6–8, 5–7, 6–4, 6–2, 8–6. The match ended at 8:45 P.M. in semi-darkness. The two players went to their dressing rooms, relaxed, dressed and returned more than an hour later to find most of the crowd still on hand, buzzing over the spectacular duel.

Budge followed up this triumph with an outstanding performance in the Davis Cup Challenge Round against the British that returned the trophy to the United States for the first time since 1926. He scored singles victories over Charlie Hare and Bunny Austin of Britain and teamed with Mako for another point in the doubles. The Americans won 4–1, Frankie Parker splitting his singles assignments.

The gangling Californian returned home to a hero's welcome and was acclaimed the world's Number One amateur player. He reaffirmed that position by sweeping into the final of the National Championships without loss of a set and then scoring his third straight triumph over Von Cramm.

Now strong pressure was on Budge to turn pro. An international tour against his old rival, Fred Perry, would be a tremendous success, promotors argued. But Budge resisted. He felt he owed more to the game and it would be selfish to capitalize so quickly on his fame.

There followed, in 1938, a triumph that would hence be the supreme goal of all young tennis players. Budge achieved the game's first Grand Slam. He began it with the Australian championship, then added the French. His second straight Wimbledon, without losing a set, made it three down and one to go. In the meantime he helped defend the Davis Cup, beating Aussies Bromwich and Quist at the Germantown Cricket Club. Then, completing a sweep of major titles that no one had ever accomplished, he retained his U.S. crown with loss of only a single set.

That fall, with no more worlds to conquer in amateur ranks, Budge turned pro. "I don't feel my debt to the U.S. Lawn Tennis Association has been squared in full," he said, "but I am sure they will realize I must think of my future. I want to buy a nice home for my father and mother in California. I want to provide a few comforts for those who have made such sacrifices for me."

No rancor could be found among America's tennis officials when Budge, just twenty-three, made his professional debut against Ellsworth Vines at Madison Square Garden on January 3, 1939, before a crowd of 16,000.

Though he had trouble adjusting to the indoor conditions, he won his opening match and went on to take the cross-country series from Vines, 21 matches to 18. Then he played a series with Perry, his old amateur nemesis, winning 18–11.

In 1940, Budge emerged the victor in a tour which included Perry, Bobby Riggs and Frank Kovacs. In 1941, just before the United States entered the war, he crushed an aging but brilliant Tilden, 51 matches to 7. He joined the Air Force and after five years returned to the circuit. Overweight and over-age, he lost to a spryer Bobby Riggs, 23–21, and that was the signal for him to quit.

Walter Pate cited Budge's ability to make tough assignments look easy as proof of his greatness. "His footwork and body control were so perfect he seldom made a jerky motion," Pate said. "He just flowed into his shots. In all the matches I saw him play he never fell once."

That Budge never lost a crucial match during 1937 and 1938 is "one of the great all-time sports achievements," according to Pate.

"I think this rates even above Bobby Jones' Grand Slam in golf. It's fantastic that a man should be able to go through two years without losing a match except for two contests at the tail end of 1938 when Budge had already decided to turn pro and wasn't half trying."

"When Budge was in his prime, no player, past or present,

could have beaten him," Sidney Wood said. "It was like playing against a concrete wall. Don used a tremendously heavy racket weighing about 16½ ounces. It felt like a telephone pole. He wasn't a wristy player and he didn't seem to swing hard. But the ball came back like a rock."

Bobby Riggs called the California redhead "the most devastating and impressive player I have ever seen."

Riggs summed it up: "Tilden often toyed with his opponents—he would tease them by letting them get close. Vines was inconsistent, a world-beater one day and a patsy the next. Not Budge. He was not only extremely steady, he was explosive. He could blow you off the court 6–0, 6–0, 6–0 before you knew it."

TWO
8

The War Years

World War II interrupted what may have been a long reign by Don Budge and perhaps also significantly changed the complexion of the game. With no war how far might Bobby Riggs have gone? Would Joe Hunt, as many predicted, have climbed to the top of the ladder, leaving Jack Kramer to languish in his shadow?

Riggs, a little craftsman for whom tennis was a thinking man's game, won the first of his two national championships in 1939 at the age of twenty-one, battled into the final the next year losing to Oklahoman Don McNeill, and in 1941 beat talented Frank Kovacs for the title.

Bobby was one of the most underrated players ever to swing a racket. Lacking the big power game, he nevertheless had no weakness. He was quick, clever and deceptive and he chopped the big guys down to his size.

Both Don Budge and Jack Kramer acknowledged that they preferred to play anybody other than the canny Riggs. Asked shortly after the war whom he considered the best modern player, Big Bill Tilden replied unhesitatingly, "Riggs."

Riggs was followed by Ted Schroeder, Joe Hunt and Frank Parker.

Schroeder, who teamed with Kramer to win the national doubles in 1940 and 1941, won the singles crown in 1942, defeating Frank Parker in the final. Built like a middleweight fighter, with a bulldog face, strong arms and shoulders and a pair of bandy legs that refused to quit, he hit the ball well, was agile and quick. But his forte was determination and he was toughest when he was down.

Hunt also came from California, a tall, handsome youngster who, if he had stayed in Hollywood, might have made millions as a movie star. Fair-complexioned, blond and lean, he moved over the court with effortless grace. His strokes, taught him by his father, were classic. He had a beautiful touch at the net and an unerring overhead.

He won a series of junior and intercollegiate titles and was twenty-five when he faced Kramer in the 1943 final at Forest Hills. The two players were alike in many respects. Both had the fresh appearance of All-American boys, and both possessed the "Big Game" with powerful services and good net attacks. Although not at his best, Hunt—relentless in the final set—beat Kramer 6–3, 6–8, 10–8, 6–0.

But Hunt's promising career was cut short when he was killed February 2, 1945, in an airplane training accident in Florida.

He was succeeded as national champion by Frank Parker, a slender protégé of Mercer Beasley. Unlike Kramer and Hunt, who had natural ability, Parker achieved fame through hard work and dedication.

Under Beasley's watchful eye, Parker drilled himself hours at a time until he was able to hit a serve on a dime and knock a forehand drive through a twelve-inch hole. He lacked the big guns of his opponents but usually levelled them with rapid rifle fire.

Parker, slender, bespectacled and normally unemotional, won the national crown in 1944 and 1945, both times defeating Bill Talbert in the final.

William F. (Billy) Talbert came out of Cincinnati and established himself first as a player bucking overwhelming odds, then as Davis Cup captain, adviser to young players and author of numerous books on tennis.

He was a diabetic, one of the first to prove he could succeed in a tough competitive sport. He ranked among the U.S. Top Ten for fourteen years, was four times winner of the U.S. grass court doubles championship with Gardnar Mulloy, held the national mixed doubles crown with Margaret Osborne for four years and won numerous other national and international honors.

He was cut from the same bolt as Riggs, although of a less bombastic personality. A court strategist, he lacked raw power but compensated for it through knowledge and superior tactics.

Talbert was instrumental in helping develop Tony Trabert, a fellow Cincinnatian who won the Wimbledon and American championships and teamed with Vic Seixas to win the Davis Cup from Australia's Lew Hoad and Ken Rosewall in 1954. Talbert, a Wall Street executive, was an adviser to many young players and was one of the country's most popular Davis Cup captains.

But as the war years drew to a close, Parker and Talbert had to move aside with the advent of Jack Kramer and the "Big Game" in 1946.

TWO
9
Jack Kramer — They Called Him "The King"

They called him "The King"—and no one in tennis better fit the mold.

Jack Kramer's record as an amateur—two national titles

and only a single Wimbledon—fell far short of successes hung up by Bill Tilden, Don Budge, Fred Perry and Rod Laver. His career was interrupted by a war and plagued by injuries and bad luck.

Yet in any roll-call of the all-time greats, his name is always near the top. Most students of the sport rank him with Tilden, Budge and Laver, in varying order, as one of the best players ever to pick up a racket. No one has ever questioned his vast influence on the game.

Jack Kramer's era was 1946–1954. During that period he helped wrest the Davis Cup from Australia, which had held it since 1939 with a six-year hiatus because of World War II. He won both the amateur and professional championship of the world. Taking control of the pro tour, he became its most prosperous and controversial promoter. More than any other man, he was responsible for the removal of barriers to open tennis.

He could wreck a nation's Davis Cup team with a stroke of the pen—and he frequently did. He tossed $100,000 and $150,000 contracts around as easily as some people did quarter tips and he collected the greatest players of his time, manipulating them like puppets on a string. He enjoyed the fear and respect of the national amateur associations. His voice carried weight in the highest tennis councils.

For close to a decade, they called tennis "the big, green world of Jack Kramer."

One of the most astute businessmen in sports, Big Jake as he became known, was a man of contrasts. Perennially boyish-looking, handsome in an All-American way with a warm, bubbling personality, he turned killer whenever he faced an opponent across the net. He was cold and calculating in his dealings, although his sternest critics admitted he was completely honest. There was no way to be neutral about Jack Kramer. You either adored or disliked him tremendously.

Although men served hard, went to the net and practiced a forceful attack as far back as Dick Sears in the 1880's,

Kramer was credited with introducing the modern game of the big serve and volley. He didn't actually introduce these tactics but, according to Bill Talbert, he utilized them better than anyone before. He became the first symbol of power tennis.

Jack had a crackling service, not as hard as that of Pancho Gonzales and Ellsworth Vines, but he managed to get an inordinate number of first deliveries in court. This put his foes immediately on the defensive. He was a master volleyer but his big weapon was his forehand, which he hit with a little spin for control and which he could drill through a keyhole.

A natural athlete, six feet, one inch in height and about 175 pounds in his heyday, Kramer took up tennis reluctantly through the persuasion of his parents.

Born August 1, 1921, in Las Vegas, Nevada, son of a railroad engineer, he was sports-minded from the beginning. His ambition was to be a major league baseball player and at the age of seven he owned half a dozen bats, seven mitts, a catcher's mask and a bucketful of baseballs. He spent his spare time playing baseball, basketball or football with the other kids in a corner lot—but not tennis.

It was actually football that introduced young Kramer to the game. He came home one afternoon from a particularly violent skirmish, his nose broken, a few ribs cracked and blood streaming down his chin.

His mother was appalled. His father was shaken.

"This simply can't go on," said Mrs. Kramer. "If you want to play sports, why don't you find something less brutal?"

"You should play tennis," advised Papa Kramer. "It's a good, fast game and a lot of exercise."

"Tennis?" exploded Jack. "That's a sissy game."

Further persuasion by his mother influenced Kramer to give tennis a try and the bitterness of the pill was allayed somewhat when the family moved from Las Vegas to San Bernardino, California.

At first Jack was ashamed to be seen on the street with a

Tom Brown, Jr., also just out of the service. Brown had been the tournament sensation, eliminating defending champion Frank Parker in the quarter-finals and sweeping to a straight-set triumph over Gardnar Mulloy, the star of the grass court circuit, in the next-to-last round.

"Can Kramer beat Brown?" That's what everybody was asking as the two California comets clashed in Forest Hills' first post-war final.

The first set was a battle of heavyweight hitters swapping mortar shells. Brown rallied from behind to go ahead 7–6 only to be broken in the fifteenth game. From then on, it was a cinch for Kramer, who won 9–7, 6–3, 6–0. He had finally arrived.

In December, Kramer and Schroeder crushed Australia 5–0 to recapture the Davis Cup. They not only defeated Bromwich and Dinny Pails in singles but teamed for an avenging doubles triumph over Bromwich and Quist, winning in straight sets.

No tennis player can claim greatness without winning Wimbledon. Conscious of this, Kramer invaded England in July, 1947, and leaving no doubt that he was the best amateur in the world, demolished his old friend and rival, Tom Brown, in the final. The match, witnessed by King George, took only forty-five minutes. Jack returned to the United States and in September scored his second straight American victory, turning the tables on Drobny in the semifinals and beating two-time winner Frank Parker in the last round.

By this time, Kramer's ears had become sensitive to the pleasant clang of cash registers.

Bobby Riggs had defeated Don Budge in the 1946 professional tour and promoter Jack Harris was looking around for a fresh face. His eyes had not missed the exploits of Jack Kramer.

Just in case Kramer might be hesitant, Riggs chose to stir the pot a bit by boasting publicly: "I can beat Jack Kramer on grass, on clay, on cement, indoors or outdoors."

Kramer didn't need to be goaded.

He called Riggs' hand, turning professional in 1948 for a guaranteed $50,000. "Riggs is a defensive player," Kramer retorted. "I don't think there's a defensive player in the world who can beat me."

This made good grist for the publicity mill. Spectators came out in droves to watch the rookie pro crush the boastful Riggs in their cross-country tour, 69 matches to 20. Jack collected an extra bonus of $37,000.

He was now on the escalator of success.

"I had been scratching out a meager living in amateur tennis," he explained later of his move into pro ranks. "I had a side job for $60 a week with a meat-packing company. When I started catching cold, I decided I had had it."

Riggs succeeded Harris as promoter in 1949 and signed Pancho Gonzales, who had replaced Kramer as national amateur champion, for a tour against the new pro king. Now twenty-eight and at the peak of his game, Kramer also smothered Gonzales, 96 matches to 27, and in 1951 overwhelmed Pancho Segura 64–28.

It was in 1952 that Kramer took over the pro reins, after a contract dispute with Riggs, and began his long and lucrative promotional career.

Kramer found it expedient later to divest himself of his promotional responsibilities, but maintained a close association with the game. He became a television commentator for tournaments at Wimbledon and Forest Hills. He bought real estate, a stable of race horses and engaged in other enterprises.

He traveled the world—mostly at his own expense—to preach the advantages of open tennis. As the sport moved into the 1970's, there was world-wide agitation for a man to rule tennis with an iron hand, a virtual czar.

The name most mentioned: John A. Kramer.

Pancho Gonzales — Latin Fire and Fury

When Jack Kramer decided to turn pro after sweeping the Wimbledon and U.S. titles in 1947, it was feared the bottom would drop out of American tennis. There were a number of competent players but none conceivably in position to don Big Jake's mantle as undisputed king of the amateur game.

The heir apparent appeared to be Kramer's closest friend and regular doubles partner, Frederick R. (Ted) Schroeder, Jr. Like Kramer, Schroeder grew up under Perry Jones' wing in Southern California.

Schroeder won the junior singles championship in 1939, the year Kramer, never a junior singles titleholder, teamed with C.E. Olewine for the doubles crown. Schroeder and Kramer won the national doubles in 1940 and 1941 and, after serving in World War II, came back to capture their third title in 1947.

Schroeder had also won the national singles championship at Forest Hills in 1942, while Kramer was just maturing, so he seemed a natural successor to his old buddy.

Schroeder was a stocky, athletically-built young man of tenacity and determination. He walked with a quick, bow-legged gait, his shoulders hunched and his head thrust forward like an angry bulldog's. He looked like a man impatient to get to the next shot.

Besides Schroeder, main pretenders to Kramer's throne included Frankie Parker, a stylist who won the Nationals twice during the war years; tall Gardnar Mulloy and steady Bill Talbert, renowned as doubles players; bandy-legged Pancho Segura, a left-handed little court master named Art Larsen and Herbie Flam, another Los Angeles native who had mopped up in the junior ranks. The player most everyone figured was destined for greatness—blond, handsome Joel Hunt—had been killed in the service.

No one gave notice to Richard (Pancho) Gonzales.

Yet this Mexican-American, born in modest circumstances in Los Angeles, a school drop-out and a temperamental fire-brand, was destined to make an indelible mark on the game both as an amateur and a professional. He became one of tennis' greatest craftsmen and most controversial champions.

"Pancho's no saint," Gonzales' closest friend and fellow competitor Pancho Segura once said. "But whoever saw a saint with a tennis racket."

If anything could be said of Pancho Gonzales, it was that he was no saint—on or off the court.

As a schoolboy, he played hooky regularly, causing his parents considerable concern. While still a teen-ager, he was suspended by the Southern California Tennis Association. When he reached maturity, he continued to explode in the middle of matches. He carried on running feuds with of-ficials and fans alike, kindled the ire of galleries and battled his contemporaries—particularly Jack Kramer, with whom he waged his own version of the Seven Years War.

Once he left the court in a steaming rage to assault a spectator who was riding him unmercifully in Boston. An-other time, in Australia, he slammed his racket against a microphone at court side, inciting newspaper charges that he had attacked the umpire.

"Pancho is very even-tempered," a friend once said. "He's always mad."

For many years he served the U.S. Davis Cup team as coach and he was a stern disciplinarian. His pupils respected but feared him. He demanded hard work and near perfec-tion. His sharp tongue was a crackling whip. Once in Australia, while coaching the team, he became incensed over the lackadaisical play of Dennis Ralston, whom he had taught and nurtured as he would his own son, and walked off the court in a huff, taking the next flight back to the United States.

Gonzales, in his prime, possessed a magnificent game with few flaws. His service was like a rocket, timed officially at 110 miles per hour. He moved over a court like a jungle cat, effortlessly and quick. He had tremendous reflexes. The racket, which he held with the eastern or shake-hands grip, always looked like the extension of his right arm. He was a grim fighter, had remarkable concentration and possessed—according to his fellow players—perhaps the keenest tactical knowledge the game has known.

Pancho—called "Gorgo" by his contemporaries—was a handsome figure—6′ 3″ and 185 pounds, with no paunch even as he reached his forties. Raven-black hair curled around his dark, coppery features. A scar across his left cheek—the result of a childhood car crash—seemed to ignite into a sliver of flame when he became angry.

Perhaps no tennis player ever had greater sex appeal. Women adored him. They would come out by the thousands to watch him play, even after his cannon-ball service lost much of its smoke and his lean, hairy legs slowed a step. Some fans enjoyed needling him just to see him explode. But they always came. He was one of tennis' outstanding gate attractions.

Richard Alonzo Gonzales was born May 9, 1928, in a small apartment near Wrigley Field in Los Angeles. His father and mother had moved to California from Chihuahua, Mexico, and the father, a shop worker, had difficulty supporting his seven children.

"We had few luxuries in our house," Pancho recalled. "Food wasn't abundant, but it was simple and filling, and we never went hungry. Our clothes were just clothes—inexpensive but clean. We wished for many things that never came."

The elder Gonzales worked hard, moved often and sought to give all his children a full education. But Pancho presented a problem. He hated school. He played hooky whenever possible. He hung around the neighborhood playgrounds and picked up an interest in tennis through a close friend, Chuck Pate.

When he told his mother and father of his new interest, Papa Gonzales was upset. He felt tennis was just a distraction, a vice that might prevent his son from becoming a success. Pancho, an avid movie-goer with a passion for Westerns, despaired of ever achieving his first two goals—to be a crooner or a dancer.

He was twelve when his mother bought him his first tennis racket. It was a frail, butterfly-net type of implement which cost 51 cents at the local cut-rate store. Chuck Pate showed Pancho how to hold the racket and Pancho was bitten. Every day he would take his cheap racket and race over to the tennis court where he would play for hours. During off periods he would wander over to the Exposition Park Shop run by Frank Poulain, and watch Frank string rackets.

As days passed, Pancho found it increasingly difficult to attend school. Truancy grew more frequent as did visits to the tennis court. The Mexican-American boy became very close to Poulain, often slept in the room back of his shop. It was Poulain who interceded with Pancho's father to get permission for the boy to devote more time to the game.

"My son doesn't need tennis," Papa Gonzales insisted. "He needs an education."

"The boy will have made more money from tennis by the time he's thirty than you will make in your lifetime," Poulain argued.

With the reluctant approval of his parents, Gonzales began playing in junior tournaments. Soon he was winning his share of matches. It wasn't long before he was introduced to Perry Jones through the good graces of Poulain.

Jones ruled the sport in Southern California with an iron fist. He designated the players who went East. He gave assistance to those who needed help. He was counselor and patron to scores of young men anxious to make tennis their career.

Gonzales fell under his aegis only to discover that Jones was a stern disciplinarian. When the tennis czar learned Pancho had been skipping school he suspended the youngster, thus preventing him from playing in big tournaments and temporarily scuttling his chances for national ranking. By and by the suspension was lifted. After trying five high schools Pancho had had his fill of geometry and American history and had quit to concentrate on tennis. Hence he was no longer subject to truant officers or, for that matter, to Perry Jones.

His first big break came when he was nineteen. Playing in the Southern California Championships, he battled his way to the men's final and found himself facing Herbie Flam, winner of the national junior crown two years before. Mama Gonzales didn't want her boy appearing in front of all those elegant people at the Los Angeles Tennis Club looking like a ragamuffin. She bought him some new tennis shoes (95 cents), a white shirt (59 cents) and some shorts for a dollar-fifty. Pancho stuffed the gear in a canvas satchel and, with three transfers, hopped a streetcar to the stadium.

"It was a lonely feeling," he recalled. "I didn't see a familiar face when I started for the locker room."

Flam was not new to Gonzales. They had played each other in boys' tournaments, Gonzales usually winning. But while Pancho was sweating out his suspension, Herbie had gone East and made a name for himself. He was never a big game player. He was relatively short and stocky, with a soft but effective service. He concentrated on keeping the ball in play.

Gonzales started nervously and dropped the first set 10–8. He improved a bit in the second but so did Flam, moving into a 6–5 lead and 40–0 on Pancho's service. Gonzales had three match points against him.

Just then one of his cronies from Exposition Park let out a deafening yell:

"Come on, Pancho!"

Pancho served an ace.

Another yell: "Pancho!"

Another ace.

A third ace and Gonzales had fought his way out of trouble. He held service and, with Flam obviously unnerved, took the initiative and finally the set 8–6. Hitting with confidence while his pals cheered wildly, Gonzales won the third set and match 6–4.

His career was on its way.

Pancho played in the 1947 National Championships at Forest Hills and scored a first round victory over Derek Barton, British Davis Cup ace, before losing a five-setter to Gardnar Mulloy. In the Pacific Southwest tournament he knocked off Jaroslav Drobny, Bob Falkenburg and Frankie Parker before losing to Ted Schroeder.

People on the Coast began buzzing about the up-and-coming prospect with the blazing service, and Perry Jones promised him an Eastern tour in 1948. Pancho's first tour of the grass court circuit, however, was spotty. He beat Budge Patty at Southampton, lost to Gardnar Mulloy at Orange, bowed to an outsider named Sam Match at Newport.

It was no surprise that Gonzales was seeded Number Eight in the domestic list at Forest Hills. Kramer had turned pro and Schroeder, the man who figured to succeed him, had decided not to compete. So the tournament was wide open. Bob Falkenburg, who had won at Wimbledon in July, was rated one of the favorites, the veteran Drobny another. Frankie Parker, Tom Brown, Gardnar Mulloy and Billy Talbert all had their supporters. Gonzales was just another name.

He swept past Ladislav Hecht, Gus Ganzenmuller and left-handed Art Larsen. Frankie Parker, two-time champion and the man who had played Kramer in the 1947 final, popped up next in the draw—the tournament's top-seeded player. Pancho, playing superbly, won in four sets.

In the semifinals Pancho came against Drobny, the left-handed Czech who had defected from his Communist homeland after the war and taken up residence first in Egypt and then England. Drobny was a wonderful player—smart, tricky and left-handed.

The Czech won the first set and took a 2–0 lead in the second before Gonzales harnessed his game, finally winning 8–10, 11–9, 6–0, 6–3. Pancho then defeated Eric Sturgess of South Africa for the championship.

But there was only mild satisfaction in the triumph. Gonzales felt he had won the tournament by default because Schroeder, rated the country's best amateur, had not competed. It would be a year before Pancho could prove himself.

The tennis world looked to the 1949 U.S. Championships with anticipation. Was the tall Mexican-American with the scar on his left cheek really America's best tennis player? Or would that honor go to the stocky, hard-fighting Schroeder, one of the most popular players in all tennis? The Nationals would provide the answer.

As if following a script, Gonzales and Schroeder moved resolutely through one match after another. Pancho knocked over Jack Geller, Straight Clark and Jimmy Brink without dropping a set. Schroeder also refused to yield a set in the early rounds. Pancho survived a five setter with Art Larsen and then rallied for a victory over Frankie Parker. Schroeder was carried five sets by Australia's Frank Sedgman and dogged Billy Talbert before he finally reached the last round.

"The whole thing resembled the corny plot of a grade-B movie," Gonzales recalled.

Neither player spoke to each other in the locker room. Both appeared nervous in the warm-up, although Schroeder, true to character, behaved nonchalantly, kidding with the gallery, waving and chatting with linesmen. Gonzales was very intent.

The first set followed service for thirty-two games and the score went to 16–16. In the West Side Stadium's big concrete horseshoe the near-capacity crowd was tense.

Then in the thirty-third game Gonzales fell behind 0–40 on service. The vital break appeared imminent. Pancho unleashed three big services and the score was back to deuce. A net cord shot gave Schroeder another advantage and set point again. On the next point Pancho hit a volley down the line.

He thought the ball was good. So did many in the crowd. The linesman called "Out!" It was Schroeder's set.

Gonzales apparently was still thinking of the line call when he dropped the second set 6–2 with hardly a fight. Now Schroeder led 2–0 in sets and the match appeared over.

Pancho recalled afterwards that he was seething inside. First, he was upset over the line call that had cost him the first set. He was annoyed further when Schroeder was granted permission to don spiked shoes to offset the slippery turf. Pancho had no spikes.

"My only thought was to play as hard as I could," he said.

Pancho ran off four games in a row and won the third set 6–1. Following intermission he played with more confidence, powdering his own service while handling Schroeder's with greater ease. He took the fourth set 6–2, evening the match, then, fighting off a comeback by Schroeder, pulled out the final 6–4. He had proved he was the champ.

It was inevitable Gonzales would follow Kramer into professional ranks. The pro tour, under the direction of Bobby Riggs, was paying well. A tour involving Kramer and Gonzales was a natural. Gonzales signed for 30 percent of the proceeds.

The tour, while a financial success, proved a disaster for the newest recruit from amateur ranks. The tough, seasoned

Kramer whipped Gonzales in 96 of their 123 matches, losing only 27.

If Gonzales had hopes of duplicating his $75,000 professional earnings the following year he was doomed to disappointment. When time came to sign up principals for the upcoming season he received no offers. Seeking out Riggs to learn why, he was told: "You're dead as a drawing card, Pancho. People only pay to see winners."

It was a disillusioning experience for the hot-headed Latin. Returning to Los Angeles he bought his favorite old tennis shop at Exposition Park; Frank Poulain had retired and the property was available. The man once ranked as America's best amateur player now passed his time stringing rackets and selling balls.

Social matches and an occasional exhibition were the only tennis he played. In desperation he took to hotrod racing and at night he bowled or played poker. For three years his career appeared at an end and a national magazine drew attention to the fact with a story about him entitled "All Dressed Up and Nowhere to Go."

In the meantime Riggs gave up promoting the pro tour and Jack Kramer stepped in. Kramer, who had demolished Frank Sedgman on the 1953 tour, was looking for a new name for 1954. He was a shrewd operator. He knew Gonzales needed him and that he in turn needed Pancho's box office appeal. "Where do I sign?" said Gonzales, beginning a stormy relationship that would even be carried into the courts.

The new tour, starting with a Kramer-Gonzales match in Madison Square Garden, drew a crowd of 4,500. It hit other American cities before continuing on to Australia, Tokyo and Europe. Gonzales, skyrocketing from oblivion, was the ace drawing card. In 1954 he beat Sedgman and Pancho Segura, in 1956 Tony Trabert, 74–27, and in 1957 Ken Rosewall, 50 matches to 26.

Lew Hoad, who signed a $125,000 contract after capturing the Wimbledon and U.S. championships, was the Golden Boy fed to Gonzales in 1958. The hard-hitting Australian got off to a strong start, leading 18–9. Then Gonzales suddenly spurted, winning 42 of the next 60 matches to retain his pro crown.

It was during this period that the feud between Kramer, the promoter, and Gonzales, the star, reached the boiling point.

Pancho resented the fact that Hoad was getting a guarantee of $125,000 matched against 20 percent gross over the next two years while he was limited to 20 percent with no such guarantee. Gonzales had been given a flat $15,000 the year he played Trabert.

Gonzales contended that he personally had been responsible for increasing gates in such cities as New York, Chicago, Cleveland, Washington and Boston.

When Kramer refused a raise to 25 percent, Gonzales sued. The court upheld Kramer. Gonzales continued his long fight until Kramer finally pulled out of professional tennis promotion, leaving the business to an association of players.

Trabert became director of the association and picked up Kramer's controversy with Pancho. While crowds everywhere clamored for his appearance and the pro tour suffered, Pancho went into temporary retirement again. He bought a tennis ranch in California. He wrote a couple of books.

In 1964 he came back to win tournaments in Cleveland and New York.

By this time, the world was paying tribute to the game's newest champion, Rod Laver, a bandy-legged little Australian with a whip-like left wrist. Just to prove that the old sting from his racket wasn't completely dead, Pancho gave Laver lessons by beating him periodically.

Old Pancho might have retired on that one—as he frequently threatened to do—but he didn't.

During 1969 Gonzales announced his retirement after almost every tournament in which he played. Then he would change his mind and come back.

In the $50,000 Tournament of Champions at Las Vegas, Nevada, in October, 1969, Gonzales swept to the title by crushing Arthur Ashe, Jr., in the final 6–0, 6–2, 6–4.

"This is the end," he said. "I now will retire to my tennis ranch."

When the 1970 season opened in Madison Square Garden there was Pancho again—his bony features a bit more gaunt, his raven hair with added streaks of gray but his dark eyes flashing the fire of old.

"The difference between me, now at forty, and me at twenty-five is that I can't keep the pressure on my opponent," he said one day, as he wrapped his calloused fingers with adhesive tape and padded his aching feet. "I can't attack and keep attacking. I have to out-think the men I beat now."

He out-thought and outplayed a heavily favored Laver in their $10,000 winner-take-all match, inaugurating a professional world series. The Gonzales victory sent a near sell-out crowd of 18,000 at the Garden into a wild frenzy.

Gonzales followed this up with a victory over John Newcombe. People then began wondering: Will the old tiger ever call it quits?

TWO
11
Age of the Aussies

In the late summer of 1950 a seedy, little redhaired sports writer from Melbourne invaded the West Side Tennis Club at Forest Hills as captain of a make-shift Australian Davis Cup team. The United States, with such stars as Ted Schroeder, Tom Brown and Gardnar Mulloy, was favored to add another link to its imposing chain of recent triumphs —four straight and six in the last seven years.

The sports writer was Harry Hopman. He had played doubles back in the 1930's when Adrian Quist and John Bromwich were Australia's top singles performers. He was a quick, nervous fellow with an antipathy for the press, apparently because he was a newsman himself. There was a jest among his confrères that Hopman liked to keep all the stories for himself.

When he first emerged as a Davis Cup captain, Harry's credentials were unimposing and the calibre of his troops did little to help the image. Frank Sedgman, the ace of the team, had been crushed in straight sets the year before by both Pancho Gonzales and Schroeder. The Number Two man was a dark horse named Kenneth McGregor, a tall, handsome youth who had distinguished himself more as a soccer player. The veteran John Bromwich, using a racket as loosely-strung as a butterfly net, was brought along for insurance.

The U.S. team, captained by snow-haired Alrick Man, was stunned when Sedgman swept past Tom Brown in straight sets and McGregor upset the heavily-favored Schroeder, also not losing a set. The match ended the next day when Sedgman teamed with Bromwich to beat Schroeder and Mulloy in doubles. To make the decision emphatic Sedgman brushed off Schroeder in the final singles.

The upset signalled a new age in amateur tennis: "The Era of the Aussies." Americans, who had undergone brief slumps over the years but had always bounced back to retain their position as the Number One tennis nation in the world, saw their supremacy plummet.

"What's wrong with American tennis?" became a recurring question. In the next seventeen years the United States saw the Davis Cup only three times. From 1951 through 1967 it won its own national championship three times and

Wimbledon four times. For twelve straight years—from Tony Trabert's victory in 1955 until the U.S. Nationals went pro in 1968—foreigners grabbed off the big single prize. In ten of these dozen years the winners were Australians.

Australia is a continent equivalent in size to the United States but with a population approximating that of New York City, some ten million people. It is a land of broad, sandy beaches, superb athletes and an almost religious devotion to tennis.

Flying over the coastal cities at night, one looks down upon a checkerboard of lighted courts. In major cities such as Sydney, Melbourne, Brisbane and Adelaide, there are lighted courts every five or six blocks. Small tykes trudging to school are seen carrying rackets in neat leather cases. They may forget their lunch buckets or books but never their tennis equipment. The sport is part of every school curriculum.

Australian tennis officials, proud of their heritage dating back to Norman Brookes and Anthony Wilding at the turn of the century, have instituted a program of encouragement and development unmatched by any other country.

Even the smallest hamlets in the remotest sections of the "bush" stage regular tournaments and clinics. They hire coaches and bring in stars for exhibitions. The best prospects are given special attention. At an age when most American youths are playing marbles and reading comic books these youngsters are furnished the finest equipment and sent into tournaments for toughening.

The Australian assembly line turn out world champions as quickly as they can be gobbled up by the pro ranks. In Australia the star tennis player is a national hero, worshipped just as baseball and football stars are in the United States.

During the period of declining American court fortunes, U.S. apologists contended that the reason for Australia's superiority lay in the differing educational processes. Only a small minority of Australians went to college. The Aussies completed a high school equivalency at about age fifteen, then they went to work—or, in the case of talented tennis players, on the road. They became, some Americans argued, tennis bums, touring the world on expense accounts twelve months a year, while the top U.S. players completed college and frequently went into business.

After his spectacular success in the 1950 Davis Cup matches, Sedgman, a bowlegged, well-built athlete with lightning reflexes and rare volleying ability, forged to the top of world rankings. The next two years he added U.S. championships to his two Australian crowns and in 1952 he also won Wimbledon, though his previous bid for that trophy had been thwarted by Dick Savitt, a tall, hard-hitting New Yorker.

After successfully defending the Davis Cup a second time, both Sedgman and McGregor turned professional. The deal negotiated in secret created a furor in Australia where friends of the amateur game raised a small fortune in a vain effort to keep Sedgman pure. Fortunately there were waiting in the wings two seventeen-year-olds whom Australian authorities had been watching since they were big enough to hold a racket. One was Lew Hoad, a blond, thick-shouldered boy who hit the ball with thundering force. The other was Ken Rosewall, black-haired, frail-looking, who handled a tennis racket with the artistry of a violin maestro. He lacked Hoad's power but every shot came off with the crispness and deadly effectiveness of a sabre slash.

Hoad and Rosewall were not unprepared. In the summer of 1952 the Australian Lawn Tennis Association had sent them on a world tour as members of the official traveling team.

A few years later, after turning pro himself, Hoad related the experience in a somewhat bitter magazine article in which he confessed:

I was a tennis slave. The association demands that all players going on tour sign a contract which specifies that for travel and other expenses they will compete in tournaments and exhibitions designated by the association. The agreement runs from April, when the team leaves, until the next January 31.

The contract makes the player the property of the association. He has no independence. If I go through a rugged tournament such as Wimbledon and say afterwards I am tired and would like a rest, the association says, no, you have commitments to play here and there.

Hoad was born November 23, 1934, in Sydney, Australia. "I began playing tennis at the age of nine, barefoot," he recalled. "At eleven, I was being furnished good rackets and shoes. At fifteen I was a seasoned tournament player, and at seventeen I made my first trip around the world. I played tennis the year round, moving into Europe in April, into the United States in July and back home to Australia in October for the summer season, which coincides with most people's winter. In all my years as an amateur, I never saw a winter."

Rosewall, only five feet, seven inches tall and less than 140 pounds in his heyday as an amateur, was born in the little village of Turramurra in New South Wales. He was twenty-one days older than Hoad.

At age ten the two boys met for the first time in a school tournament, Rosewall winning 6–0. In 1946 they played an exhibition at the Kooyong courts in Melbourne where Jack Kramer, Ted Schroeder and other members of the U.S. Davis Cup team were gathered for the Challenge Round. Rosewall won 6–0 and when the crowd called for another set he repeated the feat. Hoad recalled how Schroeder came over to comfort him, saying, "Don't worry, kid, you'll beat him someday." In a later tournament, however, Rosewall defeated him again 6–0, 6–0 and Hoad was so discouraged he gave up tennis. Not until he resumed playing in 1949 did he score his first triumph over his long-time rival in the New South Wales Championships at Sydney.

The blond Sydney bomber went on to become the best player in the world. He won Wimbledon in 1956 and 1957 but bowed to Rosewall at Forest Hills in 1956. This was Hoad's greatest year. Sweeping the Australian, French and Wimbledon titles he needed only the American crown to complete a Grand Slam. A back injury suffered in the Paris tournament, however, was the apparent reason for his failure to do so. Just as Hoad never won a title at Forest Hills, so Rosewall never put his name on the Wimbledon trophy. Nevertheless, in addition to his 1956 triumph at Forest Hills, he captured the Australian championship in 1953 and 1956 and the French in 1953. The two Aussies also dominated the doubles.

It was during this period that U.S. tennis was given a shot in the arm by a husky basketball player from the University of Cincinnati and an indefatigable court fighter from Philadelphia's main line.

The former cager was Tony Trabert, a strapping, crew-cut slugger with the legs of a football halfback. A protégé of Bill Talbert, Tony parlayed power and determination into a winning formula. On the court he appeared sluggish. But he hit a service with thunderclap force and attempted to make every shot a winning one.

Stepping out front with Trabert was Victor Seixas, a handsome, dark-haired, six-footer who played the tournament circuit in near anonymity for years, failing to reach tennis maturity until he was twenty-seven. Seixas' game lacked the classic mold. His repertoire consisted of a looping forehand, a slice backhand, a variety of tricky spinners, lobs and drop-shots. His asset was superb condition. He looked as if he could run all day. He blunted superior games with his unorthodox style and tenacity.

Trabert and Seixas comprised the U.S. Davis Cup team sent to Melbourne in 1953 to recapture the trophy from

Hoad and Rosewall, each only nineteen. The Australians were led by the whip-cracking Hopman. Bill Talbert called signals for the Yanks.

Against strong odds the Americans almost pulled it off. Trabert crushed Rosewall but Hoad evened the score with an opening day victory over Seixas. Then, the panicky Hopman shuffled his doubles team, replacing the soft-serving Rosewall with Rex Hartwig. Talbert came up with a scissors play—both Trabert and Seixas occupying the same side of the court at service and crossing over only on special signals —to send the United States ahead, two matches to one. The next day, in a drizzling rain, Trabert and Hoad engaged in one of the most dramatic duels in Cup history. Hoad finally won 7–5 in the fifth. Rosewall came back to beat Seixas in the deciding match.

The two Americans got their revenge in Sydney in 1954, playing before the largest crowd ever to see a Davis Cup match (over 26,000). Trabert beat Hoad while Seixas walloped Rosewall in opening singles and the two Americans clinched it on the second day by taking the doubles. It was a severe blow to Hopman and the Australians, a titanic triumph for Captain Bill Talbert and his favorite tandem.

Hoad had become disgusted with tennis by then and was considering retirement. He disliked the Australian system. He resented Hopman's strict, often unnecessary discipline. Australian newspapers were riding him about his association with Jennifer Staley, the pretty Australian girl he later was to marry, and his slump.

Hoad and Rosewall won back the Davis Cup and defended it at Adelaide in 1956. Afterwards Rosewall signed with promoter Jack Kramer but Hoad demurred, holding out until he had won his second Wimbledon crown in 1957. Then he signed a three-year contract for $125,000, the biggest ever offered a tennis player.

Trabert and Seixas continued to shine. Trabert won the U.S. Championship in 1953 and again in 1955, beating

Seixas for the first of these and downing Rosewall in the second. He captured Wimbledon in 1955 and won the French in 1954 and 1955.

Seixas won Wimbledon in 1953 and the U.S. title in 1954, beating Denmark's Kurt Nielsen in the former and Australia's Rex Hartwig in the latter. After the successful 1955 campaign Trabert turned professional, losing a series to Pancho Gonzales, 74 matches to 27. Seixas chose to remain amateur. He was still giving the young tigers a stiff battle well after he had reached the forty-year mark.

Meanwhile, Australia continued to turn out champions. Replacing Hoad and Rosewall were a handsome, dark-haired stylist named Ashley Cooper; a pair of tough, sinewy Queenslanders enough alike to be twins, Malcolm Anderson and Roy Emerson, and a judge's left-handed son, Neale Fraser. Cooper teamed with Anderson and Mervyn Rose for a Davis Cup victory in 1957. In 1957 and 1958 he captured the Australian championship and in 1958 the Wimbledon and U.S. titles.

A transplanted Peruvian briefly derailed the Aussie steam engine. He was Alejandro Olmedo. Of mixed Aztec and Spanish descent, Olmedo earned a tennis scholarship to the University of Southern California where he impressed Perry Jones so much that when Jones was named Davis Cup captain for 1958 he built his plans around the Peruvian. There was some criticism about using a foreigner to play for America but since Olmedo had learned his tennis in the United States and been a resident for the specified number of years, he was eligible. For tacticians Jones called on Jack Kramer and Pancho Gonzales, both willing to repay him for his assistance over the years.

Olmedo moved with cat-like grace on the court. Though he lacked a powerful game he possessed an uncanny touch and feel. His ability to anticipate an opponent's shot was uncanny and he volleyed superbly.

Nevertheless it was a surprise when the Peruvian defeated Anderson in the first Davis Cup match at Brisbane and teamed up with Ham Richardson to beat Anderson and Fraser in the doubles for a 2–1 lead. Barry MacKay lost to Cooper in the other opening singles but Olmedo trounced Cooper for the decisive point. The irony was that Kramer had coached the Americans to whip two players he intended to star on the pro tour—Cooper and Anderson.

Three weeks later, though suffering an arm injury, Olmedo won the Australian championship, the first American to do so since Dick Savitt in 1951. In 1959, before turning pro, he captured Wimbledon. That same year, at the Davis Cup matches, he and hard-hitting Barry MacKay scored singles victories over an unseasoned Australian left-hander named Rod Laver. But Neale Fraser, winning two singles and sharing the double prize with Emerson, brought the Aussies through.

Fraser and Emerson were the next to steal the limelight. Fraser, a good-looking left-hander, boasted a slashing service and an effective spin on his shots. He won the U.S. title in 1959 and 1960 and Wimbledon in 1960. After that, going into semi-retirement, he was never a strong factor, though he continued to play on Davis Cup teams through 1963.

Emerson, strong and steady as a backboard, won the Australian championship more than any other man—six times. He captured the American crown in 1961 and 1964, the French in 1963 and 1967. In the nine years he competed for the Davis Cup, Australia only lost once. He finally succumbed to the offers of protour promoters in 1968. A gallery favorite, the modest six-foot Queenslander with slicked-down hair, gold teeth and a nut-brown physique played in a businesslike manner, never fuming over questionable calls.

In the meantime, Laver, Harry Hopman's favorite protégé, had begun to come on strong. At five-feet-eight, 150 pounds, with bandy legs, a long nose and a shock of red hair, he was far from an imposing figure. But few men possessed more destructive weapons. With a snap wrist he could cross court and send the ball down the lines from either side and among his wide variety of shots was a service that often looked as if it would spin over the fence.

The little redhead won the Australian in 1960, Wimbledon in 1961. Then in 1962 he swept all four major championships to become the first player to complete a Grand Slam since Don Budge had managed the feat in 1938. Laver went on to succeed Ken Rosewall as the best pro player in the world.

There was no letup in the production of top talent by Australia. Players such as Marty Mulligan, Ken Fletcher, Bob Mark and Bob Hewitt moved to other countries and some picked up Davis Cup assignments from their new homelands. Fred Stolle, a towering stylist, played in three Wimbledon finals, starting in 1963, and won the American title in 1966. He was followed by a pair of wreckers named John Newcombe and Tony Roche.

Winning the Wimbledon and U.S. doubles in 1967, Newcombe established himself as the top amateur in the world. When he turned pro, taking teammate Roche with him, flashy Bill Bowrey and slashing, lefthanded Owen Davidson took over for them—and both seemed promising. Throughout this period all challenges to Australian domination were temporary.

Big Barry MacKay from Dayton, Ohio, and Earl (Butch) Buchholz, Jr. from St. Louis, son of a tennis professional, attained world class but turned pro after a couple unsuccessful Davis Cup ventures. Dennis Ralston, from Bakersfield, California, seemed off to a great start when he became an eighteen-year-old Davis Cup team member in 1960. But as an amateur he never realized his full potential. Some blamed his ungovernable temper, others his poor handling by the U.S. Lawn Tennis Association. Dennis won a score of U.S. junior and senior titles, gained the final at Wimbledon in 1966 and finally turned professional in 1967.

Ralston's companion in arms was a bouncy butterball

from St. Louis named Charles (Chuck) McKinley, who led the national rankings in 1962 and 1963, yielding that position to Ralston for the next three years. McKinley, five-feet-eight and 180 pounds, had his greatest season in 1963. He beat Fred Stolle for the Wimbledon championship and led the U.S. Davis Cup team on its invasion of Australia. Teaming with Ralston under the captaincy of Bob Kelleher, he scored the vital point over John Newcombe that returned the cup to the United States for a year.

When McKinley took a job on Wall Street and curtailed his tournament activities, there was no one in sight to spark U.S. fortunes. Arthur Ashe, a stringbean Negro from Richmond, Virginia, attracted attention with his 110-miles-per-hour service but just as he was reaching a peak he was called into the military service. Charles Pasarell, Jr., a strapping Puerto Rican with great natural ability, won the National Indoors and the National Intercollegiate, grabbing the top ranking in 1968 before he too was called into service.

The two main threats to Australian supremacy in the 1960's came from players of Latin origin. Manuel Santana, a toothy Spaniard, was rated the world's best amateur player on clay. He won numerous titles on that surface—including two French crowns—but adjusted well enough to grass to win the U.S. championship in 1965, Wimbledon in 1966, and twice carry his Spanish team into the Davis Cup Challenge Round against Australia. He rejected all offers to turn pro. The other Latin was Rafael Osuna, a Mexican with the feet of a ballet dancer and the touch of a safe-robber. For nearly a decade he was a Mexican Davis Cup star. His finest hour occurred when he won the U.S. National championship in 1963, beating six-foot-six Frank Froehling III.

From 1955 until the tournament went Open in 1968, Santana and Osuna were the only men able to break Australia's hold on the American championship. During the same period, Olmedo, McKinley and Santana were the only non-Australian victors at Wimbledon. The Aussies threatened to carry their dominant role into the new opened-up game, while relinquishing little ground in amateur competition.

It was Australia's tennis generation.

Rod Laver — He Rewrote the Book

In 1938 when Don Budge was scoring his Grand Slam—the unprecedented feat of sweeping the Australian, French, Wimbledon and U.S. championships in a single year—a cattle rancher and his wife in far-off Queensland, Australia, celebrated the birth of their third son. Like Budge, he had a shock of flame-colored hair and was also destined to win the Grand Slam—not once but twice—and become the greatest tennis player in the world. In the late 1960's, after the game opened the door to pros, there were observers who said Rodney (The Rocket) Laver perhaps was the best who ever lived.

At first sight no one would suspect Laver of greatness. He was a skinny boy with sunken chest, long nose and bandy legs. Even when he grew to maturity and played before royalty, he remained comparatively puny. He stood five feet, eight inches and weighed less than 150 pounds, the antithesis of Budge, an imposing six-footer.

Rodney's father, Roy, a tennis enthusiast, held greater hopes for his two older boys, Trevor and Bob, who had good physiques and classic strokes. The first time Harry Hopman, Australia's famed Davis Cup captain, laid eyes on Laver, he blinked and exclaimed, "My, he's a little one—and we have to do something about that sunken chest."

One man, Charlie Hollis, a coach in the Laver's home town of Rockhampton, had confidence in the boy from the beginning. "Trevor's got beautiful strokes," Charlie once commented to the father. "They're better strokes than Rodney's but he's got an explosive temper like you. He's never going to be champion. Rodney's like his mother, quiet and determined. He'll make it."

It was a long, hard struggle. He lost his first two Davis Cup matches in 1959 at Forest Hills to Alex Olmedo and Barry MacKay. He was beaten by Olmedo and Neale Fraser in the Wimbledon final in 1959 and 1960. He dropped successive straight-set matches to Fraser and Roy Emerson in the U.S. final in 1960 and 1961. He won the Australian championship twice—1960 and 1962—compared with six triumphs by Emerson. After turning pro in 1963, he suffered humiliating defeats by Lew Hoad and Ken Rosewall. Nevertheless, within two years he had established himself as king of the pros.

Laver was no stylist. Left-handed, he relied on a spinning rather than a cannon-ball service. His wrist was strong as a steel hinge. He hit slicing drives off both his forehand and backhand and was so accurate he could spin the ball on a shilling.

His service was devastating, though not powerful. He could clip the corners and kick up the line dust with it. The delivery had such a high-bounding kick that it was almost impossible to attack it. Laver, however, was best at returning service. He moved in close and met the ball on the rise, whacking it across the net for repeated winners. Probably no other player attacked as relentlessly or effectively. In matches with such rivals as Ken Rosewall and Pancho Gonzales, Laver never played tentatively. Grabbing the net and volleying with a swordsman's fury, he went for broke. He turned tennis into a new game.

Rod was introduced to the sport when he was ten. His father had built a tennis court in the backyard. The court was surfaced with ant hills, packed hard and rolled smooth. "It was the best clay surface in the world," Laver recalled. Lights were strung up to permit night play and one evening, when he was supposed to be in bed, young Rod stole out to watch his father and brothers practicing with Charlie Hollis. Spotted by the tennis coach he was invited to hit a few balls. It was the beginning of an association with Hollis that would have lasting impact on his career.

Rod began getting up at 5 A.M. and accompanying his brothers to the Rockhampton Tennis Association courts for lessons with Charlie. They would all put in about two hours of practice before going to school. Rod usually played with his mother's racket because it was light.

Laver became Hollis' pride and joy. The red-haired youngster would hang around the coach's shop and help him string rackets. He strengthened his left wrist in this way and built up his hands and wrist by squeezing a steel spring or squash balls. Besides teaching Laver the proper grip and strokes. Hollis also drilled into him the importance of a winning temperament. The mind is what makes champions, the coach insisted, impressing upon Rod that he must avoid getting upset over mistakes. It was Charlie's theory that a player should never give an inch and should cream every opponent 6–0, 6–0 if possible.

Laver was not quite twelve when he entered the Queensland Junior Tournament for players sixteen and under. His father opposed the move, fearing a one-sided defeat might kill the boy's ambition, but Hollis insisted. Rod gained the final round where he lost to his brother Bob. Later, pairing with a schoolmate in a doubles match against a team from Townsville, Rod won easily. At thirteen he captured the Under-14 State Championships at Brisbane and he had his first experience with grass courts, playing on a private court in the gold-mining town of Mount Morgan.

Laver was sixteen when he was introduced to Harry Hopman. A teen-agers' coaching class was being held in Brisbane and the Davis Cup captain had come up from Sydney to be in charge. Rod and his coach drove the 500 miles to the

Queensland capital. Hollis could hardly wait for Hopman to see his protégé. Striding into the dressing room at the Milton courts, he began telling him about Laver.

"I'd better have a look," Harry said.

When he saw the skinny-legged kid with the mop of red hair, however, he was taken aback.

"That him?" he gulped. "Gee, he's little."

"Wait 'til you see what he can do with a tennis ball," Hollis said.

Hopman wandered over to the end of the court where Laver was leaning against the fence and said: "Okay, Rocket, let's see you serve a couple."

Unflustered, the youngster went to the service line and began putting scorchers down the lines and into the corners.

"This kid's good, all right," Hopman said. "Got all the shots. Timing is good, and he's really quick around the court."

This was high praise from a man not given to superlatives. Hopman made no effort to hide the fact that he was impressed. In time Laver was to become his favorite and the nick-name "Rocket"—a Hopman appellation—stuck.

Hopman's regard was further shown in 1956 when he agreed to accompany the eighteen-year-old Rod and another promising junior, Bob Mark, on a world tour. An Australian millionaire, Arthur Drysdale, put up $12,000 for the trip, a common gesture among wealthy Aussie sportsmen and one reason why the country was able to develop top stars.

The tour lasted five months, starting in Paris and ending in California. It was an awesome experience for the two eighteen-year-olds making their first trip away from home. Mark was a big rugged boy with dark hair and heavy eyebrows. He had talent but his career suffered from an ungovernable temper. Hopman acted like a father to the two. He taught them the proper courtesies. He spent hours banging balls with them. Both grew in poise and experience.

At Wimbledon Laver won a couple of matches in the men's division and teamed with Mark to gain round 16 in doubles. In the Junior World Championships he fought his way to the final where he lost to America's Ron Holmberg. Crossing the Atlantic, Rod won the Canadian and American Junior crowns, defeating Chris Crawford for the latter 6–3, 6–3, 6–2.

Next year Laver was named as the sixth member of the Davis Cup squad. The little redhead lacked the experience to break into a lineup that included Malcolm Anderson, Ashley Cooper and Mervyn Rose, but it was an opportunity to undergo the rigid conditioning imposed by Hopman. He spent hours, lifting weights, bike-pedaling and doing road work. His strength increased and his reflexes improved. Laver was also a member of the 1958 squad that lost the cup to the United States at Brisbane and played his first Challenge Round matches at Forest Hills in 1959, losing both.

This was the year, however, that the tennis world first took notice of the flashy left-hander. Laver gained the final in both the men's singles and men's doubles, engaging in nearly 800 games in five days. By the time he reached the singles final, he was a physical wreck and an easy victim of Alex Olmedo 6–4, 6–3, 6–4. His strength had been drained in a marathon semifinal match two days before against Barry MacKay, whom he finally beat 11–13, 11–9, 10–8, 7–9, 6–3. MacKay led 3–1 in the fifth set before Laver rallied to win six games in a row with an exhibition of phenomenal stroke-making.

"I had it won but he hit one winner after another—he didn't give me a chance," MacKay commented afterward.

Enroute to the Davis Cup Challenge Round, Laver scored a decisive victory over Tony Palafox of Mexico in the American Zone final and defeated the crafty Nicola Pietrangeli of Italy in the Inter-Zone. However, against the United States at Forest Hills he appeared tense and nervous, losing 7–5, 6–4, 6–1 to MacKay, who he had outlasted at

Wimbledon, and 9–7, 4–6, 10–8, 12–10 to Olmedo.

"There is a big difference in playing for yourself and playing for your country," Rod said later, a traditional complaint of all Davis Cup competitors. "When the umpire announces 'Australia' instead of your name and they start playing the national anthem, it is impossible not to get a lump in your throat."

It seemed Laver was destined to be one of the sport's perennial bridesmaids—having lost five finals in a row—by the time he returned home after the arduous 1959 campaign. Then the road suddenly turned. Laver won his first major title by capturing the Australian championship in 1960. The tournament was played in Brisbane, the capital of Rod's home state. His opponent was Neale Fraser, who the year before had won the U.S. championship. Laver fought off one match point and Fraser saved six before the smaller of the two left-handers survived 5–7, 3–6, 6–3, 8–6, 8–6.

Laver's bridesmaid complex was hard to shake, however. In 1960 he lost the finals at both Wimbledon and Forest Hills to Fraser. The little Queenslander still suffered from a bad temper and impatience. He sought to make every shot a winner and, when they didn't turn out that way, he tended to get rattled.

In 1961 Rod injured his left wrist in the Australian national and lost in the final to Emerson. At Wimbledon, he played superbly through the early rounds and in the final against Chuck McKinley outslugged the bouncy American for a dramatic triumph. In the American final he fell victim again to Emerson, losing in straight sets.

Laver said from the moment he started playing big time tennis it was his goal to duplicate Don Budge's Grand Slam. This was a feat that had escaped the greats. Rod had believed he might attain the mark earlier—in 1960 or 1961—but there were always road blocks.

Starting the 1962 season, he felt physically and mentally

ready. He worked on his game during the Australian summer. He listened to Charlie Hollis and his advisor and em-
ployer, Adrian Quist, a former Australian Davis Cup ace
who directed the sports division of the Dunlop Company.

The first leg of the Slam was the Australian Championships, played that year on the White City courts of Sydney.
Laver swept through the early rounds without losing a set,
dropped a single set to Bob Hewitt in the semifinals and
then went into the last round against his arch rival Emerson.
Laver won in four sets.

In Rome, Laver was behind two sets to one before rallying to score a 5-set victory over Emerson for the Italian
crown. In Paris, for the French title, he staved off a match
point beating Martin Mulligan in the quarter-finals and
rallied from 4–5 in the fifth with service against him for a
narrow triumph over Fraser. Again he faced Emerson in the
final but he had his fellow countryman's number, winning
6–2 in the fifth set.

At Wimbledon as the defending champion and seeded
Number One, Laver admitted he was nervous. In the
quarter-finals he ran against Manuel Santana. The gifted
Spaniard won the first set 11–9 and ran up a 5–1 lead in the
second, needing only one point to go two sets in front. Laver
saved the point, went on to win the match, defeating Fraser
in the semifinals and Marty Mulligan in the final.

Now only the American championship at Forest Hills remained. Laver sought to dismiss the thought of the Slam but
it was impossible. In every news interview reporters questioned him on the subject. One day Don Budge invited Rod
to an exhibition match in the Catskills and afterwards cautioned him: "Play the game the way you can, and don't
worry about the Slam." It only added to the pressure.

As expected Laver and Emerson swept into the final
round. Laver started strongly, winning the first two sets,
but dropped the third. After the ten-minute recess he got
a quick service break in the first game but Emerson rebroke

in the fifth. In the tenth game of the fourth set, leading 5–4 and with the advantage against him, Rod unleashed three slashing services which Emerson could not return and the match was over 6–2, 6–4, 5–7, 6–4.

Later, Laver said he was in such a daze his racket felt foreign to his hands and his mouth was dry. "I don't remember going to the net to shake hands," he recalled.

Laver returned to Australia to help his country defend the Davis Cup and then on January 4, 1963, with no more amateur worlds to conquer, he turned professional. He signed a contract with the International Professional Tennis Association guaranteeing him $100,000 over a three-year span.

The Rockhampton Rocket, however, got off to a poor pro start. Debuting in Sydney against Lew Hoad he waged a rugged match lasting almost three hours before losing 8–6 in the fourth set. Next day he lost to Ken Rosewall in straight sets. In all he dropped eight games to Hoad and eleven out of thirteen to Rosewall.

Nevertheless he refused to let setbacks shake his confidence. He had always been a slow starter, he reasoned, recalling his early amateur frustrations. "I figured my tennis education was just beginning," he said.

Persistence paid off. In 1966 and 1967 he won the major pro tournaments, compiling the best won-lost record on the tour.

In 1969, he established himself firmly as the king of all tennis by sweeping the four major championships—the Australian, French, Wimbledon and American titles, all now open—as a professional as he had done in 1962 as an amateur.

On the pro tour, he won more than $120,000. He was a winner, rich and undisputed.

Jean Borotra (right), one of France's
Four Musketeers, and his partner,
Robert Abdesselam, playing a
doubles match on the Number One
court at Wimbledon in 1949. Borotra
was a topflight player long after
he and his teammates dominated the
Davis Cup and major championships
in the late 1920's and early 1930's.

Henri Cochet (left), Jacques Brugnon (center), and Jean Borotra (far right), shown petting a dog on the racket of Britain's Fred Perry, were part of the French dynasty that wrested the Davis Cup from the United States and held it for many years.

Jacques Brugnon, one of France's Four Musketeers, demonstrates his stylish backhand in a 1929 match at Wimbledon. At the right, Rene Lacoste, Henri Cochet and Jacques Brugnon of the French Davis Cup team are all dressed up with some place to go as they prepare to sail for America in 1928.

Ellsworth Vines has been rated by many observers as the greatest player in the game for a single match. The tall Californian is shown at the left examining rackets for Frankie Parker, then a teen-ager. Center, he receives a trophy from movie actor Douglas Fairbanks in Los Angeles after beating Britain's Fred Perry (left). Extreme right, Vines demonstrates his formidable forehand to an admiring audience on one of the field courts at Forest Hills.

Wide World Photos

Fred Perry, the Briton who broke France's grip on the Davis Cup, was immaculate on or off the court. At the left, he is seen winning his semifinal match at Wimbledon against Donald Budge in 1936. Center, he is shown in happier days with his wife, actress Helen Vinson, from whom he later was divorced. At the right, Perry and France's Henri Cochet chat at the net before a match on the Roland Garros court in Paris.

Donald Budge is rated by many tennis authorities as the greatest player who ever lived. He was a gawky teen-ager when he won his first major trophy — as California state junior champion — in 1930, shown at the left. He looked more like an acrobat (right) in beating England's G. P. Hughes in the Wimbledon semifinals in 1937. A quarter of a century later, September 10, 1962, Budge, as the first man to win the four major championships — Australian, French, Wimbledon and U. S. titles — in a single year, congratulates another red-head, Australia's Rod Laver, as winner of the Grand Slam. They are the only two ever to accomplish the feat.

Tennis players were still wearing long pants when Bitsy Grant, the "Atlanta retriever," was practicing his giant-killer role in the early 1930's. Although he scored many upsets, he never won the national championship. A new era in tennis was breaking, represented by Ted Schroeder, Jr., left, and Jack Kramer, two youngsters from the Pacific Coast, who won the national doubles title in 1940.

Max P. Haas

Max P. Haas

USLTA

World War II interrupted the tennis careers of many of the United States' finest young players. Two of these are shown at the left in the midst of a heated match. In the foreground (left), Ted Schroeder stretches to attempt a return from Bobby Riggs.

The blond, good-looking athlete advancing toward the camera is Joel Hunt, a player of rare promise who was killed in the service. At the right, Bobby Riggs is shown as a young amateur. He later was king of the pros.

USLTA

One of the greatest doubles teams
ever formed was that of William F.
Talbert and Gardnar Mulloy. They
won scores of national championships
and remained active in tennis
long past their competitive prime.

Talbert served as Davis Cup
captain and tournament chairman of
the U.S. Open Championships at
Forest Hills. Mulloy was still
winning senior championships after
passing the age of fifty.

Arthur Ashe, Jr. —
The "Black Shadow of the Courts"

Arthur Ashe, Jr., rose to tennis fame at a time when his country was torn by racial strife. The unrest of American blacks was mounting and Ashe, as the first Negro man to attain greatness in the sport, found himself fighting two battles—one on the court, another as a civil rights advocate.

"Once I thought I would never look back but now I know I must," said Ashe who in 1968 achieved his greatest triumph by winning the first U.S. Open Championship at Forest Hills against the world's top professional and amateur players. "Things are happening. I am black. I have a certain responsibility to my race and I don't intend to shirk it."

Because of his tennis ability Ashe enjoys the white man's affluence and culture but he is well aware of the difficulty Negroes face in crashing the sport. "Unless a black kid has a benefactor as I did, it is impossible for him to make good in tennis. First off he has to buy a racket that costs around $40. How many Negroes can afford that?"

At most of the fashionable clubs where he played on his way up the only other Negroes were bus boys or waiters. In some tournaments he was snubbed outright, in others he was accepted—grudgingly or, worse, condescendingly.

"Some people are always bending over to be nice to me," he said. "They go out of their way to treat me differently— I suppose because I am different. I'm black. But it bugs me. I want to be accepted as a person and a tennis player—not because I'm a Negro."

Folks really didn't have much choice about accepting Ashe as a tennis player. With a racket in his hand he more than proved his point.

Not that he especially looked like an athlete. Quite the

contrary; tall and scrawny, six-foot-one and 155 pounds, he moved with a slow ambling gait, and the spectacles on the bridge of his nose gave him a scholarly appearance. Moreover, he played in such a relaxed manner that critics said he lacked a killer's instinct.

Ashe admitted that sometimes on the court when the going got rough, his concentration tended to wander and he would "start thinking about a million things—my home, my girl, getting married and mainly what the hell am I doing out here in the first place."

But, he added: "I feel that fighting qualities manifest themselves in different ways. It's true I don't want to kill anybody. But on the tennis court I want to win as much as anybody."

Arthur Robert Ashe, Jr., was born July 10, 1943, in a middle-class Negro neighborhood in Richmond, Virginia. His father, a recreation department policeman, was familiar with most of the city's playgrounds. But his son was barred from all except those set aside for colored people. Arthur, Jr., found his recreation at Brook Field and all his playmates were black.

When he was six, his mother died. He had a younger brother, twenty-one months old, later to become a U.S. Marine sergeant to serve two years in Viet Nam.

"It was tough at first," recalled Ashe, Sr., who had to be a father and a mother to the boys. "I scrubbed floors and cut grass. I prayed every night I would raise them right. They were good boys. They never fought. I taught Arthur to be patient. I told him things don't change in a day.

"Later I got a housekeeper—an elderly lady named Olis Berry. She tended to the boys while I was at work. With the help of the Good Lord, everything turned out all right. Nobody could be prouder of my children than I am."

The elder Ashe remarried and there was a stepsister, Florence Loretta, ten years younger than Arthur, Jr., and a stepbrother, Robert, eleven years younger.

Arthur, Jr., was too frail for football but he played baseball and tennis. He handled a racket with such skill that he caught the eye of Ronald Charity, a Richmond playground director and coach. Charity brought young Ashe to the attention of Dr. R.W. Johnson in Lynchburg, Virginia.

Doctor Johnson, a well-to-do Negro physician, was devoted to tennis. He built a court on the lawn of his home and was soon inviting promising Negro players for lessons and practice. One of his protégés was Althea Gibson, the gawky Negro girl who learned to play paddle tennis on the sidewalks of Harlem and who went on to win Wimbledon and the U.S. titles twice each and to curtsy before the Queen of England.

Doctor Johnson took an immediate interest in Ashe who displayed amazing reflexes and hitting power for a young teen-ager. He asked Arthur to join the tennis sessions and put considerable effort and money into developing his potential. By the time Arthur was fourteen the doctor was entering him in junior tournaments. In 1958 Ashe reached the semifinals of the 16-and-under division. In 1960 and 1961 he won the National Junior Indoor championship. At eighteen, just out of high school, he was Number 28 in his first national men's ranking.

He had made enough of an impression to gain an athletic scholarship to UCLA, which was in a mad scramble with the University of Southern California for tennis talent. For his books, board and tuition, Arthur put in 250 hours a year working around the campus.

Most of his free time was spent on the fast, concrete surface courts that are standard on the Pacific Coast. It was here he met Pancho Gonzales, the aging king of the pros. Pancho lived only a few blocks from the UCLA courts. He frequently visited the campus to sharpen his game and to help J.D. Morgan, the UCLA athletic director and tennis coach, with his pupils.

"It was the greatest break of my life," Ashe said. "Pancho

not only was the best tennis player in the world but most people agree he had the sharpest tennis mind. He could look at you hit a ball once and diagnose all your mistakes."

Pancho taught Arthur how to crack across the big service and also how to knife returns low and sharp so that the net rusher would have to hit his volley up for an easy kill. The old pro showed the kid how to lob, drop shot and stop volley.

"Everybody needs to have a hero," Ashe said. "Pancho was mine. I felt comfortable around him because his skin was nearly the color of mine. He was a terrific coach."

Ashe's progress was swift. By 1962 he had jumped his national ranking 10 notches to 18. He broke into the Top Ten—ranking sixth in 1963 after winning the National Hard Courts title. He moved up to third in 1964 and then to second, a ranking he held for three years.

He became a member of the U.S. Davis Cup team in 1963 and compiled an enviable record. Playing in seven zone matches prior to 1968, he won nine singles matches and lost only two. In 1968, his greatest year, he never lost a singles encounter in American victories over the British Caribbean team, Mexico and Ecuador. In the Inter-Zone semifinal against Spain at Cleveland he defeated both Luis Arilla and Manuel Santana.

Ashe came of tennis age during an Australian campaign in the winter of 1965–66—the Aussie summer—when the American team toured the country under Captain George MacCall. Most U.S. Davis Cup captains, influenced by Harry Hopman's success, enforced a Spartan training program including morning road work, calisthenics, gym work and long hours of practice. But Ashe preferred to go fishing or to the movies.

"I shiver every time I think of those Australians running and jumping and working out two on one," he said. "I don't go for all that wood-chopping, weight-lifting and running through parks stuff. It drives me crazy."

One morning when MacCall woke him and told him it was time to hit the road Ashe rubbed his half-open eyes and said, "Gee, Captain, can't we sit down and talk about it?"

Ashe brought the same easy-going approach to the court. When he played, every muscle in his wiry body seemed relaxed. Teammates, struck by the stealthy and effortless way he moved, nicknamed him "The Shadow."

Sometimes he relaxed too much. "I try to dangle on the court," he once said. "The ideal attitude is to be physically loose and mentally tight. I am usually loose but I'm afraid I too often get loose mentally also. It's hard for me to keep my mind on the game."

Nevertheless, Ashe's performance was impressive. Beating Australia's top stars, Emerson, Newcombe and Fred Stolle, he won three of the four state championships at Melbourne, Brisbane and Adelaide. He might have scored a sweep, plus the national title as well, had he not suffered a toe injury when he slipped on a curb in Melbourne.

At the time, Gonzales said of him: "Ashe is headed for the top in tennis. He has the fastest service in the game—the fastest since my own service. He is now rounding out his game."

Harry Hopman, the dour Australian captain not given to superlatives, said of him: "He is the most promising player in the world today. He is the biggest single threat to our Davis Cup supremacy."

Ashe's surge to the summit was delayed slightly by a three-year hitch in the army, beginning immediately after his return from Australia in early 1966. A major in business administration while at UCLA, Ashe became a lieutenant, serving in the data processing office at the U.S. Military Academy in West Point, New York.

Both the Army and the State Department felt Ashe should should be permitted to play as much tennis as possible while in the service. He was made available to the U.S. Davis Cup squad. In 1967, although he missed both the Wimbledon and the U.S. Championships, he represented the United States in the Pan American Games at Winnipeg, Canada, and in the Australian Championships he defeated Newcombe to gain the final before losing to Emerson. He lost in the final of the United States Indoor Championships at Salisbury, Maryland, to Charlie Pasarell, who also beat him out for the Number One berth in the 1968 rankings.

It was evident that Ashe was maturing and that he was only a breath away from greatness. Then came 1968—his year.

He started the year by winning the Madison Square Garden Challenge Tournament, beating Clark Graebner, Santana and—in one of his finest matches—Emerson. Then came a minor slump. He lost the Philadelphia and U.S. Indoor and also bowed to Stan Smith in an event in Sacramento, California. In the first Wimbledon Open he scored victories over Newcombe and Okker before losing to the favorite and ultimate winner, Laver, in the semifinals.

But triumphs followed. He won the Bristol Open against Cliff Richey and Graebner and the Pennsylvania Grass Courts at Merion against Marty Riessen. Playing brilliant tennis he swept through the international field in the U.S. Amateur at Brookline, Massachusetts, the first American to win the event since Tony Trabert in 1955.

Then, riding a twenty consecutive game winning streak, he came to Forest Hills. It was here he scored his sensational upset victory in the U.S. Open, surviving against the greatest amateurs and pros in the world.

Like Wimbledon, this was supposed to be the private preserve of the pros. Laver was top-seeded, rated the Number One player in the world and seeking to add the American to his Wimbledon crown. Then came three other Australian pros, Tony Roche, Ken Rosewall and John Newcombe, all of whom had dominated the game at one time or another. The chances of Ashe or any other amateur cracking through this formidable cordon were remote. A London book-maker put the odds against an amateur at 30–1.

Ashe drew a first round bye and in the second round toyed with the fifty-three-year-old former champion, Frank Parker, then scored an easy straight-set victory over Paul Hutchins. In the fourth round came Ashe's first severe test, a match against Roy Emerson, six times winner of the Australian title, with two Wimbledon and two U.S. crowns also on his belt.

In other days Emerson might have overpowered Ashe with his relentless, almost errorless attack and his superb conditioning but he found more than his match in the new Ashe with his cyclonic service, piercing backhand and deft drop shots. Ashe won 6–4, 9–7, 6–3 and still had not dropped a set. The same round saw the elimination of Laver at the hands of South Africa's Cliff Drysdale and the defeat of the second-seeded Roche by the wily, forty-year-old Gonzales.

In the quarter-finals, Ashe blunted Drysdale's two-fisted backhand and in the semifinals mowed down his Davis Cup teammate, Clark Graebner, in a battle of big services. Meanwhile, the pros continued to fall—Dennis Ralston, Gonzales and Newcombe—and Ashe came out to the last bracket against another amateur, or sort of amateur, the sensational Dutch Flyer, Tom Okker, who was building up a reputation as a pro-killer. The twenty-four-year-old Okker, lightning-quick, court-wise and brimming with confidence, erased the last remaining ranking pro, Ken Rosewall, in the semifinals.

Ashe's presence in the final brought a sell-out crowd of more than 14,000 to the West Side Tennis Club. Could Ashe's serving power overcome Okker's catlike speed and amazing reflexes? Could the Negro youth that some had labeled a marshmallow fighter come through in the big one?

The answer required two hours and forty-three minutes, but all of it was sparkling, dramatic tennis. Gunning his service as one would a 155 MM Howitzer, Ashe won the marathon first set 14–12, lost the second, then forged into control in the third. No one doubted that Arthur would stow it away quickly after the third-set intermission but Okker surprised by knotting the match at two sets each. Then Ashe, hitting the chalk with his cannonball service, applied the crusher in the final set.

"This week, at least," commented Jack Kramer, the former court king who did television commentary, "Ashe proved himself the best player in the world. His improvement astonished me."

Ashe's big weapon was his service. Some said it had been clocked at more than 115 miles per hour, three miles faster than Gonzales' blazing delivery in the latter's heyday. At any rate, it came off Arthur's racket too fast for the human eye to see and often Okker let it pass without a swing. Once, the young man from the Netherlands turned his back as if to receive the service from that position and say, "What's the use? I can't see it anyway." Ashe had 26 service aces in the final match.

But that proved only a fraction of his tennis repertoire. He showed himself to be at last the complete player. He scored repeatedly on drop shots and stop volleys, touch tennis seldom associated with the power game. He lofted lobs over Okker's head onto the back line. He volleyed magnificently.

Perhaps even more potent in the long run than Ashe's service was his slashing backhand, which he flipped, cut and spun for repeated winners. They said of Ashe that he had 17 different backhand shots and he often was caught in a dilemma of which to use—whether to chop it back at the net-rusher's feet or slam it cross-court with a full top-spin swipe the way Don Budge used to do.

He was still on his winning streak when he left Forest Hills—now with twenty-six in a row—and into the West Coast tournaments, the Davis Cup Inter-Zone matches and

Challenge Round, another campaign in Australia and in February, 1969, release from the army.

Waiting at the end of the rainbow was a professional contract for $100,000 a year. But fame hadn't blinded the young Negro to his responsibilities to his race.

"I want to work for my people," he said. "I hope to work for the Urban League, concentrating on helping black children."

And though he declined to align himself with black militants, he insisted some them are necessary "to keep people honest."

Said Ashe: "I'm not eligible to join the Los Angeles Tennis Club and in New York I probably won't be able to buy the apartment I want. My knowledge of my heritage doesn't go beyond one generation. All I know is that the Ashes—like every other American Negro family—got their name from the slave masters who owned them."

TWO
14
The Women — Petticoats to Lace Panties

Since the Gay Nineties women's rights have increased dramatically and tennis has felt the impact.

When the game was first introduced in England and the United States there was reluctance to let the ladies participate. Many prim young women themselves demurred. The sport was too strenuous. Women who engaged in it would lose their femininity. Besides, how could they prance around a court in all the paraphernalia that was the style of the day?

The ladies, as has been the case throughout history, refused to be denied. Watching their men cavort on the soft green grass, they became intrigued. They demanded a chance to try, and received it. Not only did Mary Ewing Outerbridge bring the first tennis equipment into the United

States but records show that women were playing against each other and with men as far back as the 1870's. But it wasn't easy.

The ladies wore long, frilly dresses that reached to the ankles. Underneath were layers of petticoats which rustled when they ran. Stiff collars rode on the neck and a ribbon or tie was always at the throat. On their heads were big, floppy, wide-brimmed hats, some with flowers.

The cumbersome apparel wasn't too much of an handicap in the early days since tennis was a slow game. The girls moved with delicate, mincing steps, served underhand and gave the ball gentle pats, giggling and chatting all the while.

Championships for women were inaugurated in England in 1884 and in the United States in 1887. Lottie Dod, one of the first English champions, winning the national title at age fourteen, began tearing down traditions early. An athletic girl, she said, "Ladies should learn to run, and run their hardest, not merely stride."

The first U.S. champion, Ellen Hansell, said years afterward: "We did, now and then, grip our overdraped voluminous skirt with our left hand to give us a bit more 'limb' freedom when dashing to make a swift, snappy stroke, every bit as well placed as today, but lacking the force and great strength of the modern girl."

Suzanne Lenglen of France was one of the first to resist the overly proper way of dress when she appeared on the courts in a one-piece sleeveless dress, cut low at the neck and rising to mid-calf. She wore no petticoat and was hatless, except for a bandana. At first prim galleries were shocked, then delighted.

The same shock waves went through the stands when Alice Marble appeared in the first boyish shorts in the 1930's and Gertrude (Gorgeous Gussy) Moran walked onto the center court at Wimbledon with lace trimmings peeking out from a tight-fitting pair of panties under a short ballerina skirt. Later some women's costumes became as brief as the wardrobe of the Folies Bergère. Nobody blinked.

Women's tennis in the United States created little attention until first Hazel Hotchkiss and then Molla Bjurstedt appeared on the scene.

Hazel Hotchkiss was the daughter of a pioneer who drove a covered wagon from Kentucky to California where he became a successful farmer and winery owner. A sturdy farm girl she took naturally to all sports. She played baseball and football with the boys until the family moved to Berkeley, California, where her parents encouraged her to take up tennis.

She decided to become a serious competitor after watching May and Florence Sutton in a tournament at San Rafael. There intense rivalries followed with all the Sutton sisters —May, Florence, Ethel and Violet—but it was years before she was able to beat May, the best.

Hazel won the first of her three straight women's championships in 1909 and she returned ten years later for a fourth crown. She was, by then, wife of George Wightman. Her fabulous career spanned three eras. She played women's doubles with Helen Wills and mixed doubles with Big Bill Tilden. In all, she captured forty-four national titles, the last a senior's championship when she was sixty-eight years old.

Mary K. Browne, a slender Californian who could fire a lethal forehand drive with a Western grip, took over as women's champion in 1912, ruling three years until America was introduced to the amazing Molla Bjurstedt, later Molla Mallory.

TWO
————
14
————
I

Molla and Hazel — The First Ladies of Tennis

Molla was the "First Lady" of tennis in her native Norway for ten years before she came to the United States to reign as queen of the courts. She won the national singles championship eight times—one more than the mark of Helen Wills Moody—and carried off numerous other honors, including mixed doubles victories with Tilden.

She arrived in the fall of 1914 to visit her mother's cousin in Brooklyn, and she liked the country so well she decided to stay. She had been in the United States only a few months when her interest was aroused by newspaper reports of the National Indoor Championships at the Seventh Regiment Armory in New York.

"Do you think I might enter?" she asked a friend.

"Why not?" the friend replied. "Go ahead."

For Molla it was largely a lark, and she didn't give herself much chance of winning. Although champion of Norway, she had been beaten frequently by women in Europe. She had placed only third in the 1912 Olympics. Yet she had one advantage. She was accustomed to indoor play. The glass-like floor and the glaring lights of the Armory were no hindrance to her.

Surprisingly, Molla advanced to the final where she met Marie Wagner, a very good player with sound strokes. Miss Wagner had a better service than the Norwegian but was not as fast. Molla, with indoor experience, caught the ball on the rise and this gave her a tremendous advantage. She won 6–4, 6–4.

Later in the year, the Norse girl won the first of her national championships on grass, beating Mrs. Wightman in the final. Now she was established. American women tennis players would have to deal with her for years.

Molla won the women's national title four years in a row before Mrs. Wightman broke the string in 1919. Then she came back to win in 1920, 1921, 1922 and, after three victories by Helen Wills, again in 1926. It was a fabulous record.

Undoubtedly, Molla would have made it eight championships in a row if romance had not entered her life in 1919.

That year, on a tennis excursion train bound for Palm

Beach, Florida, she met Franklin I. Mallory, a New York stock broker, who had been invited by the tennis party and was taking the trip as a vacation. They became constant companions.

When Molla won the women's trophy in the Florida tournament she had her initials engraved on it. Six months later, she and Mallory were married and set up house in a fashionable apartment on New York's Fifth Avenue.

Molla always disdained practice—tennis to her was just fun—and she all but abandoned her training in 1919 while busying herself as a housewife. Her game suffered and she lost her national title to Mrs. Wightman.

"How could I go to bed every night at 9 o'clock when my husband wanted to go out?" Mrs. Mallory explained. "Why, he would have been terribly bored and I couldn't blame him."

The following year, she was back in the tennis groove. She defeated Marion Zinderstein in the final at Forest Hills, repeated the victory in 1921 and won a hard three-set victory from Mary K. Browne in 1922. "Mary K. Browne had perhaps the best all-around game of her day," Molla said.

In 1921 Molla competed in the world's hard court championships at Paris where she was beaten by Mlle. Suzanne Lenglen. Disturbed by the loss, she confided to friends that she couldn't wait until she got another shot at the French ace, preferably in America.

Her wish was granted. The following year, Suzanne came to the United States to enter the championships at Forest Hills. As luck would have it, Molla, the American champion, and Suzanne, queen of Wimbledon, were paired in the first round.

Molla won the first set 6–2. After only a few shots in the second, Mlle. Lenglen, coughing violently, burst into tears and walked off the court. She defaulted to Mrs. Mallory because of illness.

The incident provoked an international furor. American writers accused the French girl of running out and denying her opponent a deserved victory. In the foreign press Mrs. Mallory was criticized for being too intent on beating a rival who obviously was too ill to play.

At Wimbledon, in July, Suzanne got her revenge. Playing Molla in the final, the French wizard reached the brilliant heights of which she was capable and blew the American champion off the court 6–2, 6–0.

Mrs. Mallory still was not satisfied. So another match was arranged between the two, this time in Suzanne's home city of Nice. Molla and her husband spent the evenings enjoying the sights and lights of Monte Carlo and other Mediterranean resorts. Suzanne worked diligently on her game. When they played, Suzanne was murderous, winning 6–0, 6–0.

Molla won four mixed doubles crowns—grass court and indoor—with Tilden as a partner. She shared the women's doubles title in 1916 and 1917 with Eleonora Sears. She played on the first Wightman Cup team in 1923 and piled up an imposing record in the international tournament.

Helen Wills defeated Molla for the singles championship in 1923 and started a dynasty of her own. Molla came back in 1926 to win her eighth title, downing Elizabeth Ryan in the final, but her tennis days were numbered.

Her last competitive match was in the Wightman Cup in 1928 when handicapped by a knee injury, she was beaten.

She retired in 1929. On November 22, 1959, she succumbed to a long illness in Stockholm at age sixty-seven.

"I had just one sure good shot," said Molla Mallory. "It was a strong drive and I used as much top-spin as I could. I always tried to get the ball on the rise. That way I had a split second advantage."

Talent wasn't her secret, she claimed. She won championships because she played, in her own words, "hard, steady, offensive tennis."

She was no dazzling beauty. She had a long, Gallic nose, a large mouth and long chin. She was stocky and swarthy with thick shoulders and lantern jaw. Yet she was supple and light as a cat on the court, and possessed a fiery temperament. She was the greatest tennis player of her day—many contend the greatest ever—and no woman, not even the fabulous Helen Wills Moody, made a greater impact on the game. For all her glamour, Suzanne Lenglen of France lived a life of tears and tensions. She was the daughter of triumph and tragedy.

In her heyday—the years immediately following World War I—she was the darling of the sports world. Thousands fought to get into arenas to watch her strike a ball. She was fawned over by kings and queens. She associated with princes and potentates. She filled Wimbledon Stadium every time she played there. Her exploits became front page news in journals throughout the world.

Time and progress produced a new breed of power player which undoubtedly was superior. But champions must be judged according to the competition and conditions of the day. In her era Suzanne was nonpareil. She proved this by crushing the American champion, Molla Mallory, 6–0, 6–0, dropping only 18 points in the entire match. She defeated Helen Wills in their only meeting.

Mlle. Lenglen could actually put a ball on a dime—or a franc, in this case—so phenomenal was her accuracy. She hit a coin as many as five times in a row, a trick learned in her childhood. She was the epitome of grace and style and at the same time a relentless court killer. Driven by doting parents, she begrudged every point scored against her. Tense and high-strung, she never gave an inch.

In 1919 she won Wimbledon in her first appearance at the age of 20 and went on to take six All-England women's crowns. She won six French championships over a period of seven years, six Wimbledon women's doubles with Elizabeth Ryan, two French women's doubles titles with Didi Vlasto, three Wimbledon and two French mixed doubles.

Her list of triumphs would have been far lengthier had she not been plagued with chronic illness—pernicious anemia, which took her life prematurely at the age of thirty-nine—and by parents who kept her on the verge of hysteria with their constant coaxing and reproving. She wasn't permitted to have suitors. She became a veritable tennis machine—a frail, sensitive robot always in danger of breaking down.

Suzanne became ill on her first ocean voyage to the United States and defaulted in her celebrated first confrontation with Molla Mallory. She often went into seclusion. Once, at Wimbledon she failed to show up at a match for which the King and Queen had made a special trip to the courts.

Idolized by the French and British, Suzanne was chided by the American press who accused her of being afraid to oppose the U.S. champions. She became a prima donna. She demanded limousines for transportation when other players rode trains. She had her daring costumes made by hand by top designers who fought for the privilege of dressing her free. She threw tantrums, battled with officials and bickered constantly with her parents. But once on the court she turned into a methodical destroyer. It was a trait sewn into her character from her earliest days.

Suzanne Lenglen, born at the turn of the century, grew up in Nice. Her parents were humble, provincial folk who recognized their daughter's tennis potentialities when they saw her hitting a ball on the hard courts of the Place Mozart. They resolved to make her a champion and capitalize on her talents.

Even as a small, sallow-complexioned girl, Suzanne practiced for hours while Mama and Papa Lenglen and a toy Griffon dog named Gyp watched from the sidelines.

"Stupid girl! Keep your eye on the ball!" yelled Mama Lenglen, a short, buxom figure with dark black hair framing her plump face.

"Move, move, keep on the move!" snapped Papa Lenglen, a small man who considered himself an expert at the game.

The father would place a coin on the court for Suzanne to use as a target, and she got so she frequently hit it five times in a row whereupon, with squeals of delight, she would demand double payment from her proud papa.

She was never allowed to become complacent. No matter how much proficiency she achieved, there was always Mama Lenglen upbraiding her for missing a line, serving a double-fault or hitting a ball into the net.

As a teen-ager, she became an attraction for residents and visitors on the south coast of France. Her reputation gained momentum when at age fifteen she won the Hard Courts Championship of the World in a tournament in Paris.

Just when the little French girl appeared on the threshold of a great career, World War I flared in Europe and big-time tournament competition was suspended for four years, from 1915 through 1918.

But the war allowed the Lenglens to further refine their daughter's game. While the guns roared, Suzanne worked on her game from morn 'til night, often playing men who were professionals.

By the war's end, Mlle. Lenglen was no longer a child but a full-grown woman. She was full-bosomed with a nice figure and good legs. Not particularly pretty, she possessed an undeniable attractiveness on the court. Perhaps it lay in her supple grace and speed. She had also established herself— principally in informal events on the Riviera—as the unrivalled women's champion of France. However, both she and her parents knew she had to make her mark at Wimbledon, the center of world tennis.

There was considerable trepidation in the Lenglen family when it crossed the English Channel to challenge the great but aging British star, Mrs. Lambert Chambers. The slender, slightly stooped British matron was a living legend at the famed tennis club on Worple Road. She had won the first of her titles eighteen years before, when Suzanne was only two. A determined competitor with long, sweeping strokes, Mrs. Chambers was regarded as unbeatable by the worshipful British.

Suzanne's reputation in France had preceded her, and the British were anxious to cast eyes on the twenty-year-old French mademoiselle who had the nerve to challenge their champion. Suzanne created additional excitement when she appeared on the Wimbledon courts with a low-cut, one-piece dress that dropped only to her mid-calves.

This was scandalous to the more conservative elements, accustomed to seeing their women cavort in corseted waists, long-sleeved blouses and ankle-length skirts padded with layers of petticoats. Most people found it a delight.

The British pulse quickened even more when the daring French girl swept through all opposition with systematic dispatch and emerged to challenge Mrs. Chambers for the women's title. Under the rules the champion was compelled to play only the final match.

"Can this French girl actually beat Mrs. Chambers?" the fans asked each other uneasily. The challenge created more excitement than had been experienced around Wimbledon in decades.

It was a titanic match. Mrs. Chambers, down 1–4 in the third and deciding set, fought back to lead 6–5 and 40–15 with double match point. A lucky wood shot and a slashing backhand pulled Suzanne out of trouble and she went on to win the match 10–8, 4–6, 9–7.

The triumph marked an end of the conservative, casual and strictly social age of tennis and a beginning of the "Lenglen Era." The graceful French star, with her fiery temperament and risqué attire, opened up the game to the masses. She now was Wimbledon champion, a world celebrity.

People flocked to see her. It was because of Suzanne's popularity that the All-England Club was forced in 1922 to abandon its modest quarters on Worple Road and seek a more spacious home.

It was natural that America should also want a look at this bright new star. Suzanne had beaten the American champion, Molla Bjurstedt Mallory, in the French Hard Court Championships in the spring of 1921 and there was a clamor for a return match on U.S. soil.

Socialite Anne Morgan of the J.P. Morgan clan hit upon the scheme of having Mlle. Lenglen and Mrs. Mallory play a series in the United States for charity, the main proceeds to go to the restoration of war-ravaged areas of France.

Papa and Mama Lenglen disagreed on whether Suzanne should make the trip. Mrs. Lenglen contended it was a patriotic gesture that would work not only to the advantage of France but to Suzanne as well. Mr. Lenglen felt the journey would be unwise. Suzanne was not well, having suffered from recurrences of asthma. Besides, there was little pecuniary gain. "Don't go," he advised. "You will tire yourself for nothing."

As usually happens in such cases, the mother had her way. Suzanne, her asthma worse and her nerves edgy, became ill on the boat. She was wan and weak when she disembarked, greeted by scores of newsmen.

There had also been a misunderstanding about whether she would play in the United States Championships at Forest Hills, which were imminent. Papa Lenglen had advised against it, telling her daughter she should confine herself to the charity series. Suzanne, reluctant to play, finally bowed to pressure from U.S. officials.

Tournament directors advised the French girl she would have easy opponents in the early rounds and plenty of opportunity to get in shape. She got in one practice session. Then her opening round opponent, Eleanor Goss, defaulted.

In the second round, Suzanne found herself facing the formidable Mrs. Mallory. This was the result of a blind draw, seeding not having been introduced to the tournament.

The great French star suddenly found herself the most lonesome girl in the world. Thousands poured into the stands for the match. This wasn't Wimbledon or Paris. The crowd was vocally pro-Mallory. Suzanne was weak from her illness and stricken with periodic coughing spells. There was no Papa Lenglen to signal encouragement or to toss her brandy-soaked lumps of sugar.

The American champion hadn't forgotten her loss to Suzanne in Paris. Molla Mallory was not only physically ready but fired with determination. Playing superbly, Molla ran through the first set 6–2. Mlle. Lenglen was only a shadow of the woman who had already won three Wimbledons and two French crowns.

Suzanne started the second set on service. Coughing, her shoulders sagging, she hardly made an attempt at the first point. Then she served two balls weakly into the net— double-fault, love 30! At this point, Suzanne walked toward the umpire's chair.

"I am sorry," she said in French. "I cannot continue. I am too ill." In tears she picked up her sweater and extra rackets and stalked to the dressing rooms.

The crowd was stunned. Newsmen were bitter and perhaps a bit unfair. They charged Suzanne with "dogging it," saying she quit because she could not stand the embarrassment of losing to the American titleholder. She should have stuck it out, they insisted.

A few days later Mlle. Lenglen was scheduled to begin her series with Mrs. Mallory at Glen Cove on Long Island. A large crowd gathered for the event. Suzanne failed to show. "Doctor's orders," she apologized. Again she was sharply criticized by the American press.

Upset by her experiences in the United States, the French star returned home. Papa was right—she never should have made the trip.

The question of who was the greatest woman tennis player remained unanswered—and hotly argued. Many conceded Suzanne was ill and her American performance no true criterion. Observers in Britain and Europe stoutly defended her. Americans hailed Mrs. Mallory and charged Mlle. Lenglen with fearing a head-to-head confrontation.

The argument was not allowed to simmer long. After winning the seventh of her eight U.S. titles in 1922, Mrs. Mallory sailed boldly for England to carry the rivalry to Suzanne's doorstep.

They found themselves eye-to-eye again at Wimbledon, which had moved to Church Road near Wimbledon Common. Excitement was high. The King and Queen were among the thousands drawn to the new site. The feeling between Mlle. Lenglen and Mrs. Mallory was understandably strained. A representative of the U.S. Lawn Tennis Association felt compelled to issue a formal statement denying remarks reportedly made about Suzanne by Mrs. Mallory.

The two met in the final on Wimbledon's new center court. It was no contest. Suzanne crushed the American champion 6–2, 6–0. Another match was played later at Nice, Suzanne's home, and the defeat of the American was even more devastating. Mlle. Lenglen won 6–0, 6–0, losing only 18 points.

Now Suzanne was indisputably the queen of tennis. But the strain of tournament competition and the tensions at home began to wear heavily on the French ace. She wearied of practicing. She resented her mother's tirades. Her illness became more pronounced.

In 1924 an attack of jaundice kept her out of the French Championships and the title went to Didi Vlasto. At first there was doubt Suzanne could play at Wimbledon. She showed up pale and hollow-eyed and defeated her longtime friend and doubles partner, Elizabeth Ryan, only to withdraw later upon advice of doctors. Kathleen McKane, a British girl, was the winner while the loser was the bright new star emerging in America, Helen Wills.

In the United States, newspaper columnists revived an old chant: Suzanne Lenglen had pulled out of Wimbledon because she did not want to face Helen Wills just as she had been reluctant to meet Molla Mallory three years before.

Suzanne took a long rest at her home in Nice and came back in 1925 with renewed vigor. She won her fifth French title and captured Wimbledon for the sixth time. She again was smothered with flowers and admirers.

Across the Atlantic, however, there was the lengthening shadow of Helen Wills, the "Little Miss Poker Face" in the white visor, being acclaimed as one of the greatest of all time. Such reports stung the proud Suzanne.

She was growing increasingly weary of the constant pressure. Her father was ill and, doctors said, would never be able to toss her another sugar lump or a bit of sage advice. Promoters were pestering her to turn professional. But to make her pro career a real financial success, they said she must first take care of Helen Wills.

Miss Wills issued a statement that she was willing to play Mlle. Lenglen any place at any time. Tennis commentators around the world badgered the French girl with the challenge: "When are you going to accept Helen's dare?"

Finally Suzanne agreed to meet the Yankee marvel at the Carlton Club in Cannes, a place on the Riviera operated by friends. The date was fixed for February 1926. Announcement of the match triggered wild excitement. People poured in from all over Europe and overseas.

Special grandstands were built. Still there was not enough room to meet the demand and no more than 3,000 could get in. Tickets sold for $11, a fantastic price for the period, and speculators got as much as $50 for a single admission.

Some enthusiastic fans climbed trees and others bought space on rooftops of neighboring houses.

At last, after several days of frustrating postponements because of rain, the weather cleared enabling the match to take place. An atmosphere resembling that of a world championship prize fight prevailed when the two great champions faced each other across the net—Helen Wills in her familiar visor and Suzanne in her bandeau, tied by a diamond clasp.

Helen was grim and methodical as she raked the lines with accurate drives. Mlle. Lenglen was not up to her best form but she had the advantage of experience and of a home setting—the crowd was strictly pro-Lenglen. The French girl prevailed in two hard deuced sets. It was to be the only meeting between the two magnetic tennis personalities.

Suzanne's thirst for greatness was not fully satisfied. Although contemplating a pro career, she wanted to match Mrs. Chambers' record of seven Wimbledon victories and she was anxious to solidify her position by scoring additional victories over Helen Wills. She determined to play in both the French and Wimbledon Championships in 1926.

She won the French title but Wimbledon proved disastrous.

Wimbledon's Golden Jubilee tournament had hardly started before the temperamental Suzanne got in a hassle with the organizers. After winning her opening singles match from Mary K. Browne, she found she was scheduled to play two matches on the same day, one of them a doubles match against her former partner, Elizabeth Ryan.

Suzanne balked. When the royal limousine drove up with Queen Mary, who came out especially to see the exciting French star, the organizers panicked.

While Suzanne closeted herself in the dressing room, the Queen was left waiting in the Royal Box. There was mad commotion in the Committee Room. Finally Suzanne appeared but as she passed through the portals she gave the officials a thorough tongue-lashing. Jean Borotra, Suzanne's fellow countryman, was dispatched to the Royal Box to apologize to the Queen.

The Queen fidgeted restlessly in the Royal Box while Suzanne and tournament officials bickered in the dressing room. At first, she was defaulted. Then the default was withdrawn. Finally, hours late, she made her appearance on the center court. Playing dispiritedly, she lost in singles to Mrs. J.G. Dewhurst of Ceylon. Then she and her longtime French partner, Didi Vlasto, bowed in doubles to Misses Ryan and Browne. Then the famed French star left the center court clad in a cloak of bitterness.

Later that year, Suzanne signed a $50,000 professional contract with Charles C. (Cash and Carry) Pyle, an American promoter, who also obtained Vincent Richards, Harvey Snodgrass, Howard O. Kinsey, Paul Peret and Mary K. Browne.

Suzanne was matched in one exhibition against Miss Browne, winner of three straight U.S. women's titles. The tour was such a success that Mlle. Lenglen was given a $25,000 bonus.

Said the Frenchwoman, who had been driven to the top by her parents' ambition and her own fierce pride, "At last, after fifteen years of torture, I can enjoy my tennis."

TWO   *Queen Helen — Miss Poker Face*

14

III

The Roaring Twenties spawned such sports giants as Babe Ruth, Big Bill Tilden, Bob Jones, Red Grange and Jack Dempsey. But all these rugged males had to move over and make room for a lady, Helen Wills.

This phlegmatic, racket-swinging automaton from the courts of Northern California perhaps did as much as any other single person to make women's sports equal to men's.

In that so-called period of Wonderful Nonsense—the days

of the easy dollar, the Charleston, the tin flivvers and speak-easies—the name of Helen Wills became a household word. She was the undisputed queen of women's tennis in America just as Suzanne Lenglen was the toast of Europe.

Helen was something of an enigma. Caught in off moments, she was a giggling, effervescent schoolgirl in black pig-tails, white blouse and neatly pleated skirt. To the general public, most of her opponents and newspapermen, she was an unemotional machine. She never said a word. She never made a gesture. She never froze a linesman with an icy stare. She went about her work like a grim tailor fashioning a cloak of defeat for anyone with the temerity to face her across the net.

Her trademark was a green-lined white eye-shade, pulled low over a chiseled Grecian countenance. They called her "Little Miss Poker Face."

Years after Queen Helen had retired to a quiet life at the foot of a picturesque canyon near Santa Monica, California, taking with her the trophies of eight Wimbledon and seven American ladies' singles championships plus numerous other honors, the sports world pondered her mysterious personality. Was she cold and aloof, or timid and retiring? Was the absence of passion merely an indication of tremendous calm?

The well-known educator and writer of the period, William Lyon Phelps, believed the latter. Discussing her lack of expression during a match, he wrote: "This did not mean that she was grim, or tense; it meant that she was calm. She was placid. She showed only equanimity."

Helen Wills was born in October 1905 in Berkeley, California, the daughter of Dr. and Mrs. Clarence Wills. It was her father, a fair club player, who got her interested in the game when she was a child. But at the age of thirteen Helen didn't even have her own racket. She had to haul out Dr. Wills' heavy, 15-ounce bat when she went away to boarding school at Bishop Hopkins Hall in Burlington, Vermont.

Even then, she did not play often. The school courts had been torn up for repairs and it was not until 1919 when her father returned from France, where he had served at the U.S. Army Base Hospital, that she was able to play tennis regularly. There was no Spartan training, no intense dedication. It was a fun game for Helen who liked to be outdoors. It wasn't long before she could beat her dad.

Doctor Wills recognized the potential of his daughter's game and felt it should be developed. On Helen's fourteenth birthday, he gave her a junior membership in the Berkeley Tennis Club.

Here she fell under the influence of William (Pop) Fuller, a non-professional coach. Pop treated her as he did his other pupils. He gave her pointers on fundamentals and arranged matches with other youngsters but made no attempt to be a hard-driving coach.

Helen mastered the game rapidly and was so strong that she was soon competing with boys. As a result her game developed faster.

In her first year at the club Helen played in a junior tournament and won. Team matches and other tournaments, to which she traveled chaperoned by her father, followed.

In a trip to San Francisco she happened to see Little Bill Johnston. Enthralled by the driving power of such a frail man, she tried to copy Little Bill's strokes, particularly his forehand.

"I'm Johnston," she would say, drawing back and putting everything she had behind her swing. She got so she could not only hit the ball with tremendous force but almost place it on a dime. The forehand became her chief weapon.

By the spring of 1921 Helen was the talk of California tennis. She won the Pacific Coast Junior Girls Championship and was chosen to represent the state in the National Juniors at Forest Hills. Playing on grass, a tricky surface to which she was unaccustomed, she became at 15—two years after taking up the game—the U.S. champion of girls 18-and-under.

Helen played the Eastern grass court circuit, astounding tennis buffs with her forceful style and maturity, and stayed around for the National Championships at Forest Hills where she got her first glimpse of the great Suzanne Lenglen.

She watched Miss Lenglen default to Mrs. Mallory—an act that Helen herself was to repeat years later in an historic match against Helen Jacobs.

Helen was so entranced with Mlle. Lenglen with her risqué attire and fluid grace, she neglected to take much note of Mrs. Mallory. The oversight was costly. The following year, after repeating as junior girls' champion, she shot her way into the women's final and was crushed by the formidable Molla 6–3, 6–1.

This humiliating defeat only made the little Californian more determined. Helen went home and worked relentlessly on her game under the eyes of Pop Fuller and her father. In 1923 Miss Wills was picked as a member of the first U.S. Wightman Cup team, inaugurating an international series against the best women players of Britain.

Helen met Kathleen McKane in the first match played on the center court of Forest Hills' new concrete horseshoe. She won 6–2, 7–5, scored another singles triumph and teamed with Mrs. Mallory in a doubles victory that launched a long and successful Wightman Cup career.

The National Championships followed and again the veteran Mrs. Mallory and the California teen-ager swept into the women's final. Helen, who had hitherto been playing in pig-tails, arrived for the match with her dark brown hair done up in buns. It seemed she had become a woman overnight. This was also reflected in the result. Playing powerful, almost faultless tennis, Helen crushed the thirty-seven-year-old defending champion 6–2, 6–1.

Thus the Helen Wills Era was born. During the ensuing

decade, galleries throughout the world thrilled to the business-like, destructive stroking power of the expressionless girl in the white visor.

She became the sports darling of the Golden Era. W. O. (Bill) McGeehan wrote in the New York *Herald-Tribune*:

She is powerful, repressed and imperturbable. She plays her game with a silent, deadly earnestness, concentrated on her work. That, of course, is the way to win games, but it does not please galleries. Of course, there is no reason why an amateur athlete should try to please galleries.

Paul Gallico, of the New York *Daily News*, told of an incident in which Miss Wills and a top-ranked U.S. male player, Fritz Mercur, played a practice match on an outside court during the National Championships, and Helen won.

The defeat nettled Mercur, who out of deference for Helen's sex had refused to go to the net. He asked for a return bout and got it, the two electing to play on the center court in the morning well before the regular schedule was to start.

This time, Mercur, employing all his masculine skills, redeemed his earlier loss, but not easily, and Gallico, one of the few witnesses to the informal drama, discovered a new side of Helen Wills.

"She let her hair down for this one," Gallico reported. "Gone was the so-called poker-face, the grim, impassive expression. She grinned. She laughed. She even giggled. The Queen giggled! . . . For that off-guard hour, she showed herself to be a gay, sprightly, pleasing young girl who could enjoy herself and be gracious in the process."

In 1924 Helen made her first trip overseas for the Wightman Cup matches and the Wimbledon Tournament. The tennis world was buzzing with the question: "Can this new American girl beat Suzanne Lenglen?" The answer was not to come immediately.

Helen played poorly in the Wightman Cup, losing both her singles matches. At Wimbledon she gained the final round where she opposed Miss McKane, England's best player. Helen won the first set 6–4 and led 4–1 in the second when she misjudged a lob and let the ball fall safe. Upset, she became moody and tentative. While the pro-British crowd cheered wildly, Miss McKane rallied for a 4–6, 6–4, 6–4 victory.

Helen was so distraught she burst into tears after the match. British correspondents were a bit heartless. They chided Miss Wills for her sphinx-like demeanor. They made fun of her apparel, suggesting it was undignified to wear a school uniform (middie blouse and white skirt) on Wimbledon's sacred center court. They criticized her eye-shade and one said, "We thought the effect of this strange rig-out was clumsy and uninspiring."

But Miss Wills shook off the effects of this experience, going on to win the singles and doubles at the Olympics in Paris and to retain her U.S. crown, simultaneously avenging her defeat by Kathleen McKane.

As her tennis conquests multiplied, demands grew for a head-to-head duel between Helen and Suzanne Lenglen to determine the best woman player in the world. Strangely, their paths had not crossed. Miss Lenglen, ill and moody, was accused of avoiding a confrontation. Some said she ducked tournaments which Helen might enter and played in those Miss Wills would avoid.

None wanted the match more than Helen Wills. She felt certain she could beat the French ace and was eager to prove it. The opportunity came in January 1926. Helen learned Mlle. Lenglen was campaigning in the south of France. Taking leave of her studies, she headed for the Continent to meet with Suzanne.

Rumors exploded like Chinese firecrackers. One report said Miss Wills had made a deal to help exploit tourist trade in the Riviera, another that a motion picture company had paid $100,000 for the rights to film the match. Someone claimed Mlle. Lenglen had become so panicky that she was ready to flee home under the pretense of renewed illness.

Ultimately the two queens found themselves in a tournament at the Carleton Club in Cannes. Excitement reached a fever pitch.

Suzanne, sleeveless, wearing a calf-length skirt with no petticoat and a low-cut blouse, played brilliantly and won the match 6–3, 8–6 although Miss Wills held set point at 5–4 in the second set.

"I never had such a thrill in my life," Helen graciously commented later. "It was our only meeting and the greatest match I ever played." She was stricken with appendicitis later that season and Mlle. Lenglen shortly afterward turned professional.

Helen won six U.S. women's titles in seven years, starting in 1923 and losing only in 1926 because of her appendicitis attack. In 1931 she added a seventh crown. At Wimbledon she won four consecutive titles, beginning in 1927, repeated in 1932, 1933 and 1935 and then came back in 1938, at the age of 32, to capture her eighth British championship.

Her victim on the final occasion was Helen Jacobs, and the victory climaxed a long and controversial rivalry.

Helen Hull Jacobs came from the same tennis incubator that produced Helen Wills. She grew up in the San Francisco Bay area, learned tennis at the knee of Pop Fuller and became heir apparent to the older Helen's throne.

Miss Jacobs was stockier than Miss Wills, much faster afoot and perhaps had greater natural talent. The older Helen worked hard to perfect her game and became almost mechanical in her stroke production. Miss Jacobs had quick reflexes, a good serve and backhand. But her forehand—her rival's big weapon—was weak. They met often, even as youngsters, with the more poised and experienced Miss Wills always the victor until the late 1930's when her game began to slip as the younger Helen's was on the rise.

In 1932, Helen Wills, now Mrs. Helen Wills Moody, passed up the National Championships, and Miss Jacobs won the first of her four straight ladies' titles, defeating Carolin Babcock 6–2, 6–2.

A year later, Helen Wills Moody was back in competition, and there was little excitement when she reached the final with Helen Jacobs. After all, Helen Moody was Queen Helen. Helen Jacobs, although defending titleholder, was regarded as only a mild threat.

The 13,000 seats in Forest Hills' concrete horseshoe were only half filled when the two Helens came onto the center court for what was to be an historic match.

The first set was furiously waged. Little Helen was a fighting tiger. She raced for every ball. She spun, she leaped, she rushed to the net behind almost every shot. Helen Jacobs won the first set 8–6. It was the third set Queen Helen had lost in the last six years.

A buzz went through the crowd. In the press marquee the sports writers stopped their chattering and leaned over their typewriters. History was being made. Tension relaxed when the older Helen rallied to take the second set 6–3.

Interest crackled again when Miss Jacobs broke Mrs. Moody's service in the first game of the final set. It intensified when the younger Helen held her own delivery and broke Queen Helen a second time for a 3–0 lead.

At this point Queen Helen strode to the umpire's chair, put on her sweater and without a word to her opponent advised the official that she could not continue. She had to default.

The spectators were stunned. The newsmen, once they had recovered from the original shock, were outraged. They called her a quitter and a poor sport. They accused her of depriving Miss Jacobs of her moment of glory.

The reason Queen Helen gave for her default was that she had injured her back in the spring of 1933 while lifting heavy rocks in her garden. She had treated the ailment with heat and massages and had managed to win at Wimbledon that year at the cost of severe pain. Returning to the United States she had undergone X-rays and had been informed she was suffering from a sacroiliac condition. She had skipped the Wightman Cup matches but, desirous of chalking up her eighth U.S. women's title, she had been unable to resist entering the Nationals.

At the time, Queen Helen refused to make an explanation, fearing it would be interpreted as an excuse. In her autobiography, written years later, she said she became so dizzy on the court that the stadium seemed to swim around her and she almost fainted before she reached the umpire's chair. "My choice was instinctive rather than premeditated," she said. "Had I been able to think clearly, I might have chosen to remain. Animals and often humans, however, prefer to suffer in a quiet, dark place."

Helen returned to the Pacific Coast for an operation and treatments that kept her idle through the 1934 season. She sought to keep in shape by swimming and walking in the hills around San Francisco but the layoff affected her speed and reflexes.

In 1935 she returned to Wimbledon for the critical test. The occasion gained added significance because the woman she had to beat for her seventh Wimbledon title was Helen Jacobs who had become a favorite of tennis galleries. Queen Helen trained hard to get herself in peak physical and mental shape. Perhaps there was never a match she wanted to win more.

The "Battle of the Two Helens" excited the world and became one of the great matches of all time. It was a titanic triumph for the elder Helen, 6–3, 3–6, 7–5, and the woman they called Miss Poker Face departed from the script when she let out a delighted scream, threw her racket into the air and raced to the net, laughing happily, to throw a friendly arm around her defeated opponent.

Queen Helen then went into virtual retirement for the

next three years and emerged in 1938 for one last fling at Wimbledon. Again she met Little Helen in the final and the latter, suffering a sprain in her right heel midway of the opening set, proved little competition. Queen Helen bowed out gloriously 6–4, 6–0.

In 1937 she turned down a professional contract for a reputed $100,000. That same year she divorced her first husband and two years later married Aidan Roark, writer, polo player and a steward at Santa Anita racetrack. Her life was full of activity. She wrote mystery novels, the first entitled "Death Serves an Ace," as well as tennis books. Her paintings and etchings were exhibited in galleries throughout the world. She sketched for a newspaper syndicate and created fashion designs for a New York department store and interiors for ocean liners.

But as for tennis, she virtually disappeared from the big court scene. She played social matches in Santa Monica but was never seen at the Los Angeles Tennis Club or the West Side Tennis Club in Forest Hills.

The U.S. Lawn Tennis Writers Association sought for years to have Helen come East and receive a trophy awarded annually to tennis immortals. She always declined with thanks, pointing out that she disliked to fly. Visitors to the Roark home said there were no signs that a great tennis champion lived there. The place was bereft of the usual trophies, plaques, pictures and newspaper clippings.

"I don't have a trophy room," Helen usually apologized. "It's too much a problem keeping trophies polished. I have them all packed away in a closet."

TWO   *Alice Marble — The Golden Girl*

14

IV

Years after Helen Wills had abandoned the court and settled down to her painting, writing and housewifely duties as Mrs. Aidan Roark, she was asked whom she thought was the greatest woman tennis player.

Helen, never impetuous and always guarded in her comments, reflected a moment and then replied:

"Alice Marble."

To people who followed tennis closely in the decades before World War II, this was not such a shocking reply. Many able critics were convinced the golden-haired and silver-voiced blonde from California was the best ever, superior to Helen Wills, Helen Jacobs and Suzanne Lenglen.

Alice, a farmer's daughter who was the home-run queen of her neighborhood and at one time the mascot of the San Francisco Seals, took up tennis at thirteen when her brother bought her a racket as a graduation present.

"He said go out and play," Alice recalled later. "I think he wanted me to stop playing baseball with the boys."

Ten years later in 1936 Miss Marble won the first of her four national championships. She captured the Wimbledon title in 1939. She excelled as a doubles player, winning the national women's doubles crown four times with Mrs. Sarah Palfrey Fabyan, taking the mixed doubles four times with as many different partners and capturing the mixed doubles at Wimbledon on three occasions.

In 1939 and 1940, U.S. sports writers overwhelmingly voted her outstanding woman athlete of the year.

Besides being one of the first girls to wear boyish shorts at Forest Hills and Wimbledon, Alice brought a strength to the women's game that had been missing before. A powerfully built girl, five feet, seven inches and 133 pounds, she hit a cannonball service as fast as that of many men. Missing her first delivery, she served an American twist for the second. The twist, requiring a very strong wrist, was almost unreturnable.

A serious illness threatened Miss Marble's career just as she was approaching her peak under the patient coaching of the well-known California instructor, Mrs. Eleanor (Teach) Tennant.

In 1934 while playing a match in Paris, she collapsed on

the court. A physician ordered her to take a complete rest. Not until the spring of 1936 was she well again. Even then, her game lost its edge in 1937 and she suffered a series of frustrating defeats. However, she bounded back to end her career on a high note, signing a professional contract for $25,000 in 1940.

She participated in a nationwide tour with Don Budge, Bill Tilden and Mary Hardwick of England, drawing 12,000 spectators to the inaugural performance at Madison Square Garden.

Alice was born September 28, 1913, on a farm in Plumas County in northeastern California. Her family moved to San Francisco when she was a child. Her older brother Donald, who gave her the racket, was a nationally known handball player. The younger brother Harry, was good enough as a baseball shortstop to receive a tryout in the Pacific Coast League.

She was eighteen before she won a tournament. She shared in a national girls' doubles title in 1931, gained a Number Two ranking among U.S. women in 1932 and in 1933 traveled East to play the grass court circuit, winning several events and capturing national attention for the first time.

In August 1933 while playing in the Maidstone Club Tournament at East Hampton, Long Island, she suffered a grueling experience that led to her physical breakdown. Against her will she was entered in both singles and doubles and as a result of a postponement because of rain, she was compelled to play the semifinals and finals in a single day.

In the morning she won her singles match—an unusually long one—and also her doubles as a partner of Helen Wills Moody. After lunch, with the temperature around 104 degrees, she played the finals in both singles and doubles, winning neither.

Leaving the court, she fainted. She had played 108 games throughout the humid day. Her doctor ordered her to rest.

She skipped the Wightman Cup matches but played in the National Championships, making a poor showing.

The following year, when she collapsed again while playing in Paris, the seriousness of her condition could not be ignored. Detailed examinations were ordered. What originally was thought to have been anemia proved to be tuberculosis, and Alice's tennis career had to be shelved as she underwent months of rest and treatment.

She was strong and fit when she returned in 1936. Hitting the ball better than ever, she swept through the fields at Longwood, Seabright and other Eastern grass court stops and slammed her way into the singles final at Forest Hills. Her opponent was Helen Jacobs, who had held the crown for four consecutive years.

It was an exciting match. Miss Jacobs, who herself at one time had been forced to quit tennis because of pleurisy, hammered away at the blonde Californian and won the first set. Miss Marble, however, serving sharply and playing a strong game at the net, won the match 4–6, 6–3, 6–2.

Alice for some unknown reason suffered a slump in 1937. Jadwiga Jedrzejowska, a sturdy Polish girl, beat her four times during the summer, and Dorothy May Bundy put her out in the quarter-finals of the Nationals won by Anita Lizana.

But those who felt her career had reached a sudden stalemate were in for a rude awakening. After hours of practice every day under "Teach" Tennant, she came back in 1938 stronger than ever. She required only twenty-two minutes to crush Nancy Wynne of Australia in the Nationals 6–0, 6–3. In the 1939 final she beat Miss Jacobs 6–0, 8–10, 6–4 and the next year smothered Little Helen 6–2, 6–3.

In 1939, losing only two games to Britain's Kay Stammers in the final round, she captured Wimbledon.

When Alice retired from tennis she kept busy by writing articles on the sport and making frequent singing appearances in nightclubs. Jill-of-all-trades that she was, she even held a dollar-a-year post as assistant director of civil defense in charge of physical fitness. But those who had faced her across a net remembered her chiefly as the best woman player of her day.

TWO   *Little Mo — Daughter of Triumph and Tragedy*

They called her "Little Mo." At the time following World War II, Americans were still talking about "Big Mo" the battleship *Missouri*. The comparison was apropos. The guns of "Big Mo" could shred a coastline or cut down an enemy fleet from miles away with deadly accuracy. "Little Mo" could crease the chalk of a sideline and chop down a tennis adversary with the same destructive precision.

Maureen Connolly might have been the equal of any woman player who ever lived and she might have set records to surpass those of Suzanne Lenglen and Helen Wills Moody, but no one will ever know. A freak accident cut short her career before it could reach its peak, and she died of cancer in 1969 at the age of thirty-four.

It was a muggy, midsummer day in 1954 and Maureen, who loved to ride horses before she had ever hit a tennis ball, decided to take her favorite roan sorrel, Colonel Merry-boy, for a leisurely gallop.

The admiring citizens of her home town, San Diego, California, had given her the horse as a tribute to her fabulous tennis success. A few weeks earlier Maureen had won her third straight Wimbledon ladies' title, and now she was looking forward to returning to Forest Hills in quest of her fourth consecutive United States championship—and she was not yet 20 years old.

It was a dream she was never to realize. As "Little Mo" rode along a cinder path beside a highway, Colonel Merry-boy became frightened by an approaching cement truck. He bolted and slammed against the side of the truck. Maureen, her right leg smashed, was thrown into a ditch.

The accident stunned the sports world. For a time, it appeared the injury might not be too serious and "Little Mo" would be able to return to tennis after a few months on crutches. However, the leg, gashed to the bone, never healed properly. Maureen, awarded $95,000 in damages, announced she would never play competitive tennis again. "If I can't play the way I used to, there is no need in playing at all," she said.

Shortly afterwards, she married Norman Brinker, an Olympic equestrian ace and Navy officer whom she had met at a San Diego riding academy. Brinker, discharged from the Navy, became an executive in a restaurant chain. "Little Mo" settled down to the life of a housewife and mother.

Her tennis was behind her. Although she missed the limelight and the excitement of big-time tournament competition, "Little Mo" resisted tempting offers from promoter Jack Kramer and others to turn professional.

Kramer sought to match Maureen with Althea Gibson, who succeeded her to the women's throne. "I wish I could play again," Maureen said. "I would like to earn the money. But I cannot. My leg still gives me too much pain."

Maureen Connolly was a cold, calculating killer on the court, and conveyed the same stony-faced impression as Helen Wills. Although bubbly and feminine off court, she was grim and businesslike once a racket was in her hand.

She gained a reputation—vigorously denied by her fellow players—of being snobbish and big-headed. Part of this criticism grew from the fact that Maureen, after winning Wimbledon in 1953, had passed up grass court tournaments at Merion, Pennsylvania, and South Orange, New Jersey. A New York newspaper headlined: "National Champion Giving Net Fathers Hard Time with Prima Donna Act." Another paper said in an editorial that the U.S. Lawn Tennis Association wanted to give Maureen some fatherly advice on the value of modesty.

The criticism became so rampant that "Little Mo" saw fit to answer her critics in a national Sunday supplement magazine with an article entitled: "I Am No Swell-Head." She denied she preferred European to American tournaments, that U.S. tournaments bored her and that she shunned sponsors who befriended her.

"I was just overly tired," she explained. "After Wimbledon, I knew I'd need some rest."

She acknowledged she was sometimes curt with photographers and newsmen, although she was a newspaper woman herself, working as a copy girl and later a columnist for the San Diego *Union*.

"I may have become irritated with some particular photographer who got too close while I was serving or running for a wide ball," she said. "And I don't like to be asked questions when I'm all keyed up before or after a match. Give me fifteen minutes to calm down, and I can answer."

On the court, "Little Mo" gave the impression of being short and dumpy, although she wasn't. Actually, she had a very nice figure—five feet, four inches tall and 130 pounds with trim legs. She had kinky blonde hair, a long nose and a puckish face.

She was a deadly sharpshooter off both sides in back court and seemed to take the net less than some of her more aggressive successors, such as Althea Gibson, Maria Bueno and Billie Jean King. There was little explosiveness about her game. She didn't leap and slide, smash and swat. Instead, there was a clinical quality in the way she sliced up her opponents. She was cool, meticulous and relentless.

Eleanor (Teach) Tennant, the famed California coach who developed Alice Marble, Bobby Riggs and Pauline Betz before taking Maureen under her wing, considered "Little Mo" the perfect pupil.

"She had the ability to assimilate what was taught and to execute it properly," the teacher said. "She practiced and practiced. She had no mental blocks or resistance to rigid training. She was extremely responsive and I never once heard her say, 'I can't do that'."

Maureen was born in San Diego on September 17, 1934. She was only two years old when her father, Martin J. Connolly, a chief petty officer in the U.S. Navy, was killed in an automobile accident. She was reared by her widowed mother, an accomplished organist, and a great aunt.

As a child, Maureen was a talented equestrienne who won prizes in horse shows, riding English saddle. Then when she was ten years old, the family moved to a house near the Balboa municipal courts.

Often Maureen wandered over to the courts and watched the tennis games through a wire fence. Her constant presence attracted the attention of Wilbur Folsom, a tennis pro employed by the city. One day he invited the small, curly-haired girl to come inside and hit some balls.

Folsom was immediately impressed with the girl's natural coordination and he invited her to join his pupils. Maureen was thrilled.

"But you're a left-hander," he said. "You will have a lot of problems. I suggest you try playing right-handed."

Maureen agreed. It was hard at first but within three months the converted southpaw could play on equal terms with anyone in her age group. Although not yet eleven, she reached the final round of the thirteen-year-old division in the LaJolla tournament. Shortly afterwards, she won the junior high title in the Harper H. Ink Tournament.

Ink was a retired Ohio businessman whose hobby was helping young tennis players in the San Diego area. He became keenly interested in Maureen and promised to aid in the young girl's development. However, just as a career was beginning to open for her, Maureen was stricken with a series of allergies. She had to give up tennis while doctors sought a cure.

After several months, Maureen returned to the Balboa

Park courts to resume play. She quickly regained her old form and began competing in junior events around Southern California.

It was on one of these tournament excursions, while practicing at Griffith Park in Los Angeles, that Maureen's fluid style and forceful strokes caught the eye of Mrs. Daisy Tree, a leading Southern California player and enthusiast.

"That girl is simply marvelous," exclaimed Mrs. Tree to a companion. "She has wonderful talent. She would be a fine pupil for Teach Tennant."

An interview was arranged with the well-known teacher, renowned as a tennis pro, analyst and psychologist, and Maureen became a Tennant protégé.

Miss Tennant brought her along slowly and never let her play out of her class. Maureen was a perfect pupil. "She grasped the picture of what we hoped to attain in each tournament," Miss Tennant said later. "She improved 25 percent every year."

In 1949 Miss Tennant decided her little protégé was ready for the big time. She brought her East to make her debut in the national girls' championship at the Merion Cricket Club outside Philadelphia.

It was a tremendous challenge for the San Diego girl, just fourteen. She had never played on grass, a tricky surface with a low and inconsistent bounce, nor had she ever been in a national tournament. But from her performance one would have concluded just the opposite.

Playing with remarkable poise, Miss Connolly swept easily into the final where her opponent was a pretty blonde girl being hailed as the new "child wonder" of the game, Laura Lou Jahn from Florida. No one expected Maureen to give Laura Lou much of a battle. Spectators were astounded when Maureen coolly polished her off 6–4, 6–3 and became at fourteen the youngest junior girls' champion in history.

By this time, Miss Tennant had determined to give her prodigy a full baptism of fire. Maureen was entered in the ladies' division of the National Championships at Forest Hills. Crowds leaned over the green fences to watch the little girl with the grown woman's prowess. Maureen lost in the second round to the more experienced Barbara Scofield Davidson.

The following year, 1950, the pace was intensified. Maureen was sent East for the complete grass court circuit. She surprised everyone by beating Helen Pastall Perez for the Pennsylvania title. She gained the final in the Maidstone Invitation and successfully defended her national girls' title, again defeating Laura Lou Jahn 10–8, 6–0. She ranked tenth nationally.

By the 1951 summer season Maureen was recognized as a player of the future. But no one imagined she was capable at sixteen of usurping the women's throne. Mrs. Margaret Osborne duPont had won the title the last three years in a row. Doris Hart, a spindly-legged girl from Florida, had won Wimbledon and was regarded as the Number One woman player in the world. Louise Brough, who had won the U.S. title in 1947 and three straight Wimbledons starting in 1948, was still a formidable factor. Beverly Baker, Patricia Todd, Nancy Chaffee, Barbara Scofield Davidson and Shirley Fry all ranked above Miss Connolly.

Nothing occurred to indicate a coup d'état was imminent in the women's division. Maureen successfully defended her Pennsylvania title but she lost to Pat Todd in the Eastern Grass Court final and the Maidstone Invitation semifinal, although carrying each match to three sets. She bowed to Miss Hart in the semifinals of the Essex Invitation, also in three sets.

What observers did not know was that Miss Tennant was merely pacing her protégé for the National Championships. Maureen was held out of the girls' championship at Philadelphia in order to be rested for the big test at Forest Hills.

She swept through the early rounds and before reaching the semifinals, had already been christened "Little Mo" by inventive sports writers. She was the darling of the gallery when she took the center court against Miss Hart as a distinct underdog.

It was an exciting match but one dominated by Miss Connolly. "Little Mo" raked the sidelines with her ground strokes, never permitting Miss Hart to gain the initiative. When Doris rushed to the net, she often was passed or sent scurrying to the base line by a well-placed lob. Maureen won 6–4, 6–4.

Shirley Fry proved a more difficult obstacle in the final. Maureen obviously suffered a psychological letdown after her victory over Miss Hart. She started strongly but lapsed in the second set, losing it to Miss Fry's powerful attack. However, she managed to rally her game and eke out the victory 6–3, 1–6, 6–4.

"Yeeow!" yelled "Little Mo" as she tossed her racket high in the air and rushed to the net to shake hands with her victim.

She was the youngest player in almost half a century to capture the ladies' crown. The triumph came two weeks before her seventeenth birthday. Helen Wills was seventeen years and eleven months when she won the first of her seven titles in 1923. May Sutton, a British-born Californian, was sixteen years and nine months old—ten weeks younger than Maureen—when she won the championship in 1904.

Maureen repeated at Forest Hills in 1952 and 1953, each time crushing Miss Hart in straight sets. She won at Wimbledon in 1952, 1953 and 1954, beating Miss Brough twice and Miss Hart once.

In 1953 Maureen became the first woman to score a Grand Slam—that is, to win the Australian, French, Wimbledon and U.S. titles in a single year. Australia's towering Margaret Smith came closest in 1963, winning all but the French, taken by her compatriot, Lesley Turner.

There is no telling how many Grand Slams "Little Mo" might have strung together had not Colonel Merryboy become fractious and banged into the cement truck on that tragic day in 1954.

Maureen was disappointed but not bitter. "I've tried everything," she said. "Rest, treatment and the best specialists. But the main artery in my leg was damaged. It can never get much better. I am lucky that the accident was not worse."

TWO
14

Althea Gibson —
From Harlem's Sidewalks to Wimbledon

VI   Overhead, the skies glowered menacingly. People in the stands seemed to realize that history was in the making. At one end of the court was Louise Brough, tall, blonde, classic in her strokes; only a few months before, she had won the second of her four Wimbledon championships. At the other end, a leggy, dark-skinned girl from Harlem—obviously tense and nervous, obviously trying too hard.

"Knock her out of there! Knock her out of there!" came a shrill voice from the gallery.

Althea Gibson gave the offender a steely stare and moved back to her position on the court. This was no time to blow up. It was the greatest opportunity of her life. She couldn't fail now.

It was a landmark in tennis. It was the turning point in the life of Althea Gibson, who had finally cracked the color line and become the first Negro to play on the center court of the West Side Tennis Club at Forest Hills.

It had been a long, hard fight upward from the poverty of the ghettos, from obscurity to the center of one of the world's most famous sports arenas. Tennis, a snobbish, stuffy sport, had yielded grudgingly. Finally, under the pressure of growing indignation, it had given the Negro girl her chance.

It was a second round match. Althea had made her historic debut in the tournament on the most obscure of the field courts—Number 14, the farthest from the old brick clubhouse. The clubhouse clientele, who sat underneath broad umbrellas sipping Martinis, had the pleasure of watching Ginger Rogers, a blonde movie star whose lady-like service wouldn't knock over a pot of tea.

The crowd hardly blinked an eyelid when Miss Brough, serving strongly and attacking the net at every chance, raced through the first set 6–1. A reporter later described Althea as looking "scared to death." A murmur of surprise swept through the gallery when Miss Gibson won the second set 6–3. "Louise just relaxed," one spectator said to another. Newsmen under the marquee, who had been munching sandwiches and engaging in small talk, hustled back to their seats.

Althea now was hitting away, slamming her services into the little square and belting the ball confidently off both wings. She now was playing strong, sure tennis. The man who said she looked scared swallowed his words.

The clouds overhead thickened. The girls swapped services—2–2, 3–3, 4–4, the score went. Althea held service in the 13th game to lead 7–6. The Wimbledon champion was only four points from elimination.

The tension was suddenly broken by a violent thunderstorm. Players and officials grabbed their belongings and ran for the dressing rooms. Spectators sought shelter beneath the concrete stands. A bolt of lightning sheared one of the huge concrete eagles and sent it crumbling to the ground below.

The match, with black-skinned Althea Gibson four points away from beating the best woman tennis player in the world, had to be postponed until the next morning.

"The delay was the worst thing that could have happened to me," Althea recalled later. "It gave me the whole evening and the next morning to think about the match. By the time I got through reading the morning papers, I was a nervous wreck."

A large gallery gathered for the finish. Newsmen and photographers were out in clusters. Newsreel and television cameras were set up to record the event.

Her back to the wall, the poised Miss Brough ran up a quick 4-0-0 lead on service. Althea won two points with good service returns and then Louise half-volleyed for a winning point. Miss Gibson, tense and jittery, got down 15–40 on her own delivery but rallied to play six deuces before finally yielding. Althea saved one match point on the next game but hit a backhand out of court on the second one and that was the match. Miss Brough had won 6–1, 3–6, 9–7.

It didn't matter. The lightning bolt that had toppled the concrete eagle that tempestuous August day in 1950 had signalled a new era in tennis.

Miss Gibson went on to win consecutive Wimbledon and U.S. championships in 1957 and 1958, travel the world and play before the Queen of England and other royalty. She represented the United States on the Wightman Cup team and made tours sponsored by the State Department. For those two years she was undisputed ruler of women's tennis.

Even so, her suspicion and reserve never completely melted. She didn't forget the barriers that had been placed in her way or the fact that her family still lived in a ghetto. She had only a few close associates, and there were only a handful of newsmen who could gain her confidence. Big, sometimes gawky-looking, Althea was largely a loner.

As a tennis ace, however, she had the big game. She served with the power of a man. Long, sturdy legs carried her to all reaches of the court. She hit the ball off the ground with great force and volleyed with killing decisiveness. But her principal forte was fighting determination. Her credo, which she also used as the title of her autobiography, was "I always wanted to be somebody."

At the height of her tennis career Althea turned professional. She hired a lawyer and public relations man, accepted a job fronting for a New York bread firm, gave clinics and exhibitions and got married. To realize a long-held dream she sang on Ed Sullivan's television show. Then, restless to remain in competition, she took up pro golf.

"I want to be the first woman ever to win national championships in both tennis and golf," she declared.

Althea Gibson was born August 25, 1927, in Silver, South Carolina. She was the oldest of four children, two other girls and a boy. Her father Daniel was a sharecropper, a powerfully-built man of 190 pounds and a stern disciplinarian. Her mother Annie was a strong woman who once boasted, "I could jump on a cow or a hog just as if it was a horse."

Silver was "a three store town," according to Daniel Gibson, and the family had tough going. Althea's father and uncle worked five acres of corn and cotton. One year the father estimated his total yield as a bale and a half of cotton, about $75 worth. It didn't take much to persuade the family to move to New York City on the advice of Annie's sister, Aunt Sally, who lived there. Althea, three at the time, went first and stayed with her aunt who, incidentally, made ends meet by selling bootleg whisky.

Almost from the beginning Althea was a difficult, headstrong girl who joined other kids in stealing fruit and vegetables. "In a neighborhood like ours the only way to prove yourself was at games or fighting," she said, and she was good at both. A tomboy, she played marbles and stickball and, at the corner playground, tossed basketballs through the hoop. When she was twelve her father taught her to box and she could lick all the girls and most of the boys on her block. Her attitude towards book learning was considerably less enthusiastic.

"I hated school," she recalled.

From junior high she went to Yorkville Trade School but was soon skipping classes regularly. Her father would give her a licking but she learned to take it without a whimper. Finally she quit school and worked at various jobs, running an elevator or cleaning chickens in a butcher shop. Leaving home, she eventually wound up on the welfare rolls.

There was one ray of hope: Althea had become adept at paddle tennis. She attracted the attention of Buddy Walker, known as Harlem's "Society Orchestra Leader," who bought her some second-hand tennis rackets and started her hitting against the wall of a handball court. She showed tremendous promise and when Juan Serrell, a schoolteacher, saw her on the Harlem River courts he was so impressed he got her admitted to the Cosmopolitan Tennis Club, which catered to some of Harlem's better-heeled citizens. After seeing the strong Negro girl trade shots with Fred Johnson, the one-armed club pro, members chipped in to buy her a junior membership.

Althea was fifteen when she entered her first tournament —the New York State Open, sponsored by the American Tennis Association, at the Cosmopolitan Club. She won the girls' singles. Later that year—1942—the club sent her to the A.T.A. (Negro) national girls' tournament at Lincoln University in Pennsylvania. Though she lost to Nana Davis, she returned to win in 1944 and 1945.

In 1946, now eighteen, Miss Gibson made her debut in the A.T.A. national women's singles at Wilberforce College in Ohio. Battling her way to the final she lost a heart-breaking three-set match to Roumania Peters. Nevertheless the event had its compensations, for it was here Althea caught the eye of two Southerners, Dr. Hubert A. Eaton of Wilmington, North Carolina, and Dr. Robert W. Johnson of Lynchburg, Virginia, interested in assisting Negro tennis players. Encouraged by these two men, Miss Gibson moved South and resumed her education. The next time she entered the A.T.A. women's nationals she won and went on to capture the title ten times in a row. She graduated from high school in Wilmington and, one of the best female tennis players in the world although she still had little opportunity to prove it, enrolled in Florida A. & M. U. on a scholarship.

Although Althea was invited to the National Indoors in 1949 and again in 1950, the National Championships at Forest Hills remained closed to her. Had she chosen to make an issue of it she might have gained acceptance sooner. But she was too proud to be shoved down anybody's throat. "I have never regarded myself as a crusader," she said. "I don't consciously beat the drums for any cause, not even the cause of the Negro in the United States."

Nevertheless she had her supporters. Pressure was brought to bear on tennis officials through news editorials. Alice Marble, one of the country's great women's champions, launched a campaign. "If tennis is a game for ladies and gentlemen," she wrote in the July 1950, issue of American Lawn Tennis, "it's also time we acted a little more like gentlepeople and less like sanctimonious hypocrites."

Such words did not go unheeded. Althea's entry for the Eastern Grass Courts Championships was accepted by the Orange Tennis Club in South Orange, New Jersey; she lost to Helen Pastall Perez in the second round. In the National Clay Courts at Chicago she reached the quarter-finals before bowing to Doris Hart, 6–2, 6–3. Then at last she was admitted to the Nationals. With her near victory over Louise Brough she had realized her goal: Althea Gibson was a "somebody."

Still, although solicitous tennis officials now saw to it that she was given proper instruction, including a session with the famed Jean Hoxie at Hamtramck, Michigan, the next few years were lean ones. Receiving her degree from Florida A. & M. in 1953, she took a job teaching physical education at Lincoln University in Jefferson, Missouri. Maureen (Little Mo) Connolly, a California girl who could thread a needle with her drives down the sidelines, dominated women's tennis, winning Wimbledon and U.S. championships three consecutive years. When she suffered a riding accident Doris Hart and Shirley Fry moved into the picture. Discouraged with her failure to win a major championship Althea decided to give up the game in favor of a career in the Women's Army Corps.

The man who prevented her from doing this was a Harlem taxi driver and part-time tennis pro named Sydney Llewellyn.

"You've got a great future ahead of you," Llewellyn insisted.

"If I was any good I'd be champion now," Althea lamented.

"Give me a chance," Llewellyn said. Althea, protesting she was sick of tennis, reluctantly agreed.

Llewellyn's hack business suffered as he took Althea out on the courts and began remaking her game. He changed the grip she had used for years. He showed her how to get more whip into shots with her wrist. He taught her court tactics. And, most of all, he put new life into her mental attitude.

In 1955 Althea got another important break. Through the help of the U.S. Lawn Tennis Association, principally Renville McMann, then president of the organization, she was chosen on a squad named by the State Department to make a tour of Southeast Asia. Other members of the group were Karol Fageros, a stunning Florida blonde, Ham Richardson and Bob Perry, both secondary U.S. Davis Cup players.

The tour carried the group through India, Burma, Ceylon and Pakistan. When it officially ended in January 1956 the girls extended it with visits to Sweden, Germany and Egypt.

"The experience was teriffic," Althea acknowledged. Her devotion to the game was rekindled, but she still had not won a major title.

The goodwill group's itinerary led to Paris, and Althea entered the 1956 French Championships at the Roland Garros courts. Here she won the plaudits of the French galleries by sweeping into the semifinals where she beat

Angela Buxton, and then into the final to win over another British rival, Angela Mortimer, a longtime jinx, 6–3, 11–9.

Althea was the first Negro ever to win the French crown.

Miss Gibson seemed tennis-weary by the time she reached England to prepare for Wimbledon. In the Northern Club tournament at Manchester, she beat Shirley Fry 6–3, 6–8, 7–5 but when she met Miss Fry in the quarter-finals at Wimbledon it was a different story. Shirley was the victor 4–6, 6–3, 6–4. Again Althea felt she was perhaps doomed to mediocrity.

Scottie Hall, writing in the Sunday *Graphic,* slapped the wrists of the Wimbledon galleries for showing bias against the colored girl from America.

"It wasn't anything that was whispered. It wasn't anything that was shouted," he wrote. "It was just the atmosphere, tight-lipped, cold." He claimed this aloofness was responsible for Althea's defeat.

Althea herself never complained, but vowed to come back and redeem herself. "I was disappointed, mad at myself," she said.

The opportunity came a year later. Althea arrived in England for the usual tune-up tournaments and won handily at Surbiton, Manchester and Beckenham.

At Wimbledon she opened with a straight-set victory over Hungary's little Suzy Kormoczy and then moved methodically into the semifinals where she faced the newest idol of the British tennis fans, Christine Truman. Christine was only sixteen but she was a six-foot girl who hit the ball with tremendous power.

The crowd was naturally pro-Christine. British tennis fans had had little to cheer about since the days of the great Fred Perry. Strong and steady, however, Althea won in straight sets.

Miss Gibson's final opponent was another American, Darlene Hard from California. Darlene was a waitress with short-cropped hair and a powerful, mannish game. She hit every ball as if she wanted to put it out of its misery. It was a tough test for Althea.

Serving superbly and showing considerable poise, Althea won the first set 6–3 in twenty-five minutes. Darlene sought to turn the tide but Althea was on top of her game. Everything the Negro girl did was right and the match was over in less than an hour.

At the traditional Wimbledon ball, Althea danced with the men's champion, Lew Hoad, as well as the Duke of Devonshire and, at the insistence of her American teammates, sang two songs for the fancily-attired guests.

"Shaking hands with the Queen of England was a long way from being forced to sit in the colored section of the bus going into downtown Wilmington, North Carolina," Miss Gibson commented afterwards in her autobiography.

Her victory was followed by a ticker-tape parade along New York's Broadway and a luncheon in her honor at the Waldorf-Astoria.

Althea helped defend the Wightman Cup at Sewickley, Pennsylvania, then prepared for the other half of her coveted tennis slam, the U.S. Nationals at Forest Hills.

The tall Negro girl swept through preliminary matches without loss of a set and found herself in the final against Louise Brough, the three-time Wimbledon champion who had beaten her at Forest Hills seven years before.

It was Sunday. Althea had a special hair-do, and all her friends turned out for the match. Although very tense she was convinced it was her day.

Louise was only a ghost of the player who had won the U.S. title in 1947. Althea played well within herself, keeping the ball and letting Miss Brough make the errors. The final was mercifully quick, 6–3, 6–2.

Vice-President Richard M. Nixon made the presentation. "Nothing quite like it ever happened to me before," Althea said, "and probably never will again."

It did happen again, but the bloom was off. Miss Gibson returned to Wimbledon in 1958 and won her second straight title by beating Angela Mortimer 8–6, 6–2. Again the Queen was in the audience.

The championships at Forest Hills ended with a match between Althea and Darlene Hard. Miss Hard surprised by winning the first set 6–3. Then Althea snapped out of her temporary lethargy and ran off the next two sets in 45 minutes, 6–1, 6–2.

Nobody doubted at that moment that Althea Gibson was Number One woman tennis player in the world and a "somebody."

TWO   *Billie Jean King—*

14   *She Played and Spoke with Abandon*

VII   Decades from now when historians are comparing the greats of women's tennis they may not be inclined to rate Billie Jean King alongside such immortals as Suzanne Lenglen, Helen Wills Moody, Alice Marble and Maureen Connolly, but they will not have forgotten she was around.

No question, the bouncy daughter of a California fireman left an impression on the game not only with her racket but with her tongue, which was uninhibited and sometimes vitriolic. She challenged all comers on the court and with equal recklessness tackled the lords of tennis and their stuffy traditions.

Billie Jean was a chubby, girl-next-door type with 140 pounds distributed over a five-foot-six frame, short-cropped hair, harlequin spectacles and a face full of freckles.

She played the game with a dynamic gusto. She pounded the ball as a man would, never tentatively. She was a female Chuck McKinley, leaping, running, bouncing all over the court, rushing the net and hitting every ball as if she had a personal grudge against it. In the heat of a match, she glowered like a prizefighter as she battled for points, berating herself in tones loud enough for the bleachers to hear.

"Keep your eye on the ball, stupid!" she would scream at herself. "Nuts!" "Boy, you've got the touch of an ox!" "Think, Billie, think!"

"Winning is the name of the game," she once said. "I'll admit I hate to lose." On the court she became a tiger, oblivious to everything else around her. It was as if she had been tossed into a gladitorial arena with the admonition to kill or be killed. Billie Jean had no desire to be killed.

Her climb to the top was not meteoric and when she got there her reign was not absolute. Her ascendancy was made easier because Margaret Smith, the big, hard-hitting Australian girl who won two Wimbledon and two American championships between 1962 and 1965, fell in love, and temporarily retired from tennis while her other chief rival, Brazil's Maria Bueno, winner of four U.S. and three Wimbledon titles, was sidelined for a time by a series of ailments.

Nevertheless, Billie Jean was indisputable queen of tennis in 1967 and 1968 before turning pro. She won Wimbledon, traditionally regarded as the world championship, in 1966 and 1967, the last two years the event was amateur. In 1968, the inaugural open, she repeated her victory and scored a rare triple sweep, the first in sixteen years, by also winning the women's doubles with Rosemary Casals and the mixed doubles with Australia's Owen Davidson.

Wimbledon was strictly Billie Jean's cup of tea and she enjoyed her greatest success there rather than at Forest Hills or in her native California. "I love Wimbledon," she said often. "It is a tournament for the players. Forest Hills is a tournament for the officials. It is easy for one to get inspired at Wimbledon. You know it is the best."

Billie Jean shared the Wimbledon women's doubles four other times, winning it first with Karen Hantze in 1961 at age seventeen. She repeated with the same partner the following year, with Maria Bueno in 1965 and Miss Casals in 1967.

Her Forest Hills record was less lustrous. In 1966, after winning her first Wimbledon, she blew her second match in the U.S. Nationals to Australian teen-ager Kerry Melville because she had a grudge against the umpire. She won in 1967 but in 1968, bothered by a leg injury which she declined to use as an excuse, she bowed to Virginia Wade of Britain in the final 6–4, 6–2.

Shortly afterwards, Billie Jean announced plans to join George MacCall's professional troupe.

"People are indoctrinated to pro sports," Mrs. King said. "If a person wants to dedicate himself to a sport, he should be a professional. There has always been too much hypocrisy and double-dealing in amateur tennis. We were not true amateurs at all."

Usually after winning an important match, Billie Jean would repair to the press quarters where, her feet on the table, she would talk about the imperfections of her favorite sport.

"Tennis," she said, "takes stamina, so much stamina, but you never think of it as a sport. You picture people sipping mint juleps under an umbrella, and it's not that way. People think of tennis as a sissy sport. That's what we must get away from."

On another occasion:

"Tennis is a very good sport but you've got to get it away from the club atmosphere and into public places, the parks, arenas like Madison Square Garden. You've got to get tennis in places where everybody feels welcome."

Billie Jean lamented the fact that tennis is restricted by stuffy traditions handed down from centuries past.

"In basketball or football," she said, "the players are cussing out there like troopers. But if you're a tennis player you have to be proper all the time. It's the same with the spectators. They can't yell and whoop it up as in other sports. They must hold their breath while play is in progress."

Once she chided U.S. men players for their lack of dedication. "I don't think they really want to be the best in the world," she said.

Billie Jean Moffitt, born November 22, 1943, grew up in sports. Her father, a fireman in Long Beach, California, played baseball and basketball besides being a crack runner in track. Her mother was a swimmer. A younger brother, Randy, once pitched three no-hitters and one one-hitter in a Connie Mack baseball tournament.

"When I was younger, I played baseball and football with boys," Billie Jean recalled. "I thought tennis was a stupid game." At the firemen's picnics she was always one of the first chosen when sides were picked for a softball game. At ten she played on a girls' softball team which won the Long Beach city championship.

It was Billie Jean's father, fearing she might become a tomboy, who suggested she take up tennis. Billie Jean balked at first. "What's tennis?" she asked.

She paid eight dollars for her first racket with money saved from doing odd jobs and sought out a professional, Clyde Walker, who gave group lessons in five city parks.

Walker was delighted to find that, unlike others, the little, freckle-faced girl was not forever eager to play matches. She would often take a bucket of balls onto an empty court and hit for hours by herself.

When Billie Jean did play, she differed from the other girls in that she was not content to stand at the base line and wait for the ball to bounce. She liked to charge up to to the net and hit the ball on a fly.

"You get in the back court and learn those ground strokes first," the professional told her. Billie Jean obeyed but she didn't like it. Years later she was grateful that Walker had forced her to ground herself well in fundamentals.

From the first, she was a stickler for training and conditioning. She preferred to walk to school, some three miles away, to strengthen her legs. In summers, when most young-sters were sleeping late and taking life easy, Billie Jean would rise at 8 A.M., practice all morning, take a break for lunch and return to play until dusk.

She first attracted attention in 1958 by winning a South-ern California 14-and-under tournament. Long Beach tennis fans raised money to send her to the National Girls Championships at Middletown, Ohio, where Billie Jean lost in the quarter-finals.

The bug, however, had bitten. The fireman's daughter had decided not to be a female Joe DiMaggio but the best woman tennis player in the world. In 1959 she went East to play in the grass courts, and there she met the Wim-bledon champion, Maria Bueno. Maria won, but not easily, and Billie Jean caught the eye of a tennis coach, Frank Brennan. Brennan gave her advice and arranged for her to get some better equipment, and she was on her way.

In 1960 she gained the final of the National Girls 18-and-Under Championships, losing to Karen Hantze. In 1961, at age seventeen, she made her first trip to Wimbledon and though beaten early in the women's singles, she paired with Miss Hantze, eighteen, to win the women's doubles crown, the youngest team ever to do so.

The following year, Billie Jean gained the quarter-finals at Wimbledon, upsetting defending champion Margaret Smith in the opening round, and in 1963 the bespectacled Californian battled her way into the final, beating Maria Bueno, the veteran Ann Haydon Jones of Britain and Aus-tralia's Lesley Turner, only to lose in the final to Margaret Smith.

Meanwhile, she had met Larry King, a blond, good-looking law student and suddenly didn't know whether she wanted to be the world's best woman tennis player any more. They became engaged in the fall of 1964. King, a reasonably good player, encouraged Billie Jean to continue her tennis and offered no objections when his fiancée decided to take off for Australia and the campaign Down Under.

When the winter chill begins its bite in the United States, summer is awakening in Australia where seasons are reversed and Christmas, in effect, is celebrated in July. Australia is a tennis player's paradise. The courts are good. Interest is keen. Competition is tough. Teachers are plentiful. Such players as Dick Savitt and Chuck McKinley credited Australian campaigns with bringing them Wimbledon victories—Savitt in 1951 and McKinley in 1963.

Billie Jean spent three months there, training, playing tournaments, receiving coaching tips from Mervyn Rose, a left-handed Australian professional and former Davis Cup player. Rose made several revisions in the girl's game, improving her service and teaching her quicker racket action. However, Billie Jean received her greatest gain from the rigorous conditioning and the bolstering of her confidence.

She was a different player in 1965 when she battled her way into the women's final at Forest Hills, losing a tough match to Margaret Smith 8–6, 7–5. "I knew then I could beat any player in the world," Billie Jean said afterwards. Miss Smith must have recognized the inevitable. She told Billie Jean: "You have all the shots. You just let me wear you out."

The tide turned in 1966. Billie Jean overtook Margaret Smith in the South African Championships and captured her first Wimbledon. By the time she won her second in 1967 she was Mrs. Billie Jean Moffitt King, housewife and overseer of a one-bedroom apartment in Berkeley, California, where her husband was studying law.

In 1965 she achieved the Number One national ranking but was compelled to share the top spot with Nancy Richey of San Angelo, Texas. The rivalry between the two became intense.

Nancy was a year older than Billie Jean, about the same size but cut of a different mold. The daughter of a well-known Texas professional, she was a grim, base-line sharpshooter who only ventured to the net when there was no other alternative. Her father taught her well. She could rake the sidelines with placements off both forehand and backhand. She was cold and deliberate, a court killer of the Helen Wills Moody stripe. Her favorite surface was clay, on which she had been reared. Billie Jean, who trained on hard courts, found that grass gave an advantage to her bold, attacking style.

Nancy had won five straight National Clay Court championships, starting in 1963. She ducked the grass court circuit as if it were a plague. Billie Jean, on the other hand, spurned the clay court competition and concentrated on grass and hard courts. People began whispering that the two girls were involved in a feud—similar to that between Helen Wills and Helen Jacobs in earlier years—and that they purposely stayed out of each other's way.

Their equal billing in the rankings added fuel to the rumors. Nancy, as defending Number One, felt she did not deserve to lose it. Billie Jean's supporters contended her record at Wimbledon and at Forest Hills made her undisputed top woman player in the United States.

The U.S. Lawn Tennis Association ranking committee for 1965 gave the Number One spot to Billie Jean with Nancy Number Two. Al Bumann, president of the Texas Lawn Tennis Association, objected. He contended the Number One spot should go to Miss Richey. He carried his fight to the floor of the USLTA convention, which must approve all rankings, and the result was the unusual compromise of co-leaders.

This was not a satisfactory judgment, particularly to a pepper-pot such as Billie Jean.

After winning Wimbledon in 1966, she returned to Forest Hills to make a bid for the American crown. When she took the center court in the second round against the young, unrated Aussie, Kerry Melville, she noticed Bumann in the umpire's chair.

"I want another umpire," Billie Jean told the officials. There were consultations on the court. The Texan, who had been assigned to the chair, refused to budge.

Billie Jean started to stalk off the court then thought better of it. However, she could hardly see the ball through tears of rage and found it difficult to pull off winning shots with smoke pouring from her ears. She lost to Miss Melville 6–1, 6–2, a shocking upset.

A confrontation with the actual source of this unpleasantness, Miss Richey, did not take place until almost two years later. Billie Jean, on the verge of signing a professional contract, and Nancy Richey, still an amateur, found themselves competitors in an Invitation Tournament at Madison Square Garden. It was late in March 1968.

Strangely the two girls had not faced each other in three-and-a-half years. Although Billie Jean was acknowledged the best woman player in the world, Nancy was skeptical. The last time the two had met was in the quarterfinals of the U.S. Nationals at Forest Hills in September 1964. On that occasion, Nancy had won 6–4, 6–4—and on grass. The Texan held a 6–1 edge over her rival.

Billie Jean's friends were quick to point out that this superiority was achieved before the Californian had developed her game fully. In the last three years, while Mrs. King was dominating the grass court circuit, where had Nancy been? Nancy grinned and said she had been around.

As fate would have it, the two girls waded through all opposition and gained the final. Tension was heavy when they took the green rubberized court under the glaring lights of Madison Square Garden.

Billie Jean, applying pressure with a strong service and net-rushing attack, won the first set handily 6–4 and rushed to a 5–1 lead in the second. At match point in the ninth game of the second set, leading 5–3, Billie Jean flubbed an easy overhead. It was the opening Miss Richey needed. Nancy won the game, then another. Soon Billie Jean was jittery and tentative. Her confidence collapsed. Miss Richey, on the other hand, became a sullen jungle cat, moving in for the kill. Before she finished, she had reeled off twelve straight games—a phenomenal feat against the world's best player—and pulled out the match 4–6, 7–5, 6–0.

It was enough to destroy the spirit of a lesser girl. Billie Jean, unshaken, stormed back to win her third Wimbledon. In the Nationals at Forest Hills, Nancy Richey declined to challenge and Mrs. King's Number One world ranking remained firm.

Larry King usually was on the sidelines, taking notes or recording the match into a tape recorder. Then they would discuss strokes and tactics over dinner.

Billie Jean admitted she listened to Larry. Larry confessed he also listened to Billie Jean—everybody did. "She's a ham," said the husband, "but she knows what she's talking about, and she's great."

TWO *Margaret Smith Court —*

14 *The Athletic Phenomenon*

VIII When Maureen "Little Mo" Connolly won the Australian women's championship in January 1953, thus gaining the first leg of what was to be the first ladies' Grand Slam in tennis, Margaret Smith was a scrawny, skinny-legged girl of eleven, living in the country town of Albury near the borderline of New South Wales and Victoria.

She already had been playing tennis two years, and she was interested enough to follow the progress of the famous American invader on the sports pages of the Sydney *Telegraph* and Sydney *Mirror*, which arrived by train a day late. Her father was foreman in an Albury cheese and butter factory. Margaret had learned to play tennis on a public clay court just across the road from her family's modest two-bedroom house.

Margaret never dreamed at the time that some day—17 years later—her name would be bracketed with that of Miss Connolly, not only as the only other woman to win the Australian, French, Wimbledon and American titles in a single year but also as the undisputed queen of the courts —one of the game's immortals.

"Whenever you talk of great woman tennis players," said Marty Riessen, who shared numerous mixed doubles titles with the tall Australian, "you have to start with Margaret. She should go down as the finest woman player of all times."

Few were inclined to disagree after Margaret, overcoming a case of mid-match jitters, scored a forehand winner that gave her a 6–2, 2–6, 6–1 triumph over tiny Rosemary Casals of San Francisco in the final round of the 1970 U.S. Open at Forest Hills.

Maggie had her slam. Nine months earlier she had crushed Kerry Melville for her ninth Australian championship 6–3, 6–1. At Paris she made short work of the pretty German fraulein, Helga Niessen, 6–2, 6–4. At Wimbledon, she survived a marathon battle with her greatest rival, Billie Jean King, winning 14–12, 11–9. Billie Jean underwent a knee operation shortly afterwards and was not around at Forest Hills to challenge Margaret's bid for the final leg of her sweep.

Three times before Margaret had won three of the four major crowns but had been thwarted in her attempt to take them all. Now, at 28 and playing so superbly that no one got more than three games a set on her through her first five matches, she had finally attained the goal of all tennis players.

Did she feel exhilarated?

"I feel flat," she said afterwards in that familiar Australian cockney twang. "I don't think I can appreciate it now. I will have to wait until tomorrow to realize what it means.

"It has been a long, hard grind and the pressure built up tremendously. In that final match, Rosie and I were both so tense neither of us played our best tennis. In the second set, I lost everything momentarily. I didn't know what might happen. Thank God, I won in the end."

It was the nineteenth major championship—the nineteenth victory in Big Four events—for the tall, athletically-built country girl, more major titles than any other woman had ever won. The total might be considered 20 since Margaret defeated Maria Bueno of Brazil for the U.S. amateur grass court championship in Brookline, Massachusetts, in 1968, the year tennis went open. Margaret was then an amateur.

Margaret's credentials are phenomenal. Through the decade of the 1960's and into the first year of the 1970's, she won nine Australian, three French, three Wimbledon and four U.S. titles (five U.S. if the 1968 amateur is counted). She bowed in the final of the French, Wimbledon and American championships once, giving her a 19–3 record in Big Four showdowns. In addition, she won the Italian championship three times, the German three times, South African twice and the Canadian once.

The record undoubtedly would be even more gaudy had she not retired at the end of the 1966 season, declaring: "I just got tired of traveling, of packing and unpacking suitcases all the time. I got tired of chasing tennis balls." She opened a boutique called "The Peephole" with a friend in Perth, Australia.

It was in Perth, the beautiful and lazy capital of Western Australia, that Margaret met a tall wool broker and yachtsman named Barry Court, whom she married in October 1967. Barry was responsible for getting Margaret back on the tennis circuit.

"Barry said he was bored and would like to see some of the rest of the world," Margaret explained later. "So off we went on the tennis tour."

Margaret Court is an athletic phenomenon who probably will rank alongside the late Babe Didrikson Zaharias and Holland's Fannye Blankers-Koen of 1948 Olympic fame as the outstanding sportswomen of the century.

Dr. Reginal Whitney, who conducted a series of tests on Margaret in London prior to the 1970 Wimbledon tournament, said she was "greatly above average" as a feminine athletic specimen.

"Mrs. Court is a big girl with a good pair of legs, relatively long arms and wider hands than average," Dr. Whitney said, "but she's no amazonian."

Although five feet, eight and three quarters inches tall and 157 pounds, Margaret remained strikingly feminine. Blonde and soft-featured with large blue eyes, she always impressed galleries with her trim and leggy figure and smooth, womanly grace. The width and strength of her shoulders seemed to pass notice.

Dr. Whitney, in releasing the findings of his tests, indicated that Margaret could have been a great champion in any athletic field she might have chosen—a runner or jumper in the Olympics, a great swimmer or gymnast.

Here are some of the results of Dr. Whitney's tests on grip dynamoter and other machines:

BODY SIZE	HEIGHT	WEIGHT
Ten women athletes	5-6¼	146 pounds
Mrs. Court	5-8¾	157

"These characteristics undoubtedly have a pronounced effect on her opponents," the report said. "They feel dwarfed by her size and strength. She has the advantage of serving from a greater height and from being able to kill smashes at the net."

World Tennis Magazine

World Tennis Magazine

Jack Kramer exercised a tremendous influence on the game. After serving in World War II, he won both the Wimbledon and U.S. Championships, turned pro and became the king of the touring mercenaries. Later he took over as entrepreneur of the pro tour where he waged a long and bitter feud with his rival, Pancho Gonzales, with whom he is shown at the right during more friendly days.

Thelner Hoover

Jack Kramer and his pretty wife give their one-year-old son, David, a dunking in the famed Davis Cup which Jack helped bring home from Australia in 1946. Another defender, slated to succeed Kramer as national amateur and pro champion, was Pancho Gonzales, shown in action at the right.

D. D. & E. P. Schroeder

Keen rivals for professional honors in the 1950's were Lew Hoad of Australia, left, and Pancho Gonzales, shown in the upper left-hand photo. Gonzales' intentness and determination are reflected in the center picture while the photo at the right depicts a part of the Australian breed that dominated tennis in the 1950's and 1960's. They are, left to right, Roy Emerson, Fred Stolle, John Newcombe and Tony Roche.

E. D. Lacey

Ed. Fernberger

Melbourne Herald, Australia

Australia, a country at the bottom of the world with a population about equal to that of New York City, has a faculty for turning out champion tennis players. It dominated the Davis Cup and world championships during the 1950's and 1960's and had the top players entering the 1970's. One of the best young players was left-handed

Tony Roche, seen in the top right photograph sipping a soft drink between court changes. Roy Emerson and Margaret Smith Court, holding huge trophies representing Australian national championships, were two other products. Mrs. Court was rated the world's Number One woman player. Rod Laver, demonstrating his devastating left-handed

drive in the center, twice
won the Grand Slam and rated
Number One in world rankings. He
is shown, bottom right, holding the
U.S. National Championship trophy
after beating Roy Emerson in the
final to complete his first Grand Slam
as an amateur in 1962. He repeated
in 1968 as a professional.

E. D. Lacey

After winning the Grand Slam in 1968 (capturing the Australian, French, Wimbledon and U.S. titles in a single year), Rod Laver, seen at the right in a typical action shot, ran into an obstacle in 1970 from a fellow countryman whom he and others had felt might be past his peak. He was classic stylist Ken Rosewall (above), hitting one of his fluid backhands, who went to the finals at Wimbledon and won the U.S. Open to be named "Player of the Year."

E. D. Lacey

Wide World Photos

Arthur Ashe, Jr., was the first man to break through tennis' color barrier and win the U.S. Championship. At the left, Arthur is shown with his father, Arthur Ashe, Sr., from Richmond, Virginia, a truant officer who saw that his son got every advantage. Arthur's backhand (above) is rated one of the most potent weapons in tennis history. His thunderous serve (right), clocked at 112 miles per hour, is one of the game's deadliest.

Helen Wills Moody and Helen Jacobs
were the bitterest of rivals, but they
were teammates on this U.S.
Wightman Cup team of 1928, shown
above in an official team photo.
Members were, standing left to right,
Helen Jacobs, Helen Wills and
Penelope Anderson; seated,
Eleanor Goss and Molla Bjursted.
At right, Miss Jacobs is shown on the
center court at Wimbledon in 1930.
Left, Mrs. Beamish, a British
player.

Two of America's finest women
players in the game's early years were
Molla Bjurstedt and Hazel Hotchkiss,
both of whom later married to
become known as Molla Mallory and
Hazel Wightman. The photo at the
far left shows Molla Bjurstedt,
center, looking on as May Sutton

Edwin Levick

receives a trophy in a women's final at Long Beach, California. Hazel Hotchkiss displays her stylish forehand in the center picture. At the right, Suzanne Lenglen, the great French star, leaps to hit an acrobatic overhead.

Suzanne Lenglen (second from left), a turban on her head and her pleated skirt falling just below the knees, smiles prior to taking the court for a mixed doubles match at Nice. On her right is her partner, Jacques Brugnon, and on her left are her two French opponents, Mr. Pierson and Mlle. Marjollet.

HAND SIZE	HAND LENGTH	PALM BREADTH
U.S. Service Women	6-7¾	2⅝-3⅝
Mrs. Court	7⅞	3⅜

"Margaret has relatively large and strong hands, the right being appreciably longer and stronger than the left," the doctor said.

HAND STRENGTH	RIGHT HAND	LEFT HAND
Average women (under 30)	76½ lbs.	64½ lbs.
Athletes (fivc tests)	92 lbs.	85 lbs.
Mrs. Court	121¼ lbs.	73¾ lbs.

"Margaret's right hand grip strength was found equivalent to average found in 10 physical education men from St. Mary's Teacher Training College."

STANDING JUMP	AVG. JUMP	RANGE OF JUMPS
Normal women	15¼ ins.	10½ to 19 ins.
Athletes	19¾ ins.	15 to 22 ins.
Mrs. Court	21 ins.	19 to 22¾ ins.

"Margaret is greatly above average. She made the highest jump of all the women we tested."

Margaret was not always so remarkable a physical specimen. When she was a young teen-ager, she was very skinny and seemingly awkward. Her father feared she never would have the strength to play tournament tennis.

However, by the time she was fifteen, she could beat every boy her age in Albury. She had collected more than fifty trophies for junior tennis achievement.

She was only fifteen and was already attracting attention in a country where good boy and girl players never escape notice when friends in Albury encouraged her to make a trip to Melbourne, the capital of the state of Victoria and the headquarters of the Australian Lawn Tennis Association.

The spindly-legged girl from the country fell under the wing of Frank Sedgman, Wimbledon champion and Davis Cup star of the early 1950's. Sedgman and his wife took her into their home.

"You're going to have to get some muscle on those bones," Sedgman told her.

Margaret started going to a neighborhood gymnasium. There she lifted weights, exercised on the bars and trampolines, jumped rope and engaged in calisthenics. The change was phenomenal. She developed powerful shoulders and arms. Her toothpick legs sprouted shapely calves and thighs.

In 1960 at the age of seventeen Margaret won the Australian women's championship, beating Maria Bueno in the final. The next step for a player of such promise in Australia is a chaperoned world tour. Margaret was on her way.

In 1962 she won the French and Italian championships before coming to Forest Hills where she upset Darlene Hard 9–7, 6–4 for the American crown. She won her first Wimbledon in 1963, beating Billie Jean 6–3, 6–4 in the last round.

Margaret won with a classic tennis game. She served with tremendous pace for a woman. He ground strokes were almost flawless. Not a relentless net attacker, she moved into the forecourt only behind an aggressive shot and then she followed with a volley or smash that often ended the point.

"She frightens you when you look at her from the other side of the court," said Rosemary Casals. "She seems to be all arms and legs. You can't get the ball out of her reach."

"The thing about Margaret," said Nancy Richey, "is that she never has anything wrong with her. She is a physical marvel."

"She simply overpowers most opponents," said Billie Jean King, one of the few women players not in awe of Mrs. Court. "You have to get on top of her at the start and never let her get away. If she breaks on top, her confidence soars and she is murderous."

Margaret's fellow countryman, John Newcombe, had another explanation for her success.

"Most of us let up against an opponent at times," Newcombe said. "Not Margaret. It's not in her make-up. She is determined to win every point, no matter who she is playing."

RECORDS

MARGARET COURT
Australian Champion—1960, 1961, 1962, 1963, 1964, 1965, 1966, 1969, 1970
French Champion—1962, 1964, 1970 (Runner-up 1965)
Wimbledon Champion—1963, 1965, 1970 (Runner-up 1964)
U.S. Champion—1962, 1965, 1968 (Runner-up 1963)
U.S. Open Champion—1969, 1970
South African Champion—1968, 1970
Italian Champion—1962, 1963, 1964
German Champion—1964, 1965, 1966
Canadian Champion—1970
Major women's doubles championships—Wimbledon 3; U.S. 4; French 3; Australian 6
Major mixed doubles championships—Wimbledon 5; U.S. 6; French 5; Australian 2

THE FOUR MUSKETEERS

RENE LACOSTE
U.S. Champion—1926, 1927
Wimbledon Champion—1925, 1928
French Champion—1925, 1927, 1929

U.S. Indoor Champion—1926
Wimbledon Doubles—1925 (with Jean Borotra)
Davis Cup Challenge Round—Singles, won 4, lost 4; doubles, won none, lost one

JEAN BOROTRA
Wimbledon Champion—1924, 1926
French Champion—1924, 1931
Australian Champion—1928
U.S. Indoor Champion—1925, 1927, 1929, 1931
U.S. Mixed Doubles—1926 (with Elizabeth Ryan)
Wimbledon Doubles—1925 (with Lacoste); 1932, 1933 (with Jacques Brugnon)

HENRI COCHET
U.S. Champion—1928
Wimbledon Champion—1927, 1929
French Champion—1922, 1926, 1928, 1930, 1932
Wimbledon Doubles—1926, 1928 (with Brugnon)
French Doubles—1927, 1930, 1932 (with Brugnon)
French Mixed Doubles—1928, 1929 (with Eileen Bennett)
U.S. Mixed Doubles—1927 (with Eileen Bennett)
Davis Cup Challenge Round—Singles, won 10, lost 3; Doubles, won 3, lost 3

JACQUES BRUGNON
Wimbledon Doubles—1926, 1928 (with Cochet); 1932, 1933 (with Borotra)
French Doubles—1927, 1930, 1932 (with Cochet); 1928, 1934 (with Borotra)
French Mixed Doubles—1925, 1926 (with Suzanne Lenglen).
Australian Doubles—1928 (with Borotra)
U.S. Indoor Doubles—1927 (with Borotra)
Davis Cup Challenge Round—Doubles, won 3, lost 3

ELLSWORTH VINES
U.S. Champion—1931, 1932
Wimbledon Champion—1932
U.S. Clay Court Champion—1931

U.S. Doubles—1932 (with Keith Gledhill)
U.S. Mixed Doubles—1933 (with Elizabeth Ryan)
U.S. Clay Court Doubles—1931 (with Gledhill)
Davis Cup Challenge Round—Singles, won 1, lost 1; Doubles, 0–0

FRED PERRY

U.S. Champion—1933, 1934, 1936
Wimbledon Champion—1934, 1935, 1936
French Champion—1935
Australian Champion—1934
U.S. Mixed Doubles—1932
Wimbledon Mixed Doubles—1934, 1935 (with Dorothy Round)
Davis Cup Challenge Round—Singles, won 8, lost 0; Doubles, 0–0

BILLIE JEAN KING

U.S. Amateur Champion—1967
U.S. Hard Court—1966
U.S. Doubles—1964 (with Karen Hantze Susman); 1967 (with Rosemary Casals)
U.S. Mixed Doubles—1967 (with Owen Davidson)
Wimbledon Champion—1966, 1967, 1968 (Open)
Wimbledon Doubles—1961–62 (with Susman); 1965 (with Maria Bueno); 1967–68 (with Rosemary Casals)
Wimbledon Mixed Doubles—1967–68 (with Owen Davidson)
South African Champion—1966, 1967
Argentine Champion—1967
Irish Champion—1963
South African Doubles—1967 (with Casals)
Irish Doubles—1963 (with Carole Graebner)
French Mixed Doubles—1967 (with Davidson)
South African Mixed Doubles—1967 (with Davidson)
U.S. Indoor Doubles—1966 (with Casals)
U.S. Hard Court Doubles—1966 (with Casals)
U.S. Clay Court Doubles—1960 (with Darlene Hard)
U.S. Indoor Mixed Doubles—1966–67 (with Paul Sullivan)
Wightman Cup Record—Singles, 10–2; Doubles, 4–2
Federation Cup Record—Singles, 15–4; Doubles, 16–0

ARTHUR ASHE, JR.

U.S. Amateur Champion—1968
U.S. Open Champion—1968
U.S. Clay Court Singles—1967
U.S. Hard Court Singles—1963
U.S. Intercollegiate Singles—1965
U.S. Indoor Doubles—1965 (with Charles Pasarell)
U.S. Intercollegiate Doubles—1965 (with Ian Crookenden);
   1967 (with Pasarell)
U.S. Interscholastic Singles—1961
U.S. Junior Indoor Singles—1960, 1961
No. 1 U.S. Ranking—1969
Davis Cup Record—Challenge Round, won 1, lost 1; Zone
   Matches, Singles 7–2, Doubles 1–1

DONALD BUDGE

U.S. Amateur Champion—1937, 1938
U.S. Doubles—1936, 1938 (with Gene Mako)
U.S. Mixed Doubles—1935 (with Sarah Palfrey); 1938 (with
   Alice Marble)
Australian Champion—1938
French Champion—1938
Wimbledon Champion—1937, 1938
Wimbledon Doubles—1937, 1938 (with Gene Mako)
Wimbledon Mixed Doubles—1937, 1938 (with Alice Marble)
World Professional Champion—1939, 1940, 1941
U.S. Junior Champion—1933
Davis Cup Record, Challenge Round—Singles 4–2, Doubles
   (with Gene Mako) 1–1

JACK KRAMER

U.S. Amateur Champion—1946, 1947
U.S. Doubles—1940, 1941 (with Ted Schroeder); 1943 (with
   Frank Parker); 1947 (with Schroeder)
U.S. Mixed Doubles—1941 (with Sarah Palfrey Cooke)
U.S. Indoor—1941
U.S. Indoor Doubles—1947 (with Bob Falkenburg)
U.S. Clay Court Doubles—1941 (with Ted Schroeder)
U.S. Interscholastic—1938

Wimbledon Champion—1947
Wimbledon Doubles—1946 (with Tom Brown); 1947 (with Bob Falkenburg)
World Professional Champion—1948, 1949, 1951, 1953
Davis Cup Record, Challenge Round—Singles 4–0, Doubles 1–1

SUZANNE LENGLEN

Wimbledon Champion—1919, 1920, 1921, 1922, 1923, 1925
French Champion—1920, 1921, 1922, 1923, 1925, 1926
Wimbledon Doubles—1919, 1920, 1921, 1922, 1923, 1925 (with Elizabeth Ryan)
Wimbledon Mixed Doubles—1920 (with Gerald Patterson), 1922 (with P. O'Hara Wood); 1925 (with Jean Borotra)
French Doubles—1925, 1926 (with Didi Vlasto)

HAZEL HOTCHKISS WIGHTMAN

U.S. Champion—1909, 1910, 1911, 1919
U.S. Indoor Champion—1919, 1927
U.S. Doubles—1909, 1910 (with Edith Rotch); 1911, 1915 (with Eleanora Sears)
U.S. Mixed Doubles—1909, 1911, 1920 (with Wallace Johnson); 1910 (with Joseph Carpenter); 1915 (with Harry Johnson); 1918 (with Irving C. Wright)
U.S. Indoor Doubles—1919, 1921, 1924, 1927 (with Marion Zinderstein); 1928, 1929, 1930, 1931, 1933 (with Sarah Palfrey)
U.S. Indoor Mixed Doubles—1923 (with Burnham Dell); 1924 (with Bill Tilden); 1926, 1927 (with Peabody Gardner, Jr.); 1928 (with Henry Johnson, Jr.)
Wightman Cup—Doubles, won 3, lost 2

MOLLA BJURSTEDT MALLORY

U.S. Champion—1915, 1916, 1917, 1918, 1920, 1921, 1922, 1926
U.S. Indoor Champion—1915, 1916, 1918, 1921, 1922
U.S. Clay Court Champion—1915, 1916
U.S. Doubles—1916, 1917 (with Eleonora Sears)
U.S. Mixed Doubles—1917 (with Irving Wright); 1922, 1923 (with Bill Tilden)
U.S. Indoor Doubles—1916 (with Marie Wagner)

U.S. Indoor Mixed Doubles—1921, 1922 (with Tilden)
Wightman Cup—Singles, won 5, lost 5; Doubles, won 1, lost 1

HELEN JACOBS
U.S. Champion—1932, 1933, 1934, 1935
Wimbledon Champion—1936
U.S. Girls' 18 Champion—1924, 1925
U.S. Doubles—1932, 1934, 1935 (with Sarah Palfrey)
U.S. Mixed Doubles—1934 (with George Lott, Jr.)
Wightman Cup—Singles, won 13, lost 7; Doubles, won 5, lost 3

HELEN WILLS MOODY
U.S. Champion—1923, 1924, 1925, 1927, 1928, 1929, 1931
Wimbledon Champion—1927, 1928, 1929, 1930, 1932, 1933, 1935, 1938
French Champion—1928, 1929, 1930, 1932
U.S. Doubles—1922 (with Mrs. Marion Jessup); 1924, 1928 (with Mrs. Hazel Wightman); 1925 (with Mary K. Browne)
U.S. Mixed Doubles—1924 (with Vincent Richards); 1928 (with John B. Hawkes)
Wimbledon Doubles—1924 (with Mrs. Wightman); 1928 (with Mrs. H. Watson); 1930 (with Elizabeth Ryan)
Wimbledon Mixed Doubles—1929 (with Francis T. Hunter)
U.S. Girls' 18 Champion—1921, 1922
U.S. Girls' 18 Doubles—1922 (with Helen Hooker)
Wightman Cup—Singles, won 18, lost 2; Doubles, won 3, lost 7

BILL TILDEN
U.S. Champion—1920, 1921, 1922, 1923, 1924, 1925, 1929
Wimbledon Champion—1920, 1921, 1930
New Zealand Champion—1920
U.S. Doubles—1918, 1921, 1922 (with Vincent Richards); 1923 (with Brian Norton); 1927 (with Francis T. Hunter)
U.S. Mixed Doubles—1913, 1914, (with Mary K. Browne); 1922, 1923 (with Molla Mallory)
Wimbledon Doubles—1927 (with Hunter)
U.S. Indoor Champion—1920

U.S. Clay Court Champion—1918, 1922, 1923, 1924, 1925, 1926, 1927

U.S. Indoor Doubles—1919, 1920 (with Richards); 1926 (with F.C. Anderson); 1929 (with Hunter)

U.S. Indoor Mixed Doubles—1921, 1922 (with Molla Mallory); 1924 (with Mrs. Hazel Wightman)

Pro Champion—1931, 1932, 1933

Davis Cup Challenge Round—Singles, won 17, lost 5; Doubles, won 4, lost 2

PANCHO GONZALES

U.S. Champion—1948, 1949

U.S. Indoor Champion—1949

U.S. Clay Court Champion—1948, 1949

Pro Champion—1954, 1955, 1956, 1957, 1958, 1959, 1960, 1961

Davis Cup Challenge Round—Singles, won 2, lost 0; Doubles, 0–0

THREE

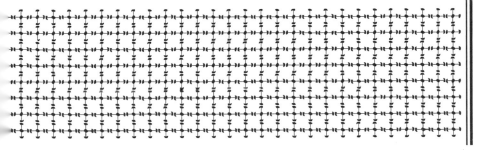

A visitor attending Wimbledon for the first time cannot help being smitten by the split personality of the dowager queen of tournament tennis. She is as majestic as the Royal Family, which has attended the matches with dedication down the years, and she is as earthy as the burly stevedores and little old ladies of Piccadilly who also descend upon the tree-lined acres at the foot of Church Road.

The All-England Championships are a combination of an English lawn party and a state fair carnival. There are ladies in silks and ruffles, and gentlemen in country frocks and top hats, who come as much to be seen as to see. There are the store clerks, secretaries and businessmen who come to watch the world's greatest players, and sip tea and munch English hamburgers called "Wimpies."

Commuters taking the train from teeming London to picturesque Wimbledon Common find the cars jammed with fans discussing the tournament as animatedly and knowledgeably as members of the exclusive tennis clubs. The game's great and near-great start eyeing the event months in advance. "It is the tournament every player wants to win above all others," said Helen Wills Moody. She won eight. "There is a flavor about Wimbledon and a greatness that puts it on a pedestal by itself," commented Billie Jean King who ascended the women's throne three decades after Mrs. Moody. "There is only one Wimbledon," said Big Bill Tilden.

It is more than a mere tennis tournament. It is a spectacle, one of the foremost sports events in the world. When play starts, British newspapers cover it with the enthusiasm they would give a Coronation. They dub it the "Dedicated Fortnight."

Wimbledon's birth can be traced to a trio of Englishmen

who hated to see broad stretches of magnificent turf wasted on croquet. Croquet had been played in Languedoc, France, during the thirteenth century and had found its way across the Channel to England where by the mid-1850's it was a part of almost every lawn party.

Clubs devoted to the game sprang up all over. One of the best was the All-England Croquet Club founded in 1870 at Worple Road in Wimbledon. Here on sunny days ladies and gents could be seen knocking balls around the beautifully manicured lawns and one afternoon, it seems, three sportsmen were beguiled by the velvety turf.

"What an ideal court this would make for sphairistike," Julian Marshall, an authority on court tennis remarked to his companions, using the Greek name for lawn tennis.

"Indeed it would," agreed Henry Jones, also a recognized sports authority who had become a devotee of the racket game.

"This would be an excellent place to hold a lawn tennis tournament," said the third member of the party, C.G. Heathcote, the stipendary magistrate of Brighton and quite a good tennis player. "Let us see what we can do about it."

The three gentlemen sold the idea to J.H. Walsh, editor of *The Field* magazine, who became the fourth member of the organizing committee. The four met in the magazine offices at 346, The Strand, in London and drew up the details. Through Walsh's efforts, the club became the All-England Croquet and Lawn Tennis Club, Wimbledon.

On June 9, 1877, it was announced that a championship would be staged at Wimbledon. The notice was signed by Henry Jones, honorary secretary, and it read:

The All-England Croquet and Lawn Tennis Club, Wimbledon, propose to hold a lawn tennis meeting open to all amateurs on Monday July 9 and following days. Entrance fee, one shilling. Two prizes will be given—one gold champion prize to the winner, one silver to the second player.

We are indebted to C.M. Jones, editor of *Lawn Tennis*, the official magazine of the British Lawn Tennis Association, for details surrounding the birth of the All-England Club and the holding of the first Wimbledon Championship.

The three organizers—Heathcote, Jones and Marshall—decided that specific tournament rules should be determined in advance. Although such rules had been drawn up in 1875 by the Marylebone Cricket Club tennis committee, English players had been using almost any standards that met their fancy. As a result there was no concrete agreement on the layout of the court, the height of the net or the type of scoring.

One of the main principles laid down by the organizing trio was that court tennis scoring in the "15's" be used instead of the racquets system—one, two, three etc., up to fifteen. It was also decreed that the court not be shaped like an hourglass but be rectangular, twenty-six yards long and nine yards wide, with the net extended from poles three feet outside the boundaries, and that one service fault be permitted without penalty no matter where the ball was hit. These regulations have stood until this day.

Twenty-two players answered the invitation to compete. There was keen interest.

The gold prize—and Wimbledon's first title—went to a Harrovian named S.W. Gore, who was considered an all-around athlete particularly adept at racket games. Gore was a big, strong man with natural reflexes. His opponents marvelled at his extraordinary wrist shots.

C.G. Heathcote, who was runner-up, wrote of the final match:

Gore was the first to realize, as the first and great principle of lawn tennis, the necessity of forcing his opponent to the back line, when he would approach the net and, by a dextrous turn of the wrist, return the ball at considerable speed, now in the forehand, now in the backhand court, till, to borrow the ex-

pression of one of his opponents of the year, his antagonist was ready to drop.

Modern fans would have found this first Wimbledon final a bit confusing because both players served side-arm, as in racquets. It was not until the next year, 1878, that the overhead delivery came into use. A.T. Myers was the man who introduced it. Soon everybody was serving that way.

In the first Wimbledon, the serve had little advantage. Editor Jones' research disclosed that of the 601 games played in the tournament, 376 went with service and 225 against. Today the ratio of winning services is about 10–1 with the men players, less among the women.

About 200 spectators turned out for the inaugural tournament, paying one shilling each. The event was adjourned one day for the Eton-Harrow cricket match, a social highlight of the era. There were no deuce sets. When the score reached 5–5, the next player to take a game won the set. Players changed court at the end of each set instead of on odd games, as later became the practice.

In 1878 Gore more than met his match in P.F. Hadow, another Harrow graduate who had been producing tea in Ceylon. Gore created a sensation by moving so close to the net that he frequently reached over it to hit the ball. This tactic caused consternation among officials, who had failed to anticipate it. They had no choice but to rule Gore within his rights. Not until two years later did they decide that no part of the racket or a player could cross the net.

Hadow refused to be discouraged by the liberties allowed the defending champion. The tea-grower stayed near the base line and lofted well-placed lobs over Gore's head. The strategy was successful and Hadow won the second championship 7–5, 6–1, 9–7, the deuce set having been adopted in the interim.

All Wimbledons until 1922 were Challenge Round affairs, such as the Davis Cup competition. The champion, permitted to sit out the tournament until eliminations provided a challenger, had to play only one match.

The early hero was a stylist named Willie Renshaw. Possessed of tremendous stamina and back court skill, he became a legend. In 1881 he defeated the Reverend J.T. Hartley in thirty-seven minutes, a speed record never threatened in subsequent years. He won seven titles, six in a row, between 1881 and 1889. That was more than greats such as Big Bill Tilden, Fred Perry and Don Budge were able to amass, but the number fell short of the record eight set by America's Helen Wills Moody in the women's division.

After Renshaw came the "Doherty Era," dominated by a pair of brothers who won nine titles between them from 1897 through 1906. The elder, R.F. Doherty, won four in a row before the string was broken in 1901 by A.W. Gore. The younger brother, Lawrie, took up the cudgel in 1902 and won five straight.

The formative years produced other high spots. A fifteen-year-old girl named Charlotte (Lottie) Dod crushed the defending champion, Blanche Bingley, with the loss of only two games in 1887, becoming the youngest ever to take the crown. An Irishman, W.J. Hamilton, was the first "outside" winner in 1890. William Baddeley won in 1891 at age nineteen, the youngest male victor. A.W. Gore won in 1909 when he was forty-one years and seven months, the oldest ever to take the men's singles.

By this time, Wimbledon had established itself as one of the world's top sports events. The invasion of Americans —particularly Davis Cup champions Dwight Davis and Holcombe Ward—added lustre to the tournament. It became a social as well as a sporting spectacle and royalty soon began attending.

The aging Gore was succeeded by a handsome New

Zealander named Anthony F. Wilding who attended Cambridge University. Wilding, dark-haired with chiseled features and strapping physique, was called "Little Hercules." He practiced incessantly, trained hard, won four consecutive championships starting in 1910.

Wilding's final triumph in 1913 was over Maurice E. McLoughlin, the "California Comet," 8–6, 6–3, 10–8. Interest was so keen that scalpers demanded and got as much as $25 a ticket. Wilding's great promise was cut short when he was killed in World War I.

Another player who captured the imagination of British fans was Norman E. Brookes, a slender, hawk-faced left-hander from Australia, later to become a knight and an eminent administrator of the sport. Brookes won in 1907 and again in 1914, just before competition was suspended for four years because of the war.

During the pre-World War I period Wimbledon was described by Miss N.G. Cleather in her book, *The Wimbledon Story,* as resembling "a delightful vicarage garden-party with tennis as the chief attraction."

Its ingredients were "players in trim, conventional flannels, or in neat dresses with skirts of modest length, an atmosphere of unhurried enjoyment in a typically English setting, and the spectators donning their party clothes to be admired by others as much as to admire the game."

This traditional casualness and straight-laced dignity was shaken with the resumption of play in 1919 and the cataclysmic appearance of a saucy mademoiselle from across the English Channel, Suzanne Lenglen. The French player electrified British galleries not only with the classical grace of her strokes but also with daring attire.

Since the start of the game lady champions had been content to compete in dresses that consisted of corseted waists, long-sleeved blouses and frilly petticoats. Mlle. Lenglen danced about the court in a loose one-piece garment with arms and ankles daringly revealed. She became front-page news. Men and women who had never given more than passsing interest to the game suddenly became tennis fans—the men to look and admire, the women to express their shock.

The old and the new were arrayed against each other in the 1919 women's singles Challenge Round, pitting Mrs. Lambert Chambers against the pretty French invader. Mrs. Chambers was a legend. She had won her first women's title nineteen years before. She had dominated her division for the last ten years, winning seven championships in a row. Suzanne was just twenty years old, dark, full-bosomed, but with the effortless movements of a lioness.

Eight thousand enthusiasts, including the King and Queen, turned out for the drama. The match proved to be one of the greatest in tennis history. Playing two hours under a bright sun, Mlle. Lenglen finally won 10–8, 4–6, 9–7. Mrs. Chambers, her petticoats flying, fought magnificently but she gave away too much in years.

The victory for the young Frenchwoman signalled the dawning of a new era at Wimbledon. There were five new champions and all from overseas, Gerald Patterson of Australia succeeding to the men's throne. Before the war, for nearly half a century, only six non-British players had crashed through to titles. In the following decades, however, the United States, France, Australia, Germany, South Africa, Belgium, Japan and Spain all scored victories on the center court while British triumphs diminished to a trickle.

Wimbledon was truly an international spectacle, the center of world tennis. More than that, it had opened the door to an unending string of court personalities.

The next to capture the fancy of Wimbledon devotees was Big Bill Tilden, who made his center court debut in 1920. He was a tall, hawk-faced man from Philadelphia's Main Line who had a powerful cannonball service and a repertoire of shots such as the All-England Club had never seen before. Like Suzanne Lenglen, he had more than a tennis game. He had class and color. A frustrated Shakespearean actor, he carried his instinct for drama onto the court and kept galleries constantly delighted with his flair for the unusual.

Tilden was destined to win the men's crown three times over a decade. Mlle. Lenglen, meanwhile, captured six women's titles, five in a row, before bowing out in 1925. Together they did so much for the popularity of the game that in 1922 it became necessary for the tournament to move to larger quarters. The last championship at the famed old stand on Worple Road was played in 1921, and it was only fitting that shapely Mlle. Lenglen should hit the last ball on the center court. This was in a women's doubles match won by her and Elizabeth (Bunny) Ryan, and Suzanne clinched the victory with a smash that almost knocked the racket out of her opponent's hand.

The new grounds were located in a picturesque hollow at the foot of Church Street near Wimbledon Common. Whereas the old club had only 500 bookable seats at first and maximum space for about 8,000 people, the new center court was in an amphitheater seating 14,750. There were stands at Court Number One, where the second most important matches were played, seating 5,000, later enlarged to 7,000. There were fifty separate entrances.

The grand opening was to be a gala occasion. King George V and the Queen were to preside over ceremonies. But on inaugural day, Monday, June 22, 1922, the skies exploded. Their Majesties, nevertheless, rode to the club from Buckingham Palace and waited until the rain subsided at 3:30 P.M. A court covering was removed, the band struck up "God Save the King" and the first match began between Leslie Godfree and Algy Kingscote. Only two matches were played that day.

The Challenge Round was abolished, defending champs being required to play from the opening rounds on, and that year also saw the initiation of seeding. In 1926 the Fiftieth Anniversary Jubilee Championship was played with George V and Queen Mary presenting the mixed doubles trophy to a husband-wife team, Mr. and Mrs. L.A. Godfree. The King's son, the Duke of York, later King George VI, played in the men's doubles.

Little Bill Johnston, Tilden's chief rival in the United States, won his only Wimbledon in 1923. Then followed the reign of the so-called "Four Musketeers" of France, who also dominated Davis Cup competition. They were Jean Borotra, Rene Lacoste, Henri Cochet and Jacques Brugnon. In the six years from 1924 through 1929, Borotra, Lacoste and Cochet each won the men's singles title twice and only Brugnon failed, though he shared in four men's doubles crowns between 1925 and 1933.

The French streak was finally broken by Tilden who won in 1930 at age thirty-eight. By then Wimbledon was drawing 200,000 spectators. Later crowds passed 300,000 and, with the great pros competing in the open, climbed towards 400,000.

The early surge in attendance was spurred by still another electrifying personality, Helen Wills. Following on the heels of the glamorous Suzanne Lenglen, the American girl received a tepid welcome when she made her first appearance in England with the Wightman Cup team in 1924.

She was heavy and rather awkward-looking, dressed in her white school uniform, a stiff white skirt and a middie blouse. She wore a white, green-lined eye-shade which later became her trademark. Helen won her first women's title in 1927. Before she was through, she was to win eight, the last against Helen Jacobs in 1938.

Sidney B. Wood and Ellsworth Vines kept the United States at the top with triumphs in 1931 and 1932, only to see Australia's Jack Crawford dethrone Vines in a great match in 1933. Fred Perry, with three straight men's victories, and Dorothy Round, with two women's championships, restored British tennis prestige in the mid-thirties. Don Budge was unbeatable in 1937 and 1939, launching an American era that saw the Yanks win every men's title but one between 1937 and 1951, with six years out for World War II.

An even greater dynasty was begun in the women's division by the magnificent Alice Marble. American women held the championship without serious challenge through 1958. During this period Louise Brough and Maureen (Little Mo) Connolly each had three-year winning streaks and Althea Gibson came out of Harlem's ghetto to win twice, in 1957 and 1958, the first Negro to curtsy before a queen on Wimbledon's center court.

The 1950's and 1960's were Australia's decades in the men's division as an assembly line succession of stars from Down Under won eleven of the seventeen titles between 1952 and 1968. Maria Bueno, a little tiger from Brazil, and Margaret Smith, an Amazon from Australia, overshadowed the women's competition until Billie Jean King entered the scene in 1966.

Frank Sedgman, a curly-haired slugger with lightning reflexes, began the Australian assault on Wimbledon in 1952. As one Aussie after another turned pro others came off the assembly line: Lew Hoad, winning twice, Ashley Cooper, Neale Fraser, Rod Laver, Roy Emerson and John Newcombe. In 1968 the inaugural Wimbledon Open was won by the redheaded, left-handed Laver who thus became the first man to take the title as both an amateur and a professional.

Although Wimbledon was a complete success as an amateur showcase, it was the All-England Club that led the successful fight for open tennis.

On October 5, 1967, the British Lawn Tennis Association recommended that Wimbledon become an open event. It was a surprising move, for during the 1930's when the United States had clamored for open tennis, England had opposed the experiment.

Now, however, Britain's court barons were disturbed by the growth of sham amateurism. Amateur players were faking expense accounts and accepting bonuses from sponsors to enter tournaments. The best way to end these abuses was to eliminate the distinction between professionals and amateurs, categorizing all entrants as merely players. Wimbledon could not be a truly world championship if it continued to exclude the pros.

The International Lawn Tennis Association, which had earlier rejected the proposal by a vote of 139 to 83, threatened to expel the British if they went ahead with their plans. Nevertheless, on December 14, 1967, the British Association voted 295–5 to stage the 1968 All-England Championship as an open event. At the same time it abolished all distinctions between the pro and amateur. A preliminary open was scheduled for April 22, 1968, at Bournemouth, the British Hard Court Championship.

From Rome on January 8, 1868, Giorgio Di Stefani, president of the International Federation, announced that the British Lawn Tennis Association would be suspended, effective April 22.

Support for the British grew in the United States. There were rumblings in Australia and France.

On February 3, the U.S. Lawn Tennis Association, meeting in Coronado, California, under the progressive leadership of Robert Kelleher of Los Angeles, took a stand in favor of restricted open competition. The USLTA also dropped a veiled threat of withdrawal from the International Federation.

Australia joined the bolting ranks. With the rug pulled out from under it, the International Federation met in Paris on March 30 and made the momentous decision. A limited number of open tournaments would be allowed. The British had won the war.

The first Open at Bournemouth was an astounding success. A blond British amateur, Mark Cox, knocked off two ranking professionals, Pancho Gonzales and Roy Emerson, in successive rounds and gained the semifinals. The tournament winner was veteran Ken Rosewall of Australia, who beat fellow countryman Rod Laver in the final.

Nostalgia was in the air as such familiar figures as Gonzales, Hoad, Rosewall and Alex Olmedo returned to Wimbledon, the scene of their amateur triumphs. Thousands poured into the stands despite cold, rainy weather during the first five days. Talent was so plentiful that for the first time directors had to seed 16 men.

The professionals, largely drawn from George MacCall's National Tennis League and Lamar Hunt's World Championship Tennis, Inc., were expected to dominate the event. Yet, as at Bournemouth, the amateurs were not to be brushed off so easily. To the delight of the galleries, the top-name pros fell one by one.

A twenty-three-year-old Russian, Alex Metreveli, knocked off the great Pancho Gonzales. Bob Hewitt, a South African Davis Cupper, beat Hoad. Long-haired Ray Moore of South Africa upset Andres Gimeno of Spain. Herb FitzGibbon, a young Princeton graduate in the U.S. Army, ousted Nicola Pilic of Yugoslavia. Tom Edlefsen, unranked in the United States, topped Cliff Drysdale, one of the newer pros. All were early round matches.

As the tournament neared the end, Tom Okker, a sensational Dutch amateur, trounced Roy Emerson; Arthur Ashe, Jr., ousted John Newcombe of Australia, who had been "Player of the Year" in 1967; and Ashe's Davis Cup teammate, Clark Graebner, polished off Fred Stolle, former Wimbledon runner-up from Australia.

When they posted the names in the semifinal brackets, two of the survivors were pros, Laver and Roche. The other two were amateurs, Ashe and Graebner. It was almost immaterial that Laver and Roche went into the last round and Laver, playing at the peak of his game, swept to the title on a crisp 6–3, 6–4, 6–2 victory.

In the women's division, Billie Jean King won her third

straight Wimbledon crown. Playing as a pro for the first time, she defeated England's Ann Haydon Jones in the semi-finals and struggled to a 9–7, 7–5 triumph over Australia's thirty-year-old Judy Tegart in the final.

Even with dollar marks and pound notes as the new theme, it was still Wimbledon and nobody thought too much about the prize money.

"Wimbledon's different," said Laver, pocketing his $4,800 first prize. "I had completely forgotten about the prize money until someone mentioned it to me."

THREE   *The U.S. Nationals—*
—————
2   *From a Shack to Concrete Eminence*

The first U.S. National Tennis Championship was a far cry from the booming, fast-paced tournament of today. It opened August 31, 1881 at the Casino Club in Newport, Rhode Island, and it was like a casual Sunday afternoon lawn party.

There were no grandstands. The spectators—ladies with parasols and ankle-length petticoats, gentlemen in white flannels, striped jackets and straw bowlers—stood or sat around the roped-off court on folding chairs or camp stools.

Blazers, knickerbockers, long-sleeved shirts, belts and woolen stockings displaying club colors comprised the basic uniform. Most of the players wore neckties and all sported caps or round hats with a rolling brim that could be turned down to ward off the glare. Rackets were crude, lopsided bats such as those used for years in court tennis and the balls were rubber covered with white flannel.

The first tournament had resulted from a meeting held in New York the previous May to establish a regulatory body for the game and determine fixed rules. Ever since Mary Ewing Outerbridge had returned from her Bermuda vacation in 1874 with a set of equipment and introduced the sport to her friends at the Staten Island Cricket and Baseball Club, tennis had grown in popularity, especially in Boston, Philadelphia and New York.

However, there was no uniformity. Courts were of different shapes, nets of varying heights and balls of no standard size. Some players preferred old court tennis rules with deuces and advantages as in today's scoring while others scored fifteen points for each game as in badminton or rackets.

The Newport Casino had had a unique birth. Newport, a social resort at the southern tip of Rhode Island, was invaded every summer by wealthy vacationers who built palatial residences which they referred to modestly as "cottages." One such mansion, later converted into a showplace, was Cornelius Vanderbilt's "The Breakers."

James Gordon Bennett, Jr., flamboyant publisher of the New York *Herald*, was a perennial visitor. In 1878 Bennett secured for a friend a guest card to Newport's most exclusive club, the Reading Room, then bet the friend, a British army officer, that he wouldn't dare ride a horse up the steps into the club's front hall.

The Englishman took the dare and Bennett's guest privileges were immediately revoked. Miffed, the fabulously wealthy publisher decided on revenge. With the aid of friends he purchased 126,000 square feet of land fronting Bellevue Avenue, only a few blocks from the Reading Room, and turned it into a lavish sports complex with a bowling alley, billiard parlor, reading rooms, tennis courts and bachelor quarters.

This was the Casino, site of thirty-four National Championships before the event moved to the West Side Tennis Club at Forest Hills, New York. Even then, the Casino continued to play an important part in the game. Under James H. Van Alen it became the location for various invitation tournaments as well as the Tennis Hall of Fame.

Twenty-five players entered the first men's singles and

thirteen pairs competed in the doubles. The rules were British and so was the ball made by F.H. Ayres Ltd. of London. The court, rectangular instead of shaped like an hourglass, measured 78 × 27 feet. The service line was 21 feet from the net which at the posts was 4 feet high and in the center was 3 feet high. Court tennis scoring was used.

The first champion was Richard D. Sears, a protégé of Dr. James Dwight, founder of the U.S. Lawn Tennis Association and patriarch of American tennis. Sears, nineteen, was a slight man with steel-rimmed glasses and a mustache,

He was the younger brother of Fred Sears, who had played Dwight in the rain at Nahant, Massachusetts, in what some historians contend was the first tennis match in the United States. Dick Sears, a strip of a boy at the time, was a spectator on that occasion.

Under Dwight's tutelage the boy developed a good overhead serve and volley and became the first American to abandon the backcourt in favor of rushing the net. Dwight accompanied him to England where Sears picked up the strong forehand drive of Herbert Lawford, the famous "Lawford stroke." In the first Nationals he had no trouble crushing his final opponent W.E. Glynn 6–0, 6–3, 6–2.

Sears was so superior to his contemporaries that he won the championship seven straight years, losing only three sets during the entire period, and then retired undefeated. In the first tournament, he and Dwight teamed in doubles, losing to Clarence Clark and Fred Taylor of Philadelphia, who played one man close to the net and the other back.

However, Sears shared in the six succeeding doubles titles, five times as a partner of Dwight and on the other occasion in 1885 with J.S. Clark.

The first women's championship was held at the Philadelphia Cricket Club in 1887. The winner was Ellen Hansell, who grew up on Philadelphia's main line and saw her first tennis match on the estate of John Wanamaker.

Ellen recalled how as a young girl she and her friends

drove a buggy to a large flat field and laid out a primitive court. With no lime for marking purposes they left the grass uncut where the lines ran. They stretched a clothes-line for a net and braced it at each end with frogged tree branches. The rackets were small and misshapen. The balls were hard black rubber, uncovered.

In the women's final, Miss Hansell, later Mrs. Ellen Allerdice, defeated Laura Knight 6–1, 6–0. She recalled that the girls, wearing long dresses, petticoats and hats, lobbed the ball back and forth very gently as they tripped around the court in heavy shoes. Spectators stood within two feet of play.

Conditions changed rapidly, however, as one champion succeeded another. Oliver Campbell, the most effective net-rusher of the nineteenth century, won three crowns in a row starting in 1890. Robert D. Wrenn, an all-around Harvard athlete with letters in baseball, football and hockey, used a powerful left-handed attack to win four titles in five years between 1893 and 1897.

Another early multiple winner was William A. Larned, who exhibited beautiful ground strokes as he prevailed in 1901, 1902, 1907, and 1911. Newport Casino also saw Maurice McLoughlin, the red-haired Californian with the big serve, and R. Norris Williams, the former Swiss star, giants of the pre-World War I period.

The West Side Tennis Club, which would become the center of American tennis, was founded in 1892. At first it consisted of just a shack and four dirt courts on Central Park West and 88th Street, New York, and there were only thirteen members.

In 1902 the club moved to 117th Street and in 1908 to 238th Street, its membership growing all the time.

In 1913 members purchased ten and a half acres in Forest Hills, New York, for approximately $77,000 and built a club-house costing $30,000. Fifty grass and clay courts for some

600 members were installed and English-born George Agutter was engaged as head professional.

The new complex entered big-time competition in 1914 when it was awarded the Davis Cup Challenge Round match between Australasia and the United States. The Australasian team featured left-handed Norman Brookes and Tony Wilding. The series was highlighted by a marathon duel between Brookes and Maurice McLoughlin, the dashing, volatile Californian. McLoughlin won 17–15, 6–3, 6–3, but the Australasians captured the cup, holding it through World War I.

The event filled the temporary wooden stands to the 14,000 capacity, and thus spurred officials of the U.S. Lawn Tennis Association to consider the club as a site for the National Championships. Though the tournament was deeply entrenched at the Newport Casino, Julian S. Myrick, Lyle Mahan and Kark Behr led a successful campaign to transfer the Championships to Forest Hills in 1915.

By this time tennis had become more than a social game. It had developed into a major spectator sport. In 1923 the club erected a concrete stadium seating 13,500 at a cost of $250,000. The little community seven miles from Manhattan found itself in a beehive of world tennis interest.

The first men's champion at Forest Hills was Little Bill Johnston, whose head-to-head battles with Big Bill Tilden were to fill the big stadium to overflowing in the postwar era.

The men's championships shifted to the Germantown Cricket Club in Philadelphia in 1922 and 1923 but returned to Forest Hills in 1924 where they remained despite strong efforts by Californians to move the event to the hard courts of the Pacific Coast in the 1950's and 1960's.

During the twenties the championships featured dramatic duels involving Tilden, Johnston, France's Four Musketeers (Borotra, Lacoste, Cochet and Brugnon), Suzanne Lenglen, Helen Wills Moody and Helen Jacobs.

The women's singles were staged at the Philadelphia Cricket Club from 1887 to 1920 when they too were moved to Forest Hills. The men's doubles had a brief tenure at South Orange, New Jersey, and later transferred to the Longwood Cricket Club in Chestnut Hill, Massachusetts, where they became a fixture until open competition was inaugurated in 1968.

Except for the three-year sweep by Frenchmen Lacoste and Cochet in 1926–1928 and the three triumphs by Britain's Fred Perry in 1933, 1934 and 1936, Americans dominated their national tournament until midway through the twentieth century. Whenever one of the nation's stars wore out, another stepped into his shoes—Tilden, Ellsworth Vines, Don Budge, Jack Kramer and Pancho Gonzales.

In 1951 Frank Sedgman became the first Australian to capture the title, and Aussies won eleven of the next sixteen championships. America's hold on the women's title, almost solid for seventy years, was broken in 1959 by Maria Bueno of Brazil and the tournament was dominated by foreigners for the next decade.

After Betty Nuthall of England cracked the long American streak in 1930 only one outside victor, Anita Lizana in 1937, won the ladies' event until Miss Bueno cut her opposition to pieces with rapier-like strokes. Darlene Hard, a California waitress, won in 1960 and 1961 but then Australia's statuesque Margaret Court Smith and Miss Bueno took command, winning six of the next seven titles. Mrs. Billie Jean King scored her only U.S. women's amateur triumph in 1967.

The National Championships went open in 1968, amateur Arthur Ashe, Jr., winning the men's title while the women's crown went to Britain's non-professional Virginia Wade. The national amateur grass court championships were moved to Longwood in Chestnut Hill, Massachusetts, Ashe beating Los Angeles' Bobby Lutz in the final and Margaret Court taking the ladies' title to Australia.

In 1969 a move by the U.S. Lawn Tennis Association allowing non-professional players to accept prize money altered the tournament format again. This reduced the national amateur to virtual college and club player status, open only to competitors who were purely amateur.

The 1969 amateur was awarded to Rochester, New York, while Forest Hills kept possession of the big one—the U.S. Open.

In an effort to challenge Wimbledon as the tennis capital of the world, the USLTA and West Side officials imported an enterprising promoter from South Africa named Owen Williams.

"Our plan is to have every ticket sold every day before the first ball is hit," Williams announced on taking the job. "We will make this the greatest tennis tournament in the world.

"Some day we will play before half a million people, take in $1,500,000 and offer $500,000 in prize money."

THREE / 3   *The Foreign Events —*
They Live in the Shadows

Although the Australian and French Championships are linked with Wimbledon and the U.S. Nationals as part of the "Big Four" they have never really measured up to their fellow tournaments.

The French event—the first was held in 1891, its winner listed in the record books only as "Briggs"—is played on the red clay courts of the Stade Roland Garros outside Paris. Perhaps this is one reason for its semi-major status, since traditionally great championships must be won on grass, the original surface. Moreover the tournament is held in late spring, prior to Wimbledon, when many players have yet to get into top shape.

Geography is Australia's nemesis. Located at the bottom of the globe, half a world away from most thriving tennis centers, the country has an upside down season schedule.

When it is midsummer in Europe and America it is mid-winter Down Under. Australia's summer tennis season runs from November through January.

Then too, other countries have been reluctant to send players so far away. Jet travel improved this situation somewhat and between 1950 and 1970 the Aussies also profited by the fact that they virtually dominated the Davis Cup. Since the Americans, Spaniards and Mexicans had to travel to Australia anyway to challenge for the trophy over the Christmas holidays, it was no great strain to remain for the Championships in January.

Even so, there was never a substantial overseas entry and the Australian Championships, like those in France, remained second class. It was a shame. Australia is a tremendously sports-oriented continent with a rich tennis tradition. All the capital cities—Sydney, Melbourne, Brisbane, Adelaide and Perth—have broad stretches of beautiful turf courts equal to those anywhere.

So the Australians have had their own national tournament largely to themselves, with only periodic threats from the outside. Jean Borotra, the French star, won the men's singles in 1928, England's Fred Perry in 1934 and America's Don Budge in 1938, on the way to his Grand Slam.

There was not another overseas winner until New York's big, hard-hitting Dick Savitt triumphed in 1951 en route to the Wimbledon crown. The only other outsider to win in the next decade was Alejandro Olmedo, the amazing, lightning-quick Peruvian who in 1958 almost single-handedly captured the Davis Cup for his adopted United States, and then stayed around to win the Australian Nationals despite a sore arm.

The women's division has been almost as barren of non-Australian winners. Dorothy Round of England took the title in 1935 and Dorothy Bundy of the United States in 1938. Doris Hart and Louise Brough of America posted back-to-back triumphs in 1949 and 1950, Maureen Connolly in 1953, Shirley Fry in 1957 and Britain's Angela Mortimer in 1958. Australia's Margaret Smith strung seven victories in a row, starting in 1960, before Nancy Richey and Billie Jean King brought the United States back with triumphs in 1967 and 1968.

For the first forty-one years of the French Championships the mother country kept an unbroken grip on the men's singles title. Jack Crawford of Australia turned the tide with a victory in 1933 and for the next thirty-four years France won only twice.

The roll call of outside champions included such names as Baron Von Cramm of Germany, Jaroslav Drobny of Czechoslovakia and Egypt, Nicola Pietrangeli of Italy, Manuel Santana of Spain and America's Don Budge, Frank Parker and Tony Trabert plus virtually every Australian champion that came along.

After Suzanne Lenglen's bow-out in 1926, the French ladies' title was up for international grabs. Americans won most the succeeding championships. Helen Wills Moody was a four-time winner. Doris Hart and Maureen Connolly each won twice, as did Margaret Smith of Australia. Francoise Durr, a frail, red-haired mademoiselle with a "setting hen" backhand, restored her country's honor briefly with a victory in 1967.

The Canadian Championships never drew the cream of American tennis or any sizeable group of international stars. As a result its victory rolls are filled largely with home talent and secondary players from the United States.

Exceptions are: Frank Parker who won in 1938; Dick Savitt, victor in 1952; Roy Emerson of Australia, who made a detour in his normal summer campaign to prevail in 1964; and Spain's Manuel Santana, champion in 1967. Margaret Osborne is the only American women's champion to hold the Canadian title. She won in 1935.

The Davis Cup started out as a young man's dream and grew into one of the world's great sports spectacles, bringing together nations of varying races and political ideologies and building a monument to international good will.

Dwight Davis, who conceived the idea before he was old enough to vote, never dreamed his brainchild would attain such scope and that the $700 silver bowl which he contributed as a trophy would someday become the symbol of international tennis supremacy.

The cup, during its first sixty-nine years, crossed the Pacific a dozen times and made almost as many trips across the Atlantic. It has been locked up in bank vaults and guarded by armed policemen as if it were the crown jewels. Cracked three times and modified over the decades, it has nevertheless grown in value as ever more nations sought it as they would the Holy Grail.

Kings, princes and premiers have watched it change hands. Numberless times it has been filled to the brim with champagne—it holds exactly 37 bottles—as winners toasted their victory.

Dwight Filley Davis was the scion of a prominent St. Louis family. He attended exclusive Eastern preparatory schools and enrolled at Harvard University. A fine tennis player, he was only twenty when he teamed with Holcombe Ward in 1899 to win the first of three consecutive national doubles championships.

That same year he conceived the idea for an international tennis competition.

Davis was a member of the Harvard varsity, which also included Malcolm Whitman, the national singles champion, and Holcombe Ward and Beals Wright, son of George

Wright, founder of the famous sporting goods firm that became known as Wright & Ditson. Young Wright later shared both national singles and doubles titles.

This was indeed an imposing team and the elder Wright thought its talent should not be hidden. He arranged a tennis trip for the four men to the Pacific Coast in order to show them off and stimulate interest in the game. The Harvards won all but two of their matches and Samuel Hardy, one of California's top players, recalled later how the tour set Davis to thinking about organizing an international tournament along the lines of the East-West duel.

Britain would be a logical opponent for such an event since the English, having gotten a head start in the sport, considered themselves the best players in the world.

Davis, Hardy and the others discussed this attitude during the West Coast trip and, according to Hardy, the conversation went something like this:

DAVIS: "I think we could beat the British. I believe our style of play is more aggressive and better."

HARDY: "Yes, I understand the British play a strictly baseline game. I doubt that they could stand up to our net attack."

The Americans had adopted a style calling for a hard service and a move to the net as quickly as possible. They had found that a player had a much better advantage if he could plant himself in the forecourt and take the ball before it hit the ground—a volley. The Yanks had also discovered more potent service called the American twist. By catching the ball over the head and slicing the racket across it, they were able to impart a fiendish spin which was very difficult to handle.

Davis said: "I think we could beat the British. It would be great if we got a chance to try."

The Harvard undergraduate discussed the matter with his teammates and the senior Wright on the long train trip East, and the more they talked the more enthusiastic all became. Wright, who had considerable influence, promised to bring the plan before the U.S. Lawn Tennis Association.

Returning home, he immediately contacted the USLTA. There he found the idea was not entirely a new one. The president was Dr. James Dwight, five times American doubles champion and one of the pioneers of the game twenty years before. Dwight said he had been trying to arrange such a match for several years. In 1897, for instance, negotiations were near completion with America offering to pay the rival country's traveling expenses but at the last moment England had decided against the trip. The next year a proposal that the U.S. play Britain following Wimbledon was jettisoned upon the outbreak of the Spanish-American War.

Hence Dwight was receptive to Davis' suggestion. He contacted the British Lawn Tennis Association and the response was affirmative. The match was set for 1900 at the Longwood Club in Brookline, Massachusetts outside Boston. Davis, who was independently wealthy, promised to provide a trophy. He contacted a Boston jeweler and together they agreed on specifications. It was a sterling silver bowl lightly washed in gold, 13 inches high, 18 inches in diameter and weighing 217 ounces, troy weight.

The British crossed the Atlantic. They were a confident team when they disembarked, wearing neat blue jackets with gold buttons and carrying rackets under their arms. Lawn tennis was a British game, after all. Who were these brash Americans that dared to challenge them?

Davis, with the approval of the USLTA and the British visitors, drew up a format. It was astonishingly simple. There would be two singles matches on the first day, a doubles match on the second and the final two singles with the pairings reversed on the final day. The series would be best three-out-of-five. It was a format that never changed.

The British were in for a shock. In the opening match Malcolm Whitman crushed Britain's Arthur Gore 6–1, 6–3,

6–2. In the second Davis won over E.D. Black 4–6, 6–2, 6–4, 6–4. With a 2–0 lead, the Americans went out and finished off the visitors in the doubles, the championship team of Davis and Ward beating Black and Roger Barrett 6–4, 6–4, 6–4.

The sweep made the final two matches unnecessary, but under the rules they were supposed to be played nonetheless. Davis won the first set from Gore 9–7 and the second set was tied 9–9 when it was decided to quit play. The match between Whitman and Black was called off and the series went into the books as 3–0.

The British, astounded, went home to tell about the Americans: how their services took strange spins and how they moved to the net to stroke the ball before it hit the ground. Still, despite hurt pride, they stuck to their baseline tactics. But, at any rate, the Davis Cup was under way.

There was no match in 1901 but in 1902 the British came over with a stronger team. The challengers consisted of Reginald and Hugh Doherty and Dr. Joshua Pim, all multiple Wimbledon champions. The match was played at the Crescent Athletic Club in Brooklyn, New York, and this time the Americans had their hands full.

Reginald Doherty got the invaders off to a quick start, beating Bill Larned in the opening match 2–6, 3–6, 6–3, 6–4, 6–4. Malcolm Whitman leveled the score by defeating Dr. Pim 6–1, 6–1, 1–6, 6–0. The British took a 2–1 lead when the Dohertys whipped the three-time American doubles champions Holcombe Ward and Dwight Davis, 3–6, 10–8, 6–3, 6–4. However, Whitman and Larned rallied for final singles victories that saved the cup for America 3–2.

In 1903 the Dohertys came back to wrest the trophy from the Americans at the Longwood Cricket Club and this marked the last time Britain and the United States were the sole competitors. In 1904 Belgium, Austria and France entered, followed in 1905 by Australasia with a combined team from Australia and New Zealand.

For the next seven years no new country appeared, although South Africa entered in 1911 but did not compete. South Africa joined Germany and Canada as competitors in 1913. After World War I, with no play from 1915 through 1918, Holland added its bid in 1920. A year later the Davis Cup family was increased by seven additional nations—Denmark, Spain, Japan, the Philippines, Czechoslovakia, Argentina and India. Growth has been steady with the number of competing countries approaching fifty as the game moved into the 1970's.

During the first seventy years only four nations won the cup—Australia (Australasia), Britain, France and the United States—although others managed to battle their way into the Challenge Round. Belgium was a finalist in 1904, Japan in 1921, Italy in 1961, Mexico in 1962, Spain in 1965 and 1967, India in 1966, Romania in 1969, and West Germany in 1970.

After the first six years of U.S.–British domination, the Australasians stepped into the picture in 1907. They came up with a left-handed ace named Norman E. Brookes, later to become one of the administrative giants of the game, and a brilliant stylist named Anthony Wilding.

They wrested the cup from the British at Wimbledon and held it four years before England, with Cecil Parke and Charles Dixon in key roles, won it back in 1912. Norris Williams and Maurice McLoughlin figured in an American victory in 1913, but Australasia's Brookes and Wilding reasserted their dominance at Forest Hills in 1914. The cup went to the bottom of the world to remain until 1920, with no matches played during World War I.

Then came Big Bill Tilden, rated by many as the greatest player of all times, and his partner and longtime rival, Little Bill Johnston, to bring world supremacy back to the United States.

In 1920 when Tilden and Johnston recaptured the cup for the United States at Auckland, New Zealand, the silver bowl was completely covered with names. There was no space to record additional results. Whereupon Davis, the donor, added a tray which cost $400. The tray is flat and as beautifully decorated as the cup itself.

Davis had departed from Harvard and gone on to enter American public life. In 1925 he was appointed Secretary of War by President Calvin Coolidge, an office he held for four years. He then became Governor-General of the Philippines, retiring in 1932 and assuming the post of Director General of the Army Specialist Corps with the rank of major general when the United States entered World War II.

Davis died on November 28, 1945, but not before seeing his boyhood dream come to realization and the world drawn into a greater understanding through a sport he loved. In an article in 1931, he enunciated the tournament's credo:

The great success of the Cup has been due to the unselfish labours of the tennis authorities in the various countries which have competed, to the magnificent sportsmanship and marvelous skill of the great players who have participated, and to the ever-increasing sport-loving public of all nations who are united in a love for clean sport, a hard-fought contest, and a splendid spirit of sportsmanship. Good sportsmanship has no national boundaries. It speaks a universal language.

The first names carved on the beautiful new tray were those of Tilden and Johnston, and as they continued to win year after year, it appeared they might hang on to the trophy forever. Then in 1927, after seven consecutive American victories, there came a surprising turn.

Playing at the Germantown Cricket Club outside Philadelphia, a team of Frenchmen scored an astounding upset. Rene Lacoste scored singles victories over both Johnston and Tilden while Henri Cochet won over an ailing Johnston for the three points needed in a 3–2 conquest. The tennis world was appalled.

They called them the "Four Musketeers," after the heroes of Alexander Dumas' swashbuckling novel. Besides Lacoste and Cochet, the swordsmen consisted of Jean Borotra and Jacques Brugnon. Products of the red clay courts of Paris' Roland Garros Stadium, all were quick and crafty, deft volleyers and all-court tacticians. They were masters on their own slow surface, but no one had given them a chance against the power and put-away qualities of Tilden and Johnston on grass.

Once the Frenchmen got the cup to Paris and were able to defend it on their favorite surface, they repelled four challenges by the United States and one by the British before surrendering the trophy to England in 1933.

By this time Johnston had succumbed to tuberculosis and Tilden had turned professional. Britain, meanwhile, had produced the world's top player in Fred Perry, a dark-haired athlete with hardly a flaw in his repertoire. He had a good partner, too, Henry W. (Bunny) Austin.

Perry and Austin joined to capture the Davis Cup from France in 1933 and for the next three years held it against challenges from the United States and Australia.

By 1934 the cup had again run out of name space. Both the silver bowl and tray were completely covered. Davis came to the rescue. He provided a base—or plinth—8 inches high and 34 inches in diameter. It was of polished walnut on which were placed sterling silver plaques. It offered enough space to take names for the next thirty-five years.

The emergence of Donald Budge, a California redhead with an explosive game and one of the most destructive backhands the sport had ever seen, returned the Americans to court power in 1937 and 1938. However, Budge also succumbed to the lure of a fat professional contract and Australia, captained by Harry Hopman, recaptured the bowl in 1939. Adrian Quist and John Bromwich rallied after dropping the first two matches to Bobby Riggs and Frank Parker for a 3–2 victory that made Davis Cup history. Never in the competition had a team fought back from defeats in the hole to survive. Australia kept the cup through the

World War II years (1940–1945) when play was suspended.

Jack Kramer and Ten Schroeder put the Yanks back on top after the war, winning in 1946 at Kooyong in Melbourne, Australia, and the Americans ruled supreme until Hopman returned as Australian captain in 1950, inaugurating what became known as the "Australian Era."

That year the little, sandy-haired Melbourne tactician pulled off a major upset at the West Side Tennis Club in Forest Hills. He brought forth an obscure player named Kenneth McGregor, better known as a football player, to team with Frank Sedgman in singles. McGregor surprisingly beat Ted Schroeder and Australia went on to a 4–1 triumph.

This spectacular coup and subsequent victories earned Hopman the title of "Miracle Man." He was a tough captain, a disciplinarian who stressed physical fitness. He put his players through rigorous training grinds, both in the gymnasium and outdoors. He levied fines against players who broke curfew or picked up the wrong fork at the table. No one was better at raising a team to a peak mental pitch before a big match.

During the ensuing nineteen years, including 1968, he won 15 matches and lost only 4, each time to the United States. The losing years were 1954, when Tony Trabert and Vic Seixas upset Lew Hoad and Ken Rosewall at Sydney; 1958, when Peruvian Alejandro Olmedo, a California student, beat the Australians almost single-handedly; 1963, on victories by Dennis Ralston and Chuck McKinley; and 1968, when Australian ranks had been stripped bare by a mass exodus to pro ranks.

After Sedgman and McGregor came Hoad and Rosewall, who made the world tour at the age of seventeen and defended the Davis Cup successfully at nineteen. Then followed Ashley Cooper, a dark-haired court killer who lost interest after marrying Miss Australia, a beauty queen; the Queensland twins, Malcolm Anderson and Roy Emerson; left-handed Neale Fraser; Grand Slammer Rod Laver; Fred

Stolle; John Newcombe; and Tony Roche. It appeared the well would never run dry, but it did.

Emerson, six times Australian champion, was finally persuaded to turn professional early in 1968 and was soon followed by Newcombe, 1967 Wimbledon and American champion, and the promising, left-handed Roche—all stalwarts of Hopman's Davis Cup forces. The Australians were left defenseless.

The country's top players were Bill Bowrey, a rangy, erratic player who won the 1968 Australian title and then went into a sudden eclipse; Ray Ruffels, a hard-serving left-hander with no major titles to his credit; and a pair of teenagers, John Alexander, seventeen, and Philip Dent, eighteen.

"The trouble is that Australia has no one left who has been able to develop a winning attitude," said Jack Kramer, as the powerful American team moved into Adelaide eager to redeem five years of frustration. "They have been held back in the shadows of better players, who now have turned professional."

No such ailment plagued the Americans. Arthur Ashe, Jr., the scrawny Negro army lieutenant from Richmond, Virginia, had shot his way into the semifinals of the first Wimbledon Open and had captured the inaugural U.S. Open at Forest Hills, playing against the leading professionals. Clark Graebner, a New York paper executive who exploded 112 miles-per-hour services off his steel racket, had gained the semifinals in the Wimbledon and American Opens. They were backed by a doubles team from the University of Southern California, Stan Smith and Bob Lutz. They had won every American doubles title and had established themselves as probably the world's best, amateur or pro.

These, plus America's Number One ranked amateur, Charlie Pasarell of Puerto Rico, were the United States' trump cards when the Yanks made their bid under Captain Donald Dell, a thirty-year-old former Davis Cup player and attorney from Washington, D.C. Although they were overwhelming 10–1 favorites, Dell and other U.S. officials were apprehensive that the cagy Hopman, called the "Old Fox," might pull another miracle out of his floppy white hat.

There was a different atmosphere about the 1968 Davis Cup matches in Australia than had prevailed in previous years. Australians had experienced a decline in tennis interest in the past few years and the country's lack of enthusiasm was never more marked than during this Christmas holiday period in Adelaide.

American players, in their dark jackets with the red-white-and-blue emblem over the breast, could walk through the streets unnoticed instead of being mobbed by autograph seekers. Taxi drivers, maids and shopkeepers, who used to talk animatedly about the tennis matches, did not even know who was playing. The turnout at the Memorial Drive courts numbered only 5,000 to 6,000 compared with 26,000 who had jammed the White City stands at Sydney in 1954.

The results were no surprise. Opening day Graebner outlasted Bowrey 8–10, 6–4, 8–6, 3–6, 6–1, and Ashe beat the left-handed Ruffels 6–8, 7–5, 6–3, 6–3. In doubles Hopman threw in the 17-year-old Alexander but his gamble backfired as Smith and Lutz crushed the uncoordinated Aussies 6–4, 6–4, 6–2. It made no difference in the outcome that Graebner beat Ruffels while Ashe bowed to Bowrey the following day.

Almost more important than the matches was the fact that sitting in the VIP section were the tennis leaders of the four major tennis-playing nations—Robert Kelleher, president of the U.S. Lawn Tennis Association; Derek Hardwick, president of the British Association, the 320-pound C.A. (Big Bill) Edwards, head of the Australian Association, and two young progressives from the French Association, Philippe Chatrier and Bob Abdesselam.

They had elected to meet in informal closed-door sessions to discuss the future of tennis, particularly the Davis Cup. Should the cup, like the rest of the game, be opened to the pros? It was an issue that created considerable controversy.

"We must make the Davis Cup open and do it as quickly as possible," warned Chatrier, vice-president of the French Association. "It is obvious that interest will die if we do not bring in the best players."

"The Davis Cup has always been the premier event in tennis," argued the American captain, Donald Dell. "If it is to remain the premier event, it cannot be content with inferior players. We must bring in the pros."

"The Davis Cup must remain amateur," insisted Hopman. "The professional is in no position to take time away from his tour to prepare and play eight months of zone matches leading up to the Challenge Round. It would be grossly unfair to let amateurs play the earlier rounds and then call upon the pros in the bigger matches. I would be opposed to it."

Jack Kramer, former champion and longtime successful pro promoter, said he believed the Davis Cup would be compelled to go open and he suggested that several players might be used by a country in the course of a campaign.

"We are all for the open Davis Cup—it is just a matter of when and how," said Big Bill Edwards.

The Cup found itself caught up in the swirling whirlwind of change. Less than a year before, the International Lawn Tennis Federation voted in favor of a limited number of open tournaments. The body also approved a category of "registered players," tournament competitors not under pro contract who could compete in amateur events and collect prize money in the opens. Such players were permitted to enter the Davis Cup.

In order to inscribe the names of Ashe, Graebner, Smith and Lutz on the huge trophy in 1968, it was necessary to add a second plinth. This was done at a cost of $1,900, giving the Davis Cup a look of greater dignity.

The new plinth, adding nine inches to the height of the trophy, provided space for silver plaques until the year 2000.

The question was: Would those plaques carry the names of such pro giants as Pancho Gonzales, Rod Laver, Ken

Rosewall and John Newcombe, whose names had appeared previously as amateurs?

Not in 1969. The Davis Cup was played again without the names of the contract professionals although most of the competitors were professionals in every sense of the word since they accepted purses.

With Australian strength thus sapped, a surprising team from behind the Iron Curtain—Romania with a pair of flashy performers in shaggy Ion Tiriac and talented, Hollywood-handsome Ilie Nastase—fought through to the Challenge Round. Ashe and Smith, with Lutz helping Smith in doubles, withstood the Communist threat at Cleveland and the big trophy stayed in the United States.

"If they got the cup behind the Iron Curtain, we might never get it back," one tennis observer commented dourly. No one took the comment seriously.

THREE
5

The Wightman Cup—The Girls Keep It Private

After Hazel Hotchkiss, the diminutive California farm girl who was a ladies' champion in the era of floppy hats and billowing petticoats, married George Wightman and settled down as a housewife in Brookline, Massachusetts, her interest in tennis continued, and she became "Queen Mother" of the game.

She competed until she was past seventy—winning the last of her forty-four national titles at age sixty-eight—and she maintained close contact with players and officials.

In 1920 Mrs. Wightman offered a trophy similar to the Davis Cup for international competition among the ladies. She explained years afterward:

I had followed with keen interest the work of the Californians in Davis Cup play—Maurice McLoughlin, Melville Long and Billy Johnston, in particular, and soon after the World War the accomplishments of Suzanne Lenglen at Wimbledon and elsewhere increased the general appeal of women's tennis to a higher degree than ever before.

The agile and gifted French girl fired the imagination of English players by her phenomenal skill and it struck me that women's play along the lines of the Davis Cup competition would provide a new and definite objective for girls who found tennis to their liking.

Kathleen McKane had become the leading woman of the English courts and Helen Wills was just beginning to show signs of power and genius which were to make her the outstanding player of two continents. The thought struck me that ably handled meetings which brought together the chief exponents of the game in France, England and the United States would add zest to women's tennis.

When Mrs. Wightman first proposed the trophy, the idea was greeted coolly by delegates to the International Lawn Tennis Federation. It was still a man's world. The directors argued that such an event would attract only mild interest and would be very expensive. The United States was fairly enthusiastic but failed to obtain the expected support of the English and French.

Mrs. Wightman had virtually forgotten the plan when in 1923, while visiting her parents in Berkeley, California, she received a telegram, asking her if she would be available to represent the United States in matches against a British team in New York in August. She was stunned by the request. Her long-time aim was taking root.

It happened that Julian S. Myrick, president of the U.S. Lawn Tennis Association, had been working diligently beneath the surface to put Mrs. Wightman's idea in motion. A new 13,500-seat concrete stadium had just been built at the West Side Tennis Club in Forest Hills and Myrick wanted to help dedicate it with a match between the best women players of Britain and the United States. The men's singles championship was being played that year in Germantown, Pennsylvania.

Mrs. Wightman gladly accepted the captaincy of the American team. Her players were Molla Mallory, Helen Wills and Eleanor Goss. Anthony Sabelli captained the British team which included Miss McKane, Mrs. Alfred Beamish, Mrs. R.C. Clayton and Mrs. B.C. Covell. The tournament would consist of five single matches and two doubles, with the winner to be determined on a best four-of-seven match basis.

Mrs. Wightman put up a silver vase, the International Ladies' Trophy, which quite naturally came to be known by the name of its donor. The Wightman Cup was born.

The crowds were good and the interest high for that inaugural match but the series was one-sided. Despite talented Miss McKane, the Americans scored a 7–0 sweep.

Helen Wills and Molla Mallory scored two singles victories each and Eleanor Goss collected the other. Mrs. Wightman teamed with Miss Goss and Miss Wills played with Mrs. Mallory in doubles.

Mrs. Wightman had intended to make the event a truly international tournament by bringing in France and any other nation where women's tennis was on the rise. But her aim never came to pass. The French were cool to the idea and there was no assurance they would have been allowed to participate anyway, since Britain was all in favor of keeping it a two-party affair.

The tables were reversed in 1924 when the Americans trekked to Wimbledon for the second Wightman and were trounced 6–1.

The lone American point came in the final doubles as Miss Wills and Mrs. Wightman defeated Miss McKane and Evelyn Colyer 2–6, 6–2, 6–4. Miss Wills played disappointingly, losing to Miss McKane 6–2, 6–2 and to Mrs. Covell 6–2, 6–4.

Britain retained the trophy at Forest Hills in 1925 and for the next five years the series was touch-and-go. With Helen Wills absent, Elizabeth Ryan and Mrs. Marion Jessup led the United States to a narrow 4–3 victory in 1926 at

Wimbledon, and Miss Wills and Mrs. Mallory came back to defend it successfully in 1927 at Forest Hills.

Eileen Bennett and Mrs. P. Watson were the heroines of a British triumph in 1928, but Helen Wills and Helen Jacobs formed an unbeatable duo in 1929. Capitalizing principally on doubles, the British snapped back in 1930, winning 4–3 at Wimbledon.

Through the first eight years of the Wightman Cup, the British won four and the Americans four, even though the United States had such outstanding performers as Molla Mallory, Helen Wills and Helen Jacobs.

Then suddenly the bottom dropped out for the British. The caliber of their women players went into a slump while that of the United States took a sharp climb. Helen Wills and Helen Jacobs recaptured the trophy in 1931 at Forest Hills and the British were not to see Mrs. Wightman's bright silver vase again for twenty-seven years.

From 1931 until 1958 American women reeled off twenty-one consecutive victories, holding the trophy also during the six years of World War II when play was suspended. Even such gifted English players as Dorothy Round, Betty Nuthall and Katherine Stammers failed to stem the tide. The United States turned out a steady stream of world class players, including Alice Marble, Sarah Palfrey, Pauline Betz, Margaret Osborne, Louise Brough, Doris Hart, Shirley Fry and Maureen Connolly.

There was talk in the high councils of abandoning the series. However, tradition and a great respect for Mrs. Wightman prevailed.

The British had reached the depths of despondency when their enthusiasm was rejuvenated by an astonishing upset at Wimbledon in 1958.

Althea Gibson, the American Negro tennis ace, was Wimbledon titleholder and rated indisputably as Number One woman player in the world. Britain's faint hopes rested with Ann Haydon, a slashing, net-rushing left-hander, and Christine Truman, an awkward six-foot giant who hit the ball like a cannon shot.

With a fantastic flash of remarkable tennis, Christine defeated both Althea and Mrs. Dorothy Head Knode in singles and joined Shirley Bloomer in a doubles victory over Mrs. Knode and pretty Karol Fageros. Those points plus Miss Haydon's singles triumph over little Miriam Arnold were enough to give Britain a squeaking 4–3 conquest.

Interest in the Wightman Cup was again revived briefly when Christine and Ann pulled off a second coup at Wimbledon two years later. It was followed, however, by another tennis famine for the British as they lost seven consecutive matches to the Americans before rebounding, again at Wimbledon, in 1968.

Billie Jean King, the three-time Wimbledon winner, had turned professional and was not available. The United States defended with a clay court specialist, Nancy Richey, and Mary Ann Eisel, Jane Bartkowicz and Kathy Harter.

The British took the wraps off Virginia Wade, a sturdy, dark-haired girl who had learned her tennis in South Africa. She defeated both Miss Richey and Miss Eisel in singles and shared in a doubles win. The margin was 4–3, three of the British points credited to Miss Wade.

The pride and tradition of the American women in this trans-Atlantic rivalry were not to be so easily disposed of, despite the unsettled state of the game because of open tennis. Playing at Cleveland in August 1969, the U.S. girls came back to win the Wightman trophy for the thirty-fourth time in the forty-six-year-old competition. Julie Heldman of New York defeated Britain's Winnie Shaw in the deciding match 6–3, 6–4.

But whether the Wightman Cup would follow the trend and go professional as did the Davis Cup was unsure. Said Mrs. Wightman, voicing her wish that the event remain an amateur one: "This is the age of commercialism and exploitation. Yet I earnestly hope that the matches will never be stunted by too much emphasis on this phase of the competition."

THREE *The Federation Cup —*
6   *World Cup for Women*

By the 1960's, it was obvious that international competition among ladies should not be confined to the United States and Britain. Maria Bueno, a cold, efficient little shotmaker from Sao Paulo, Brazil, was busy collecting Wimbledon, American and Italian Championships. Australian women had finally received their emancipation after years of playing in the shadow of their men, and the best of them was a statuesque slugger named Margaret Smith, destined to win two Wimbledons, three U.S. titles, three Italian, two French and seven of her homeland's singles crowns before she was thirty. A stolid Czech, Vera Sukova, surprised everyone by reaching the Wimbledon women's final in 1962. Good players were also emerging from France, South Africa and countries behind the Iron Curtain.

The Wightman Cup was still a private duel between two nations. For the true world team ladies' champion, it was necessary to scan a broader horizon.

Nell Hopman, wife of Australia's successful Davis Cup captain, was among the first to start beating the drums for a truly international competition among women. She drew support in the United States from Mrs. Hazel Wightman who still regretted that her plans for such an event had never been accepted. England, France and other countries joined in support.

In 1963 the International Lawn Tennis Federation placed its stamp of approval on the project and the first tournament was scheduled for June that year at Queen's Club. Any ILTF member could send a team and sixteen did so, including Communist Hungary and Czechoslovakia, making a perfect draw. An elimination format—a condensed version of what already prevailed for the Davis Cup—was decided upon. Instead of lasting an entire year, the event would be run off in four days. Each series consisted of three matches, two singles and one doubles, on a best-of-three basis.

In the opening round Australia, Hungary, South Africa, France, Austria, England, the Netherlands and the United States respectively, beat Belgium, Denmark, Czechoslovakia, Germany, Norway, Canada, Switzerland and Italy.

Australia, South Africa, England and the United States survived the quarter-finals, and in the semifinals favored teams from Australia and America stormed through, setting up an exciting final.

Margaret Smith stunned the Americans by crushing veteran Darlene Hard in the opening match, but Billie Jean Moffit (later Mrs. King) rallied for a 5–7, 6–0, 6–3 triumph over Lesley Turner. The outcome hinged on the doubles and although the U.S. was within a hairbreadth of elimination in the second set, Darlene and Billie Jean pulled off a dramatic three-set victory 3–6, 13–11, 6–3.

However, if tennis buffs expected another American monopoly, as in the Wightman Cup, they were in for a rude surprise. The following year at the Germantown Cricket Club outside Philadelphia, the Australians captured the cup by beating the United States. Margaret Smith trounced Billie Jean with the loss of only five games and Miss Turner won in straight sets from Nancy Richey. Misses Smith and Turner repeated in 1965 at Melbourne, beating Miss Moffitt and Carole Graebner, who was substituting for Miss Richey.

America's turn came again in 1966 as it swept to a 3–0 triumph over West Germany which had surprisingly battled its way to the final. Julie Heldman, Billie Jean's singles mate, was much improved and defeated Helga Niessen while her partner, having since become a housewife, crushed Edda Buding. The doubles played in Turin, Italy, had no effect on the outcome.

Rosemary Casals of San Francisco, the bouncy bantam with the heavyweight punch, was Billie Jean's mate in 1967, and the tournament became a mini-version of the Wightman Cup as Britain made the final for the first time. Rosemary beat Virginia Wade 9–7, 8–6, and Mrs. King trounced her long-time rival, Ann Haydon Jones, 6–3, 6–4. The doubles were cancelled with the two teams at one set apiece.

The famed Stade Roland Garros in Paris was site of the 1968 Federation Cup matches, and this time the ladies played on clay, a surface that stole some of the advantage from the Americans, Australians and British who are normally sharper on grass. Russia was among the fifteen competing nations, defeating Italy in the first round but bowing to England in the second.

The United States advanced over Switzerland and France, then slipped up surprisingly against the Netherlands, a real dark horse. Nancy Richey defeated Astrid Suurbeck but, Marijke Jansen toppled Mary Ann Eisel of St. Louis 7–5, 6–0, and Miss Suurbeck and Lidy Venneboer won the clinching doubles match from Miss Richey and Kathy Harter 2–6, 8–6, 6–0. It was a blow to American prestige.

The Netherlands went into the final against Australia, whose girls appeared to have no difficulty adjusting to the clay surface. Margaret Smith Court and little Kerry Melville pulled off a 3–0 rout.

Billie Jean King and Rosemary Casals, meanwhile, had turned professional, as had Ann Haydon Jones of Britain and Francoise Durr of France.

Under these conditions, no single nation could claim distinct international superiority. It had become a wide-open fight.

The United States regained the title, however, in 1969 in Athens, Greece, where Nancy Richey won over Kerry Melville and teamed with Peaches Bartkowicz for a clinching doubles triumph over Margaret Court and Judy Tegart.

FOUR

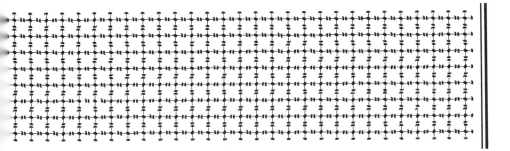

Styles of the Greats: Julius D. Heldman

When lawn tennis was first played both in England and in the United States, it was a leisurely, social game. Players generally patted the ball back and forth over the net with a gentle, ladylike stroke. They moved easily over the court with mincing steps. There was none of the mad dashing, scrambling, scooting and leaping that characterized the Chuck McKinleys of a later age. For several years, it was stylish to serve underhand.

Transition came slowly, but it came. As time went on, players learned to apply spin on their drives for control. They began to hit their services progressively harder, overhand, of course. They gained speed and mobility. The gentle, slow-paced pastime of the 1870's gave way to a fierce, attacking style that demanded lightning reflexes, power, precision and the endurance of a marathon runner. Tennis became a game for the superbly conditioned athlete.

The pioneers were handicapped by primitive equipment, an excess of attire and sticky traditions. In the early days, men bundled themselves in long, flopping trousers, blazers, long-sleeved shirts, ties and caps. The women wore dresses that fell to their ankles, layers of petticoats and hats that would have done justice to an Easter parade. The rackets were shaped like spoons and were loosely strung. The balls were solid rubber and uncovered.

As the game progressed, equipment improved, apparel became more practical and both styles and shots became more refined.

Richard D. Sears used a sweeping forehand drive that he picked up in England from the famed British player, Herbert Lawford. The "Lawford" was a stroke everybody tried to copy for years. Sears, the first American champion in 1881, also went to the net but his volley was largely a push shot which is seen in ladies' doubles almost any Monday at the local club.

Through the first two decades, play was largely defensive. Players worked on the all-around game and the object was to force the opponent into making an error rather than to take the offensive and blow the ball past the adversary. Holcombe Ward, who won the U.S. title in 1904, is credited with originating the American twist service, achieved by hitting across the ball and following through with a long swing. This imparted a high bounce.

Maurice McLoughlin, the Californian who won in 1912 and 1913, is said to be the first who capitalized on the big serve and volley. He fathered the so-called "Big Game," although it remained for successors to refine it and turn it into an instrument of destruction. Little Bill Johnston's Western forehand was a thing of beauty. Big Bill Tilden was the master of all strokes. Ellsworth Vines introduced power tennis with a service that supposedly rocketed off his racket at better than 120 miles an hour—faster than that of Pancho Gonzales.

Don Budge in the 1930's was the exponent of the game's most devastating backhand, a stroke that Arthur Ashe, Jr., perfected thirty years later. Alice Marble brought severity to women's tennis by playing with the sharpness of a man, and Jack Kramer became the ultimate master in the "Big Game." Phenomenal quickness, dexterity and left-handed power were the ingredients that converted Australia's Rod Laver into a shot-production machine that most people agreed had no match in this century.

As player and spectator, I have seen many of the great styles develop. The following accounts are one man's analyses of the all-time greats:

Bill Tilden was one of the immortal athletes of the twenties, a Golden Age which produced such figures as Dempsey, Tunney, Bobby Jones, Red Grange and Babe Ruth. Even the youngsters who never saw these stars will remember their names. In my own case, I did see Bill Tilden but only after he had passed his prime. Later I got to know him well and to appreciate his great achievements even more.

In 1931 at the age of twelve, I scraped together a few shekels and went to see Tilden play Hans Nusslein in a small ice-skating and hockey arena at Melrose and Van Ness in Hollywood. Tilden had turned pro the year before. I was too young and new to the game to have any in-depth knowledge or critical ability, but I remember vividly how imposing a figure he was. He commanded the court from the moment he stepped out to be introduced—a tall, stoop-shouldered, rather gaunt and shaggy lantern-jawed figure casually carrying a half dozen open-throat Top Flight rackets and wearing a cable-stitch sweater. I am sure now that his casual pose was studied, as were all his mannerisms and gestures. He was, in short, a real ham. But he was Mr. Tennis.

Players today warm up to unlimber and get their strokes working properly. Not so Bill. At least as a pro, and I am sure before, he gave a kind of exhibition warm-up—all the spins were put on display so that the spectators could immediately marvel at his range of talents. And his mastery of spins and control was truly marvelous. Bill prided himself on his repertoire and loved to use it. He had all the strokes: topspin drive, slice, chop (He always distinguished between slice and chop, although I could never follow the miniscule difference. Both have underspin; to Bill a chop meant coming straight down on the ball without sidespin, and a slice meant following through under and outside) on both forehand and backhand, closed stance and open stance. Change of spin and pace were almost ends in themselves for him, during a match as well as in the warm-up. No two successive balls were hit the same way unless he had some object in mind, as when he decided to show his superior ability with underspins by hitting only chops and slices against Wallace Johnson, the foremost chop artist of his day, and trouncing him at his own game.

Technically Bill's ground strokes were superb, the result of many years of practice and training. You don't get that kind of control and versatility overnight. When, after quite a few years of knocking around in the First Ten but never really making it, he decided his backhand wasn't strong enough, Bill took out a whole winter and did basically only two things: He hit backhands mostly against a practice board and chopped wood to build up his muscles. It worked. For almost a decade after that he ruled the courts, at least until the Frenchmen started to reach him in the late twenties.

Bill was tall, about six feet, two inches, and he used his height to full advantage on his serve. His action was letter-perfect but fast. Some people said he hit the ball on the up-part of the toss, but actually he timed his toss and fast wind-up so that he hit the ball when it was dead-still at the top of the toss. He knew all the spins but preferred the flat or slice. On the American twist, he got a good wrist-kick in but didn't have a really heavy ball. As we now view the game, the reason becomes clear: Bill swung his right foot over but did not follow his serve in to net, at least in singles. Remember that in those days the footfault rule was more restrictive.

Tilden did as much acing as anybody. By any standards, yesterday's or today's, he had a great serve and could call on it, like Gonzales, for big points when he was in trouble. Bill was a great believer in getting first serves in, as am I, and he always pulled back on severity until about 75 percent or more of the first deliveries went in.

When you come down to it, Big Bill Tilden was a serve and forehand player. As I pointed out earlier, he could do anything on his right side, but he loved most to roll the ball a long, full, loop sweep. The backswing was not big and the racket head was about parallel with his arm. In other words his backswing was straight or only slightly raised. On the forward swing he came down to get under the ball and then rolled up and over it, finishing sometimes with arm and racket wrapped around his neck. I think one such picture, Bill's legs twisted as well to demonstrate the full hip pivot from closed stance, is my favorite. Bill was wearing his woolly-bear, a fuzzy sweater style of the early twenties, and also spikes.

Tilden was a side-to-side artist. He loved to move the ball and his opponent around. In today's game there isn't much of that left, the sole exponents being Tony Roche on a slow court or Manuel Santana, but in Bill's day that was the philosophical pinnacle. Nowadays nobody in men's tennis (women's tennis is different, perhaps more like the techniques of the men in Bill's day) waits for a carefully-maneuvered attacking opportunity. There is not time. Instead, one takes the first ball—sometimes even return of serve—and tries to hold it on the racket long enough, with chip, spin and control to get some semblance of position at net. After that you depend on your reactions, anticipation and punch or lunge volleying abilty to win more points than you lose. Of course, on your serve you have an edge, but only if you follow it in consistently.

Bill was a competent volleyer. After all, he did win the National Doubles six times and the Wimbledon Doubles once. But he was not truly at home at net, I think because he was almost afraid of losing his feet or dirtying his flannels if he lunged. He was a volleyer like Budge, not given to exposing himself on attack. Also Bill did not like to play close in to net. He had a fine overhead to back himself up with when he was lobbed, but he was perhaps not as athletic a leaper as most of the modern breed and so hung back a little. That is not the way it is done today.

by Julius D. Heldman / 239

I don't want to dwell on Bill's personality, which was strong and complex, or his offcourt life, but they are a part of the man and deserve mention. He loved tennis and had a strong, strong ego and also wanted to be an actor. That about sums it up. He wrote several books on tennis, a bad novel and acted in two Broadway productions. He was also an avid bridge enthusiast and a successful money player. But, first and foremost, he wanted to have the center of the stage.

Tilden was clearly the greatest player of his era. All of us who know anything about the game are asked, once a week or more, how Bill would stack up against Budge or Gonzales or Laver, each at their best. Firstly, the question is moot. Any answer must be subjective. The same question is asked about other sports where there are quantifiable physical records, but even so I think similar reasoning may apply.

You cannot divorce athletic performance from its immediate milieu, either direct competition or training methods or equipment. Athletes today break all kinds of records, but nobody can say that a young John Weismuller or Ben Eastman, subjected to the regimen used today, including nutrition, would not do as well as today's stars. In tennis, where your opponent has a direct effect on your play, the situation is even more complex. Remember, Bobby Riggs, essentially an all-court tactician, consciously changed himself into a serve-and-net rusher in his head-to-head pro tour against Kramer. He had to in order to survive, and he did well enough. I think he would have done even better had he changed his game earlier, as did Schroeder and Kramer.

Bill was the kind, but there were clear signs that the style of the game was pressing him. Jean Borotra was a player perhaps ahead of his time: serve or push or do anything or run for the net and dive for a winner. And, with inferior equipment, Jean was beating Bill in the late twenties, although gamesmanship might have had a little to do with it.

If Bill had been determined to change his approach and had started young enough, he would have been great enough to have won even today. But I think our present crop, playing today's game, would mop up the players of the twenties, although Allison Danzig and Sidney Wood strongly disagree. Bill is dead, and long live Bill, but there are now greater kings.

FOUR   *Ellsworth Vines*

1

II

In 1932 a brilliant and personable nineteen-year-old slashed and whipped his way to the U.S. National Singles title. He was a lanky six foot one and weighed only 145 pounds. He shambled when he walked like the great basketball player he was, but he was beautiful in motion. Ellsworth Vines was the "players' player" of his era. He had the flattest set of ground strokes ever seen and they were hit so hard, particularly on the forehand, that they could not clear the net by more than a few inches without going out.

Vines came up the public parks route in Pasadena. He was the hardest hitter among the Juniors but also one of the most erratic. His flat strokes were gorgeous but never safe or secure. The antithesis of the Vines game was that of his doubles partner, Keith Gledhill of Santa Barbara, who was a spin artist. In their Junior years it was usually Gledhill who came out on top. Then, for some reason, Ellsworth suddenly consolidated his game and became the top amateur in the world for two successive years. He hit the Number One spot with meteoric speed, climbing from a Junior with potentiality to the top American man in the space of one year. All of a sudden the ball started to go in, and the gawky Junior who was then only a mild threat became the sensation of Forest Hills.

Vines attended the University of Southern California while still a Junior in tennis and was the star of the freshman basketball team. Tennis and basketball are the two most compatible games for men; the same physical skills other than racket handling are involved. In winter, basketball is good for every tennis player to increase or aid stamina and speed of foot. Ellsworth, otherwise known as "Hank," "Slim" or "Elly," showed the results of the double training in his excellent footwork and use of his body on the volley and overhead. He was sinuous and agile, leaping in the air for an overhead like a center on the opening jump. He knew how to make maximum use of his body, moving and stretching for volleys but still keeping his flat, hard approach.

THE SERVE

I have always likened Elly's wind-up action on the serve to that of a writhing snake. His body seemed to amass energy as he stretched up to maximum height for the first ball. Think of an Indian fakir piping a snake into standing erect and you can then visualize Vines climbing up to the top of his swing. It was a beautiful motion followed by a stinging, heavy whip at the ball.

The first serve was almost flat. It had the same heaviness of the great Budge delivery, but the motion was freer and deceptively easy. His second ball often had a heavy kick, with placement being his primary objective. The serve was the most reliable part of his game, for although his ground strokes could desert him badly, he seldom had a day of double faults. Unlike the player who resembles him most today, Barry MacKay, Vines chose to put enough heavy spin on the second ball to maintain the attack without frequent double-faulting.

I ballboyed for Vines when I was twelve years old. He was playing Fred Perry in the finals of the Pacific Southwest. A very vivid recollection is that of catching one of Vines' aces as it whizzed by Perry. It was leaden—heavy and hard, with enough spin to hurt. My hand stung for an hour. I have played against many other serves since, but none had the same leaden feeling with the exception, perhaps, of Budge, Gonzales and occasionally Savitt.

THE FOREHAND

Elly had a four-fingered grip not only on the serve but on the forehand as well. He simply extended his leverage by sliding his little finger—and sometimes his last two fingers—off the racket. It gave him the famous whip stroke but it also caused his highly erratic play. When his timing went off he had no stiff wrist shot on which to fall back. Only four fingers controlled the wiggle of the racket. They were strong as iron, but even the very slightest misjudgment produced a monstrous error.

When Vines was warming up with new balls, he would hit them so flat with his forehand that you could read the marking as they went over the net. Then, as he started to hit them harder, you could clearly see them spinning sideways, not rolling over or under. Only Kramer, following Vines, ever had this approach to the forehand, and of course he modelled his after Ellsworth. Jack at age fifteen used to practice with Vines regularly, and it was inevitable that he would pick up many of Elly's characteristics. Vines could hit an overspin crosscourt but it was not a stroke he used often or from choice. If he were pulled wide, he preferred to blast the ball from a down-the-line placement, and the trajectory would keep the ball actually wide of the court until it hit on the sideline.

Vines never temporized by hitting a foot inside the line. He made more chalk fly on grass than any player who ever lived. Rosewall's backhand passing shot, while not in the style of Vines, is also a chalk-raiser. The fact that Vines hit so flat or with sidespin meant that the ball slithered off the ground. It never set up "fat" for his opponent.

THE BACKHAND

Although Elly hit hard off the backhand, it was not the equal of his starboard side. He preferred low or waist-high balls and perhaps this was the reason he was so good on grass. He got down well. He had a little natural underspin on his backhand, particularly when he would temporize, but he played his best in hard-driving baseline rallies where he would work his opponent into an impossible position off either side. He never knew what it was to move back; he moved beautifully sideways and attacked as a natural consequence of his forcing game.

Vines' game is the direct opposite of the current "chippers." His return of serve alone would annihilate the poorly founded youngsters of today. He did not chip or block: He stroked returns of serve because his muscle-eye coordination was so good.

THE VOLLEY

Vines was a very unsafe volleyer. He had little spin clearance and he went for winners most of the time. He did not play too close in to net, and he did not mind taking balls off his shoe tops on either side, hitting almost flat, low put-aways. His volley was great but fundamentally risky. It is surprising with his almost perfect overhead that he did not play in a little closer in singles.

He was not a true net-rusher such as Kramer. He came in occasionally behind his serve, more so on grass than on any other surface. He attacked the barrier more than Tilden but he has to be considered a baseliner in comparison with today's net-campers.

Despite the fact that Vines at his best was unbeatable, his style of game made him inevitably the victim of serious slumps. After two years at the top in which he mopped up the opposition, he suffered a disastrous third season. Vines went to Europe with the Davis Cup team and literally

The rivalry between the two Helens — Helen Wills Moody and Helen Jacobs — was one of the keenest and most interesting in tennis annals. The portrait (top) of Helen Jacobs shows her sensitive beauty. Helen Wills, shown at lower right with a Roaring Twenties hat and (center) on the court wearing her familiar white eye-shade, was something of a paradox. On the court, she was cold and methodical. Off the court, she could be very warm and friendly.

With the departure of Helen Wills Moody and later Helen Jacobs, shown preparing to hit a backhand at the left, the U.S. women's tennis throne was taken over by a pretty, blonde Californian named Alice

Frank Nothaft

Marble. In the center is an
inscribed photo of Miss Marble
and in the photograph at the right,
Miss Marble (right) walks off the
court with an English rival,
Mary Hardwicke.

World Tennis

European

Maureen "Little Mo" Connolly was one of America's greatest woman tennis players, but her career was cut short by an accident and later an untimely death. Maureen follows through on a backhand at the left. She loved horseback riding almost as much as she loved tennis and it was a horseback mishap that ended her career. Here she is seen riding at the San Diego Academy in California with her mother, Mrs. Jessamine Berste. At the center, she is caught in one of her pensive moods between shots.

Althea Gibson came off the sidewalks of Harlem to become the world's best woman tennis player and to perform before royalty. She was twenty-nine when she became the first black player ever to win the Wimbledon championship, on July 6, 1957, shown at the left. She was given a homecoming parade up New York's Lower Broadway upon her return (above). At the right, she and her doubles partner, Angela Buxton of England, receive trophies and a smile from the Dutchess of Kent on Wimbledon's center court.

Wide World Photos

P. W. Trostorff

Billie Jean King, bespectacled, bouncy and outspoken, won three Wimbledons in a row and was leader of a women's tennis rebellion for higher purses in 1970. An aggressive player, she is in danger of biting her tongue in a 1968 Wimbledon match at the left. She is congratulated by her husband, Larry King, after winning the U.S. Championship at Forest Hills in 1967 (above), and she rears back (right) for delivery of a service to Ann Haydon Jones of Britain in a match at Forest Hills.

Two of the world's leading women
tennis players in the 1960's were
Brazil's Maria Bueno, shown at
the left in portrait and in action, and
Britain's Anne Haydon Jones,
right. Miss Bueno won 4 United

States, and 3 Wimbledon Women's
Championships, while Mrs. Jones, a
frequent runner-up in major events,
finally broke through to beat Billie
Jean King for the Wimbledon
title in 1969.

Le-Roye Productions Ltd.

Wide World Photos

Wimbledon is the world center of
tennis. Rich in tradition, it is the
tournament everyone wants to win.
Here (above left) is a scene of
the Wimbledon Stadium and the field
courts. Above is the Wimbledon
Cup, and at right Rod Laver is
holding the men's singles trophy after
winning it in 1968.

E. D. Lacey

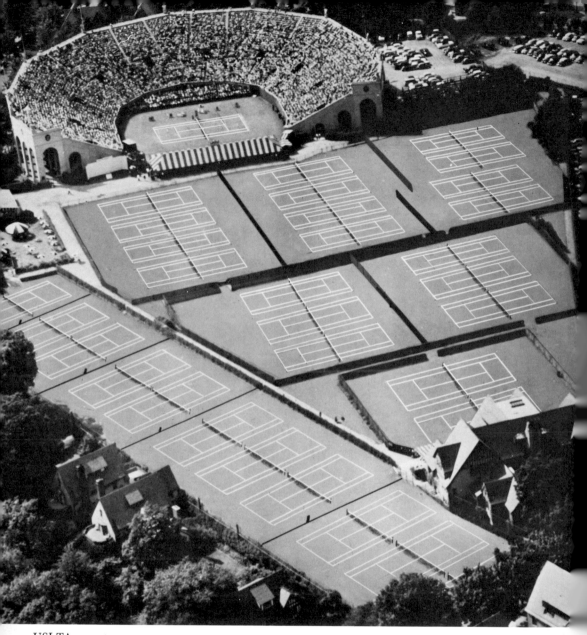

USLTA

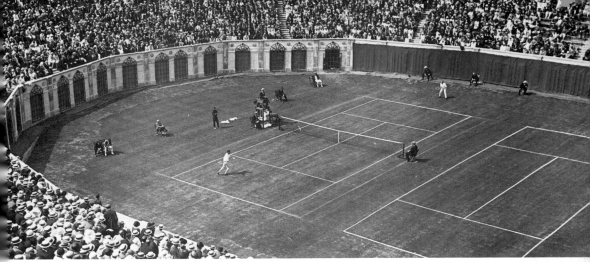

A bird's-eye view of the West Side
Tennis Club at Forest Hills, New
York, scene of the U.S. Tennis
Championships. The old concrete
horseshoe, shown at the top of the
picture, has been the scene of many a
historic court battle. Above is
an earlier picture of the crowded
stands and below, the West Side
Tennis Club when it first became site
of the Championships.

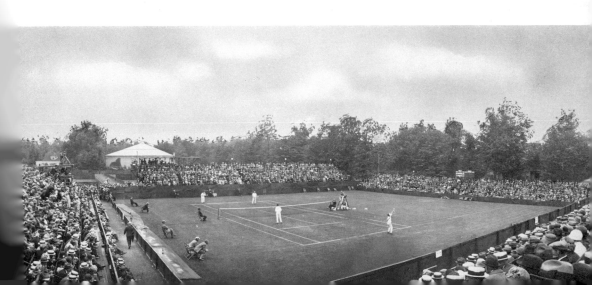

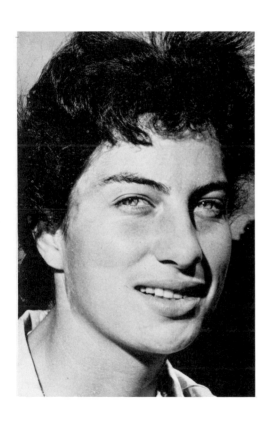

A pretty British girl, Virginia Wade,
playing an amateur, was winner of the
first U.S. Open Women's Tennis
Championship at Forest Hills in 1968.
A vicar's daughter with a strong
back court game, she is shown here in
a close-up and in action, hitting
one of her destructive forehands.

collapsed in his match against Fred Perry at Roland Garros. Then he was beaten by Jack Crawford at Wimbledon. On his return to the States, Bitsy Grant threw every ball back at him in the Nationals and Vines promptly hit every ball out. He was beaten in three straight sets. Then, in the Pacific Southwest, Elly went to pieces against Jack Tidball after amassing an almost unbeatable lead. This was his last amateur singles match. He turned pro shortly thereafter and dominated the play-for-pay group until the advent of Don Budge five years later.

FOUR   *Alice Marble — The Golden Girl*

1

III

"Meteoric" is the word to describe Alice Marble's magnificent tennis career. In 1931 she was a promising young player at Golden Gate Park in San Francisco. The next year she was Number Seven in the country and the following year Number Three. She was just approaching the apex of her career when she was stricken by pleurisy. From the medical reports it seemed that her tournament tennis days were ended, but two years later she made one of the most remarkable comebacks of all time to win her first National title. She was the Number One American player for five years, turning professional in late 1940 to tour with Mary Hardwick, Don Budge and Bill Tilden. Some years later she suffered a recurrence of her illness. A lung was removed, ending her serious playing days, but she still keeps active in the game with occasional social doubles.

I first saw Alice when she was making her comeback in 1936. She was very trim and tan from a winter of training in Palm Springs, and it was already clear that she would be the world champion if her health held out. Everything about her game had the mark of greatness. Just as in 1957 every tournament player immediately spotted the future world champion in Maria Bueno, so did all those who saw Alice recognize her fantastic talent. It was more than just athletic ability, although there are hardly four or five women in the history of tennis who have had as much. It was a knack for playing the game more aggressively than any of her competitors; it was a man's approach to the game, from the American twist serve to the leaping volleys and jump overheads. Added to this was her fierce competitive spirit and coolness under pressure. She was head and shoulders above her closest rivals, and she dominated the women's field to the same degree as did Don Budge in the men's.

Only occasionally do the leading male players come out to watch their female counterpart. The men on the circuit turned out en masse for Alice. Her appearance was trim, her manner brisk and business-like, and her style of play exciting. She managed to play like a man and still maintain her feminine appeal. She went for the kills at net, and she angle-volleyed like Gene Mako, one of her famous mixed doubles partners. She played without restraint, running wide-legged, stretching full out for the wide balls, and walloping serves and overheads. Her game was the product of her tomboy days of baseball in Golden Gate Park. The throwing action and batting stance learned there carried through directly to their tennis counterparts, the serve and forehand.

THE FOREHAND

Alice had a flat Eastern grip on the forehand which she hit with a loose wrist action. Her fingers were held close together, and she did not get that feeling of control which comes when the fingers are spread out. The combination of floppy wrist and bunched fingers resulted in more errors than necessary. Her forehand was a powerful baseball-type swing with an almost flat-back wind-up. There were no curlyques, rolls or figure eights in the backswing, which was very short. There was a snap of the wrist at the moment of impact and then, like all wristy Eastern-grip players, sidespin for the down-the-line or a pull-up, short loop action for the crosscourt.

Marble's forehand was powerful albeit not as hard as Maureen Connolly's. She used it to attack and was one of the first women players to follow her forehand to net at every opportunity. I have seen her rally from the baseline on the starboard side, but to me she always appeared uncomfortable here since she was not steady enough to maintain her dominance. Her forehand was a weapon to get her to net, but it was neither chip nor push; it was forceful in that it produced a weak return, but it was not an outright point winner.

Alice had two distinct follow-throughs. Neither was big, even when she hit her hardest. When she hit with sidespin down the line, her racket face came across the ball and the follow-through was more likely to end at waist rather than shoulder level. Among the men, Ellsworth Vines was the most famous exponent of the sidespin forehand, although his whole action was longer than Alice's. Louise Brough's sidespin drive resembled Marble's, but Maureen Connolly's famous sidespin was more like Vines'. Alice's topspin drive was a little wristy and was not the Rock of Gibraltar by any means. Sometimes she literally came over the ball, turning the racket face over after the hit, while other times she simply pulled up and ended high on the follow-through. Her wrist enabled her to become a master of the sharp angles, which characterized her style of play.

THE BACKHAND

If Alice had not had so much athletic talent, her loose wrist tendency on forehand and backhand would have been a serious handicap. Instead this same wristy action enabled her to disguise her shots, to change directions at the last minute and to give added pace to the ball. She had good body control and she stepped into the ball solidly.

by Julius D. Heldman / 247

Everything else about her game was classically executed.

The Marble backhand was also a short stroke. It was rather flat but she often added overspin by rolling her wrist slightly. When she hit down the line, she preferred to use sidespin rather than underspin. In other words, she held the head of the racket behind her wrist and let the elbow guide it down the line.

Alice could hit on the dead run on both sides, and there was nothing she liked so much as to wallop a ball and charge the net. This style was a revelation in women's tennis. She was playing in a league of solid baseliners, all of whom were sharp with passing shots, and so her approach shots had to be forceful. This philosophy led her to more ground stroke errors than her contemporaries, but she made up for it by the advantage she gained from her constant attack. Marble was the all-court player par excellence. Her movements were rangy, her ground strokes aggressive, and she leaped and jumped like a top man athlete.

THE SERVE

There have been only a few great serves in women's tennis, and among them most players would number Alice, Althea Gibson, Maria Bueno, Doris Hart, Margaret Osborne duPont and Louise Brough Clapp in her prime. To me Marble's delivery was by far the best from three standpoints: Her first serve was as hard as any and more consistent; her second serve had more bite and was better placed than the other women's; and her attack, particularly in doubles play behind the service, was incomparable. She was the most sought-after mixed doubles partner in the history of the game. Budge and Mako alternated cleaning up the major titles with her. It was a foregone conclusion that if she had a reasonable partner they would win. It was like having two men serve on the same side!

Marble was completely unrestrained on her service action. She could stretch more from the chest, bend more from the back and kick more from the knee than any other women. Her's was a free, relaxed motion. She could clout an ace on the first serve or kick a high spinner on the second. She did not follow her serve to net in singles as much as Althea did, but if she were playing in the current era there would be no problem in adapting her game to the philosophy of 100 percent attack.

The backswing on the serve was not as long as Bueno's or Gibson's. It was a fairly short action in the style of the top Aussie players of the last decade. The racket came up from the waist to the shoulder rather quickly, then was followed by the sharp elbow bend and back-scratching action. The hit was made with a wrist snap of real power or spin. She was not quite the feminine counterpart of Vines, who snaked up to the ball, but she had a definite body slither in the style of some top batters.

If a single outstanding feature had to be picked out of Alice's game, it would have to be the serve. I have a vivid mental picture of her standing up to the line, batting an ace and moving briskly into the next court to serve again. She had supreme confidence in her serve and it was thoroughly justified. The rest of her game could go off key, but the delivery was her faithful standby. There was never any rash of double faults, and when the first serve did not go in, she had that kicking American twist serve to fall back on.

THE OVERHEAD

The overhead was as good as her serve, free and unrestrained. She leapt beautifully, and this enabled her to play closer in when she attacked. Occasionally she might have a missing spell, but she never babied an overhead. It most resembled Darlene Hard's among the current players, although Alice had more wrist in the hit. She hit for the angles, and a lob from her opponent invariably meant the end of the point either way.

THE VOLLEY

Alice was a killer volleyer. She played in close and she went for the short, sharp angles. She was death on the high ones, but her wrist sometimes played her false, causing her to miss a sitter. She was a great net player because she anticipated and moved so well. She was also fearless. Technically her volleys were a little too flat, perhaps too much like a short stroke rather than an underspin punch. For this reason low volleys sometimes gave her trouble. She did have a great eye and fast reflexes, and she never lost that tomboy attitude at net.

In doubles she was a delight. She had the knack of poaching for the kill, and she ate up the other man's speed. When she played with Budge or alternately with Mako, she started the fashion of standing in on her partner's return. She was the first woman to do so, just as Budge and Mako were the first men's team to stand in on each other's returns. Alice was as good a doubles partner as any but the very top men, except for the fact that her return of serve was not consistent enough. She was also as pleasant a partner as one could hope to have.

Alice had a most attractive court personality. She was able to be warm without losing concentration, and nothing won over a gallery quite so fast as the smile and wave of the racket which she gave in recognition of her opponent's good play. She was a fierce competitor and did not like to lose, but she was never a gamesman. There were no sulks or moans or unhappy expressions during the play, but after the match was over she could cry if she lost. Everyone liked her, from her closest competitors to the linesmen and ballboys who worked her matches. She was as friendly a World Champion as the game has ever known.

Alice's record places her among the all-time greats. She won the Nationals in 1938, 1939 and 1940, Wimbledon in 1939, the National Women's Doubles four times with Sarah Palfrey and the National Mixed Doubles with Gene Mako,

Don Budge, Harry Hopman and Bobby Riggs. Following her tennis career she became a successful nightclub singer. She is currently living in Southern California where she works in a medical clinic.

FOUR *Fred Perry*

1

IV

England's greatest player since the days of the Dohertys was the flamboyant Fred Perry. Dressed in beautifully tailored white flannels and a matching white blazer, Fred looked and was the amateur champion of the world. He had the personal magnetism that is "star" quality. He dominated the scene from the moment he walked on the court, casually carrying a half dozen rackets under his arm and waving pleasantly at select acquaintances in the gallery. He was the idol of thousands of young players, though more for his poise and court demeanor than for his style, which was beautiful but highly personalized. He made the game fun for the spectators, joshing with the ballboys when he was ahead, dazzling the crowd with his tricky shots and chatting with the boxholders in between games. When the going got tough Perry got down to work and concentrated as any great champion must. He was a showman but nevertheless a magnificent competitor.

When Bill Tilden was incensed by a call, he would argue with the linesman or demand his removal. Perry never got as upset, but when he was the victim of a questionable decision he would smile at the linesman, humorously shake his finger at him and remark: "Naughty boy!" He wasn't a temperamental player. He had spark, fire and verve and an enormous amount of self-confidence. He did not "blow" because of emotional problems, and his game was so grooved that he seldom had a really bad day.

Fred Perry had the greatest running forehand the game has ever known. His serve was quite good, albeit not great, his backhand was very accurate, his net game vastly underrated and his overhead absolutely deadly. He had a cocked wrist Continental game with more wrist power than any other player before or since. His eye was superb; it had to be for he took every ball on the rise. He was fast as lightning and was always in top physical condition.

Perry won every big title in the amateur game. He appeared on the international scene during Ellsworth Vines' last amateur year. Jack Crawford of Australia was the heir apparent and won the Australian, French and British titles before losing out in the finals at Forest Hills to Perry. Fred teamed with Bunny Austin to take the Davis Cup for his country, and the two of them held the Cup against all challenges for three more years. During this period Perry was the world's best amateur, winning Wimbledon three times, the French title once, Forest Hills three times and Australia once. He turned professional to play Vines in a very successful tour. He continued to compete professionally until his late thirties, despite interludes at other enterprises. He became a well-established teaching professional, retiring in 1956 when he reached the age of fifty. His is still the magic name in England, and a few years ago when he made a rare public appearance at the Art Larsen Benefit, thousands turned out to watch the unique Perry game in action.

THE FOREHAND

Just as Don Budge had a backhand that never went "off," Fred Perry had a forehand that was aggressive and always consistent. It was a table tennis forehand, hit with an extreme Continental grip and a pronounced cocked wrist action. Fred was the World Table Tennis Champ before he ever took up lawn tennis. As a result of his background and great athletic ability, he had magnificent wrist control. He could fool his opponent on any shot on the forehand, whether he hit from an open stance or on the dead run. It was a graceful stroke, without the extra frills that many

Continental artists use. Both the backswing and follow-through were extremely short, the whole stroke being simply a wrist snap.

Footwork meant nothing to Perry on the forehand side. He could just as well hit by snapping the ball from behind him while facing the net. However, he was never off balance; his body was always right for every shot and he was never caught in an awkward stance. He was most famous for his forehands hit on the run coming into net. These were lethal. His opponents used to say it was more dangerous to run him wide on his forehand than to play the center of the court! He had complete angle control, and when he was pulled out of court he could just as easily hit a sharp, short crosscourt as a deadly down-the-line. Vines, for example, could not hit a sharp crosscourt well when forced. Budge could hit the crosscourt with as much power but not as sharp. Only a looper or a Continental artist can execute this riposte with any pace, the rare exceptions being Maureen Connolly and Dick Savitt among the classical Eastern players.

Perry generally hit a flat forehand with a wrist snap at the moment of impact. He used top spin occasionally, particularly when picking up a low ball. The topspin was manufactured by pulling up sharply, somewhat in the manner of Hoad, although Perry's stroke was much shorter. He never chipped, chopped or sliced on the starboard side. His return against a powerful service was small enough to be called a block, yet it was actually a drive. A block is merely a backboard response to a hard stroke, with the racket held stiff and essentially motionless. Perry did more than this: A short wrist flick often sent the ball back harder than it came to him. There was no arm motion to his return. All the power came from wrist action and body balance.

THE BACKHAND

Perry was a fine player in all departments but a great

player only on the forehand. In the ranking lists of most tennis aficionados, Perry's name appears among the All-Time Top Ten. To achieve this distinction a player cannot have a weakness. When I say his backhand was not in the same league as his forehand, it is not meant as a derogatory remark. His backhand would be the envy of every top junior today. It was not a defensive shot and he passed extremely well with it. However, when he was engaged in a baseline backhand rally, he was content to keep the ball deep and in the corners. He did not let fly like Budge or even Savitt, nor did he come in behind it like Rosewall. The key for him on the backhand was control. He and Vines would often have long backhand exchanges, the ball going back and forth eight to ten times in one rally, neither player daring a down-the-line to the opponent's murderous forehand.

The backhand was just as short a stroke as the forehand. All of Perry's actions were quick. There were no long, flowing motions except the sweep of his running advance to net. The rapid backhand motion was also a wrist flick, with the same cocked wrist as on the forehand. This small, neat action was capable of executing both the flat and underspin drives. He would pull his wrist under at the last minute to hit the down-the-line but would hit with relatively little spin when exchanging backhand crosscourts. It was a full-length drive rather than a chip since the wrist always snapped or came through, but it was a very short action. He never shoved the ball or hacked at it.

THE VOLLEY

Perry was essentially a baseliner who came to net when the opportunity arose. He never followed his serve in. His coming-in shots were so forceful that he seldom had to volley more than competently. Spectators rarely saw him leaping since his way to net had been so thoroughly prepared. He was no Wilmer Allison at the barrier, the latter being far more at home at the net than at the baseline.

Perry got down well for his low forehand volleys, which he took to the side of him or even hooked from behind him. His forte was his high volley on both forehand and backhand. He was a short stroke volleyer, the wrist being the dominant part of the action. All volleys above the net were stroked, the motion being quick and sharp. His net play was in keeping with the rest of his game—crisp, neat and lightning-quick. There were no false moves, no awkward pushes. Everything was done with grace and dispatch, and every shot was executed with the same flair.

THE OVERHEAD

Perry's overhead was absolutely lethal. He never bludgeoned the ball, but he never missed and he always outguessed his opponent. He was uncanny in his ability to pick the right spot. He was agile, quick and leapt well. Those who saw Fred in action will always remember him springing in the air to bring down a tough lob. His legs were as springy as a basketball player, and he always seemed to be on the balls of his feet.

The overhead action was just as small as his other shots. There was no massive wind-up. He simply brought his racket head behind him with a cocked wrist and snapped the ball where he wanted it. The shot was distinguished by his ability to leap, most other players appearing dead on their feet in comparison.

THE SERVE

Fred Perry was the quick-server of all time. His whole game was characterized by rapidity of movement during and in between points. He was always ready before his opponent, and he always wanted to get on with the next point. He was frequently accused of serving too fast, and although this may not have been deliberate, it was nevertheless a fact. He had a short wind-up and a fast action, and this undoubtedly contributed to his opponents' dismay.

Don Budge often held up his hand and asked to have a let played. I can remember myself, when playing him in the Pacific Southwest, feeling hurried whenever Perry served.

Perry had a rather flat first serve with just a little overspin to bring it in. There wasn't enough spin to call it "slice" or "twist." He hit it reasonably hard, but he depended more on accuracy than blinding pace. A very high percentage of his first balls went in; when they didn't, the second was on its way! This second ball usually had American twist, although he could slice in the right court. His American twist was not one of these big, high-bouncing balls that pulls you out of court and is hit with a back bent almost double. Again, it was a neat, short wrist-snap designed to keep him out of trouble and open a baseline rally. It was good enough to prevent his opponent from taking net off it.

Any man who made his move too soon while Perry was serving was a dead duck. Fred had a very quick eye, and his reactions were so fast that he could change direction in the middle of a stroke with accuracy. Even though his second serve was far from murderous, he would ace an opponent who tried to outguess him almost every time.

PERRY THE MAN

All champions are in excellent physical condition when they reach the top. They have to be. However, few have all the physical attributes that compose the perfect athlete. Ken Rosewall has the disadvantage of small stature; Lew Hoad is almost over-muscular; Dick Savitt is so big that it is sometimes hard for him to maneuver; Bunny Austin was too frail to stand up to a five setter; Welby Van Horn, Billy Talbert, Ham Richardson and Doris Hart had to overcome actual physical handicaps. Only occasionally does a Frank Parker, a Gardnar Mulloy, a Pancho Gonzales or a Fred Perry come along. These are perfect athletes with ideal tennis builds. They have an edge which is given only to a few. I never saw Perry tired in the course of a match. His great eye, natural talent and physical ability enabled him to compensate for any weaknesses inherent in the overly wristy Continental game.

FOUR   Don Budge

1
v

I was one of those players who grew up in the era of Don Budge. He was the king of the tennis world from 1937 until World War II, and to those of us who were on the circuit with him he was not only untouchable but the greatest player of all time. The same arguments as to who was the better, Tilden or Budge, started in 1937 and are still going on.

"Untouchable" was the right word to describe Don. He never allowed an opponent to get his teeth in the match, and his overwhelming power was not subject to bad streaks. His unfortunate victim had the feeling of complete helplessness for there was no way in which he could touch Don. The situation would be the same today if Pancho Gonzales were playing against the current crop of amateurs.

Budge grew up in Oakland, California, and was soon the best Junior in Northern California. His backhand was always sound and aggressive, but until he was nineteen he had a rolling Western forehand. He was one of those players who was anxious to improve and willing to listen. He heard enough from his tennis friends to determine him to switch to the more appropriate Eastern grip. He made the change in the winter of 1935. From then on it was only a matter of time as to when he would win the world title.

Budge, like his arch-rival Fred Perry, made a magnificent court appearance. Dressed in immaculate long flannels, carefully whited shoes, imported woolen shirts, traditional cable-stitch tennis sweater and a white Davis Cup blazer, he looked every inch the champion. In contrast to Perry, Budge was always serious and straight-forward. There were no casual quips, no light-hearted behavior, and absolutely no comments during the match. He never questioned a call during his entire amateur career, and he was always a perfect gentleman, even during those rare occasions when the going got rough. The game was everything to him and he always gave it 100 percent effort.

Don was well-liked by all the players, but his special friend during his playing days was his doubles partner, Gene Mako. Gene was already a famous young player in 1933, and when Don beat him in the final of the National Juniors it was considered a tremendous upset. After that the two became inseparable. They were inveterate jazz listeners to the extent that they never traveled without their portable record player and a large collection of their discs. I remember rooming next door to them at Westchester during the Eastern Grass Courts and hearing them shave to the accompaniment of Benny Goodman.

THE FOREHAND

Because Don's forehand was a completely trained stroke, it is unique among the strokes of all the champions. Technically it was flawless. It was mechanical in that it was not original with him, but although it did not have the personal flair of his backhand, it was a magnificent forceful weapon. Of all of the strokes of the great champions, this was the one that was always hit properly. He was drilled so thoroughly by Tom Stow, and he was so willing and apt a pupil that he never hit it in any manner but letter-perfect. He always approached the ball in the same way, hitting with a closed stance but moving forward. He did not chop, chip or hit on the dead run; he wheeled into position, aimed and fired. The result was a heavy ball to a corner followed, if there was a return, by an equally heavy ball to the other corner.

Budge's forehand was a relentless bludgeon. He took the

ball on the top of the bounce, although his eye was good enough so that he could hit on the rise if he had so chosen. He hit on the rise only when it was necessary on a deep ball. This was in strong contrast to the styles of Fred Perry and Henri Cochet, both masters of the half-volley. Budge preferred to take a careful, calculated swing that was sure to put his opponent in the soup. However, although he was no net rusher in the sense of a Schroeder, he never let a ball drop and followed all short ones into net. He hit so well on a short ball that he seldom had to hit anything but a set-up volley or an overhead.

Don's timing was fantastic. He saw the ball better than anyone else. Contrary to most professional advice, he did not "feel" the ball on his racket for any length of time. Most players will flatten or lay back their wrists as they hit in order to hold the racket on the ball as long as possible. If they then mistime the ball, they shall have a very good margin for error. There was no margin on Don's shot. The wrist was locked and not laid back, and if his eye had been poor he would have been a most erratic player. Instead he had perfect coordination and he hit the ball clean and true.

Every Budge forehand was the same. He gracefully two-stepped into position, pivoting as the wind-up started. His backswing was a compact semicircular motion, the hit was wristless, and the follow-through was over the left shoulder. On return of serve, the only forehand shot which he hit with an open stance, he was always on balance and his weight was moving forward.

Don had a slight amount of overspin on the forehand. The overspin was heavier on the crosscourts and for this reason he was one of the few men capable of hitting a sharp crosscourt with a lot of pace. While others used a slight knee-bend on waist-high balls, Don spread his legs for the low ones. The racket head never dropped, but Don never really crouched over either. He got far enough away from the ball so that he was not cramped, but he always stretched rather than bent when digging up a grounder.

THE BACKHAND

Budge's backhand is the most famous ground stroke in tennis. Technically it was very much like his forehand, but it had that extra flair, that great freedom of motion, which made it the envy of every player who ever lived. Only once in his life did it ever go "off," and that was in the early days of a Wimbledon tournament; he regained the feel for the stroke after a few worried hours and took the title handily.

The backhand was hit with a slight amount of topspin, although he often used sidespin when hitting down the line. He was capable of underspinning but he did so rarely, and then mostly in doubles play. His forte was sustained power, not touch tennis. He could hit a placement from any spot in the court to any other spot in the court. His opponent just could not possibly get Don in trouble off the backhand. No matter what you did, he would reply offensively off this wing. The player who attempted to serve and come in on Budge generally lost the point outright, but he was in even more hot water if he tried to serve to the forehand and come in! This left the contestant with no choice but to serve to the backhand and stay back. Years later when Don was past his prime, the big net rushers such as Kramer, Gonzales and Sedgman found that they could not stay on even terms with him if they tried to follow their serve in.

The backhand was a free motion which basically consisted of taking the racket back rather straight and then literally throwing arm and racket toward the opponent's back fence. The arm straightened out during the hit. It is a simple stroke for anyone to hit and does not require split-second timing—unless one hits it as hard as Budge. It has been a stroke that has been used successfully by a variety of Northern Californians such as Frank Kovacs, Tom Brown and Dorothy Knode. Practically the only other top players who hit the backhand with overspin in the game recently have been Dick Savitt and Tony Trabert. It is a pity that more players have not learned this easily timed and potent overspin weapon since the underspin fails repeatedly against the big net attack.

THE SERVE

Don served his share of aces, but not to the extent of an Ellsworth Vines or a Barry MacKay. It was a great serve nevertheless because the ball was so heavy, deep and well-placed. He had a lot of confidence in it during his amateur days, and he took a full roundhouse swing. The toss was always perfect and he used his full height. After the war he developed a slight hitch in the backswing due to a previous arm injury, and he was never quite able to regain his former freedom of motion.

Budge's second serve was hit almost as hard as his first. There was possibly a bit more spin but it was never pronounced. He was not a spin artist and he never used the American twist. He put just enough slice or overspin on the ball to give him control. It takes a lot of confidence to hit that way since the ball skims so close to the net. Don had supreme confidence not only in service but in all other strokes. When he was in his prime he never clutched because he never doubted that he would win. Therefore, there were no double faults or easing up of the power game.

Don did not take the net behind his service. He was a good athlete and could have come in, but it was not his style of play. He was not the type to scurry or scramble; he chose instead to put the pressure on from the ground, coming in only for the assured kill.

THE OVERHEAD

Budge hit the overhead just as he did the serve. He had a big, round swing in contrast to most players, who choose a smaller backswing on the smash. It was a bludgeon based on heavy rather than wrist-snap power. Behind it was the full weight of his 170 pounds, backed by perfect timing. In later years it was the first stroke to go off since he refused to temporize or shorten the swing.

Because Don's overhead was like his serve, it was hit with a small amount of slice. The average big overhead is hit quite flat since the player is always standing inside the baseline and often inside the service line. A serve must be sliced because of the distance to the net, but the smash can safely be hit without spin. This weakness in Don's overhead never appeared when he was playing top tennis. In his tournament days it was a great, if somewhat unusual, shot.

THE VOLLEY

Don was a stroke volleyer by preference. Anything above net level was stroked rather than punched. The only difference between Budge's stroke volley and ground strokes was a shorter backswing and shorter follow-through. It was lethal off both sides. This was the finishing touch of the killer who had prepared his way up to net very carefully. He could stroke volley the way other players could punch volley. In general, his volleys had no spin and were hit almost completely flat, and the fact that he was so consistent was a tribute to his magnificent timing.

Don could also slice volley. It was still a big stroke compared with most punches, but he did turn his racket head under for all low balls and for those where he was necessarily cramped. He did not get down too well but he was surprisingly good as a low volleyer. Here he proved that he could have touch, and he could drop-angle volley with the best of them. He was a great doubles player; the only time he ever really camped at the net was in a doubles match. He was also a good poacher and could leap well when required.

Budge's physical condition was always perfect. He never got tired in his life, the one exception being when he had a bad cold. He had a big chest and a wonderful breathing apparatus, but mostly it was because he hit so hard that it was his opponent rather than he who was on the run. He carried himself royally and was one of the few big men who was graceful. In his Junior days he was as thin as a Buchholz, but as he reached his prime as an amateur he developed a physique in accordance with his powerful frame.

Don Budge was the first man ever to win the Big Four. In one year he took the titles in Australia, France, England and the United States. After dominating the amateur game for two years, he turned professional with the blessings of the USLTA officials. He had stayed amateur another year at their request to defend the Davis Cup, and because he had made a personal financial sacrifice, there were no hard feelings when he eventually made the decision to tour. He dominated the pro world until he went into the Army.

Budge is still a name to conjure with in the world of tennis. When the young players come East for the first time after having fraternized with "name" players on the tournament circuit, the one personality who can still awe them simply by his presence is J. Donald Budge. The big redhead with the friendly personality is still "Mr. Tennis."

FOUR   *Bobby Riggs*

1

VI

The best founded strokes in the tennis game belonged to Bobby Riggs, a Southern Californian who came up the hard way. He did not have a power game, particularly as an amateur, but he did everything right and was capable of hitting hard when he had to. He was undoubtedly the cagiest player of all time and was a superb gamesman as well. He was small as tennis players go, standing only five feet, eight inches; he had a duck-footed walk, which is untypical of athletes; but he was speedy, enormously talented and, more than any other player, exemplified the champion's "will to win."

Bobby had the spark from his earliest days. He used to play at Highland Park wearing street clothes and a pair of sneakers, but the tiny twelve-year-old was already steady enough to win sideline bets for his brother John. At this time, one of the top local players, Dr. Esther Bartosh, spotted him and immediately realized his amazing potential. Esther and Jerry Bartosh rallied with him, drove him to tournaments, saw that he had rackets and gave him those fundamentally sound strokes. He had no other coaching, and while other young Los Angeles players were growing up with flippy Continental strokes, Bobby acquired a clean, solid, wristless Eastern game.

At age thirteen it was already clear that he was going to be a top player. None of the men players wanted to admit it since Riggs at that time could only bloop the ball. Nevertheless, he was amazingly accurate on passing shots, he lobbed perfectly and he eked out ranking Southern California men. The mark of the comer is the ability to win matches that he is supposed to lose, and Riggs always out-played the rankings and seedings. At fifteen he was winning men's tournaments. His only loss that year was in the finals of the National Boys when Bobby Harmon beat him. At sixteen he defeated Frank Shields, then the Number Two man in the country. This defeat, plus his loss to Don McNeill in the finals of the Nationals in 1940, were his only reversals in major competition. His entire tournament record is astonishing for its consistency, yet he always came back from a beating stronger than ever.

Riggs was a monkeyer in his early round matches. He frequently dropped sets to "unknowns," yet when he got to the quarters and semis he often won with the loss of only a game or two. As a result, players paradoxically boasted that Bobby beat them 6–0, 6–1, to prove that he respected their game enough to work on the match!

THE FOREHAND

Bobby Riggs' forehand was absolutely correct in every particular. It had the least wrist of all the big forehands and therefore was not as hard as some of the others. Because of the lack of wrist his accuracy was fantastic both in depth and direction. His fingers were separated well on the racket, his wrist was slightly laid back, and he had only the faintest trace of a semicircle on the wind-up. He had rather a short backswing, which helped his disguise, and he got his accuracy out of perfect timing. He did not flick his wrist for change of direction but instead hit the ball slightly earlier or later. Never in his life did he drop his racket head, which is further proof of his iron wrist.

On all his ground strokes he was not ashamed to clear the net by five feet or more. This was to get depth when his opponent was in the backcourt. When his opponent attacked he could skim the net on a passing shot, and that locked wrist and very slight overspin would put the ball just where he wanted it. With the same action he could lift lobs, which were just deep forehands to him. Occasionally he would underspin a very high defensive lob in order to get back into the game, but the lob was primarily an offensive passing shot for Bobby.

Riggs was not a bone-crusher on his forehand. He was primarily a parrier off of his opponent's thrusts. He could do something with every forehand he could touch, and he seldom made errors except when he was "monkeying" in those early rounds. His footwork was marvelous. In the early days he was not an "open stance" man. He had the old-fashioned classical approach that the Bartoshes gave him, with the left foot placed well forward toward the net.

In later years he began to chip with an open stance to get the net position.

THE BACKHAND

Bobby was just as letter-perfect on the backhand. The stroke was essentially flat, but he could apply a little overspin for passing shots or a little underspin for baseline rallies. He had a small, net backswing, he guided the ball by holding it on his racket as long as possible, and although he lacked real power, he was able to utilize his opponent's pace effectively. His ground strokes were not colorful because he never really teed off on the ball.

Riggs was a great touch artist. He could drop shot off either side, and he was always working the angles of the court. He hit short crosscourts successfully because he did not hit too hard. His backhand motion on the lob was as good as his forehand, and it was death to take the net against him. Joey Hunt at that time epitomized the attacking game, but in the hundred or so meetings between the two, Riggs only lost three times. Hunt had a big serve, a powerful overhead and a murderous volley. Bobby would lob a lot, losing points frequently in the earlier sets in order to pull Joe back from the barrier. Then the passing shots would begin to sneak by, and brother John would win another bet.

THE SERVE

Bobby never had a hard serve until he was a top amateur. He always had a competent delivery, and the first ball came in 90 percent of the time. Riggs did not see the percentage in missing and could go months without ever double faulting. His was the most underrated serve in the game. He had just enough American twist to put his opponent on the defensive. He served deep into the corners, never following his service into net as an amateur. Gradually his delivery hardened up, and by the time he was National Champion he was able to throw in an occasional ace.

The serve was also a classical action, distinguished by the fact that he used his height so well. It was competent and clean but seldom a cannon ball. He was giving his opponents at least four or five inches in height so that he could not hope to keep up with them on blistering aces. The motion was beautiful without extra frills. It came from the book and, like all his other strokes, was manufactured without a hitch.

THE VOLLEY

Bobby became a true net player only when he came up against Jack Kramer as a pro. His answer to Kramer's relentless drive to the net was to follow his own serve in every time. The game had changed and Bobby changed with it. After fifteen years of playing tournament tennis mainly from the baseline, Riggs became a volleyer. It is a great tribute to his basic ability that he was able to make this change. His height, reach and lack of power were against him, and yet he managed to beat all but Kramer with his new tactics.

Whatever Bobby did he did well. The forehand volley was practically wristless, pulled from the shoulder with an extremely short swing. He sometimes stroke-volleyed high forehands, which is practically the rule in top-flight tennis. His backhand volley was simply a foreshortened version of his backhand ground stroke, with a little bit of underspin added to control. On both sides he got down well for low balls, but he never bent his knees unnecessarily.

Riggs had always been a competent volleyer. However, as a pro he made the volley his forte. If there was ever a time when he hit the ball hard it was on a high stroke forehand volley. Generally he was a percentage volleyer who never hit harder then he had to. Bobby was interested in winning the maximum number of points, which from his point of view meant consistency.

THE OVERHEAD

Bobby knew the angles on the overhead. Again he was equipped with a good fundamental stroke, and he chose to use it as a placement weapon rather than a bludgeon. Whereas other players would leap backwards in an attempt to kill a difficult lob, Bobby would be content just to tap the ball back deeply to get into position. He was deadly on short to medium lobs and careful on the deep ones.

To beat Bobby you simply had to outhit him. Nobody could outsteady or outthink him. No one could "out-psych" him—usually the shoe was on the other foot! He had to be out-powered, and it took a consistent hitter like Budge, and later Kramer with his grooved shots, to beat the little "guts" player. Those who played him in tournaments had the utmost respect for his game. He was a clutch artist, a money player and a competitor who was never out of the match until the last point was over.

In his amateur career he won the National Juniors, the National Clay Courts, the U.S. National Singles twice and Wimbledon. At the age of eighteen, he was ranked Number Four in the men's division. He took the Nationals for the first time when he was twenty. He was unsuccessful in defending it the next year, losing to Don McNeill, but the following year he came back stronger than ever to win back the crown and to turn pro. He was out of competition during the war years. To Bobby, his biggest success was beating Don Budge in their pro tour. The margin was only one match, but Riggs had at last beaten the man who has often been called the greatest player of all time.

FOUR Jack Kramer

1
VII

The Kramer theory of modern tennis completely changed the complexion of the game. Jack popularized the terms "attack," "the Big Game" and "percentage tennis." There were many attacking players before Kramer but none who consistently came in behind every serve. The big serve combined with the big volley became known as "the Big Game." The words "percentage tennis" described a theory of play which included such Kramerisms as hitting every forehand approach shot down the line, serving a three-quarter speed to the backhand on important points, and coasting on the opponent's delivery until the opportunity came for the break.

Jack Kramer did not start to play tournament tennis until the age of thirteen. When he was fourteen he became a member of a select group of young players who were being developed by Dick Skeen. The latter, a classical baseliner, had organized a method of training for some fifteen youngsters which was designed to make them into champions. The group met almost daily at various courts, including Poinsettia Playground in Hollywood, the Palomar in Culver City (now the California Racquet Club) and private courts in Altadena, Beverly Hills and San Diego. Whenever Skeen gave a lesson on a private court he took some of the group with him. Most of these youngsters were from relatively poor families; Skeen's fee of ten to twenty dollars a month included rackets, balls and lessons. Kramer, who lived way out in Montebello, would be driven in several times a week by his mother or his aunt to work out with the Skeen group. The brush action on Kramer's forehand was a typical Skeen stroke, and the undercut backhand also bore the Skeen stamp.

Jack developed remarkably fast. He came from a family of moderate means but he was able to play the National Boys' Championships at Culver Military Academy due to the fact that his father was a railroad engineer, which entitled young Kramer to a free ticket. He played at Culver at the age of fifteen, winning the title although he had not been the pre-tournament favorite. Larry Dee and Jimmy Wade were the top seeds, but Dee was upset by Harper Ink and Wade, who was sick, was eliminated by Kramer.

Almost from the beginning Jack showed great court

presence and good match temperament. He never got flustered or fell apart under pressure. In the 15-and-Under division Jack's game was noted for its consistency in the backcourt. He was a steady player but not a soft ball artist, and he was definitely not a net rusher. He was not a great natural athlete since he was always a little heavy on his feet. He could not change directions fast or run down a ball that got behind him as could a young Vic Seixas or a Pancho Gonzales. However, he had a great eye, an infinite capacity to work on his game and a champion's determination to win.

Jack was the top future prospect when he returned from Culver as National Boys' Champion. Southern California officialdom lured him away from the Skeen group by offering him playing privileges at the famous Los Angeles Tennis Club. Here he got the opportunity of a lifetime. He worked out with Ellsworth Vines, the world's best player, almost daily. Other youngsters before and since Jack have had similar opportunities but never developed into championship calibre. Kramer stayed hungry and eager. He consolidated his strokes and learned to handle speed. Within a year he had all the earmarks of a world-beater. He was often beaten but he never played foolish tennis and never stayed disheartened.

Just about this time an automotive engineer named Cliff Roche convinced Kramer that the winning game should be played in set patterns. Roche, who played reasonably well himself, had worked in Detroit as a mass production designer and had formalized a theory of the game based on repetitive action. Every ball, he said, should be hit in a certain pattern. The forehand down the line approach shot, for example, became 100 percent automatic since it was not a function of the opponent's position or strength. Every time the "automatic player" came into net behind a forehand, he hit for an area two feet from the sideline and three feet from the baseline. Crosscourt forehand approach shots were never to be used since, on a percentage basis, they would lead to more passing shots on the return. The crosscourt forehand could be played only as an outright placement, never as a forcing approach.

Roche had been expounding his theories of the game for many years but no player had ever thought to follow his strategy religiously. Jack Kramer and his young doubles partner, Ted Schroeder, were the first Roche disciples. The court tactics in which they were drilled became the ABCs of modern tennis. Today every top player adheres to the basic Roche tenet of coming to net behind every serve and, whenever possible, behind every return. Kramer and Schroeder, from being steady baseliners, became net rushers.

The Roche strategy, as exemplified by Kramer, contains much more than the principle of attack. Coach Roche wanted Jack to limit himself to a few grooved shots. Every backhand exchange from the baseline was a deep crosscourt. The backhand down the line was to be used only for the sure winner. The term "percentage" was the key to championship tennis: If backhand crosscourts earned more points than backhands down the line, then never use the backhand down the line. Considered in the calculations were the errors and placements of the player as well as the errors and placements of the opponent. Roche did not attempt to modify Kramer's stroke technique. He was interested only in overall strategy.

Kramer became the automatic player. He served every ball to the backhand except when he saw the big opening. He never tried for an ace on an important point. His first serve went in a remarkable percentage of the time. His forehand became so grooved that he could hit the two-foot by three-foot rectangle consistently. He never learned a defensive game other than the necessary lob. He went all-out to win every service game but elected to go all-out on his opponent's service only when he felt he had a real opportunity for the break. He was tireless in a five-setter because he always conserved his strength on his opponent's delivery except when he felt the opportunity for the "kill." He played pattern tennis.

Jack's career in the game puts him in the category of one of the all-time great players. At eighteen he was selected to play Davis Cup doubles with Joe Hunt. The war interrupted his meteoric rise and he scarcely played any competitive tennis for five years. He returned to the circuit as the top amateur. Jaroslav Drobny upset him at Wimbledon in 1946, but thereafter Kramer was untouchable. He won the U.S. National Singles title twice, the Wimbledon Singles once, the U.S. National Doubles with Schroeder, and the Wimbledon Doubles with both Tom Brown and Bob Falkenburg. When he turned pro he completely dominated the pay-for-play circuit. On his first tour he defeated Bobby Riggs and thereafter he downed Pancho Gonzales, Frank Sedgman and Pancho Segura. He retired undefeated when Gonzales came into his own.

THE STROKES

Jack's strongest weapons were his forehand and serve. The volley was great only because the approach was great. Every stroke in his repertoire was thoroughly grooved, and he even had a preferential spot for his overheads. His one weakness was the undercut backhand, which did not have enough pace to be an effective passing shot. He was a good drop volleyer and knew the value of the dump shot as a winner. He played close to net, knowing that the percentage was against his opponent in placement lobs and that the percentage was with him in scoring with close-in volleys.

His forehand was hit with a laid-back wrist. When he hit down the line he pulled the racket slightly across his body. The sidespin on the down-the-line side was a heavy ball to return. When he hit crosscourt he used overspin by pulling up on the follow-through. The stroke was a relatively short one, always hit with an open stance. It was a great, grooved approach shot which forced the opponent into errors or pop-ups.

The backhand was steady but not powerful. Jack led with his elbow always, which meant that there was sidespin as well as underspin on the ball. The sidespin was on the down the line and the underspin on the crosscourt. He hit with good depth, but unless he followed the ball to net his backhand never worried his opponent. It was a small stroke, and the action and style were only slightly longer than the "chip" shot.

Although Jack did not serve as many aces as Bob Falkenburg or Pancho Gonzales, he was considered by all those he played to have one of the truly great serves. His second serve was almost as hard to handle as his first. It was a slight service with great depth and placement. The ball was heavy and invariably pulled his opponent wide, and of course Kramer was in to net waiting for the return. The action was highly stylized, and for five years every Junior attempted the Kramer wind-up. Jack leaned way back, almost on his haunches, at the beginning of the wind-up, pulling up to full height at the hit. The overhead, which was hit with the same action as the serve, had that high left hand pointing at the ball just as he pointed at the end of the service toss.

The forehand volley was hit with a laid-back wrist and resembled his down-the-line forehand without a follow-through. He did not make leap-volley kills nor did he powder the ball. He hit with great placement and consistency, not with bludgeon power. His first volley behind service was just like his forehand: It was always placed deep to the backhand unless he had a set-up kill. He did not attempt to put away the first volley but merely to set himself up for the killer second where he was in close.

The backhand volley was hit with a fair amount of underspin and had the same action on high and low balls. It carried slightly less pace than the forehand volley but he had excellent control. He never rallied from the net: When the first volley was not a put-away, he was either passed or made a winner on the second. He tried to force his opponent into hitting set-ups or errors by his great depth and blanketing of the net.

The Kramer Pros were carbon copies of Jack tactically, although individual styles and stroke techniques vary. Each one has learned that percentage tennis as exemplified by Jack is vital to survival in the top leagues.

FOUR   *Pancho Gonzales*

1

VIII

It is my belief that Pancho Gonzales is the most natural player who ever lived. He never had a tennis lesson, and he had almost no tournament competition during his formative years. When he dropped out of school in the tenth grade, the Southern California Tennis Association did not permit him to play in Junior tournaments. He was nineteen when he played his first big event, which was the Southern California Championships. He defeated nineteen-year-old Herb Flam, the National Junior Champion.

Two months later, Pancho went back East to play the clay and grass court circuit. His play was spotty, but he managed to earn a Number Seventeen ranking. The following year (1948) he was Number One in the country, beating Eric Sturgess to win at Forest Hills. The next year he again won the Nationals, defeating his old nemesis, Ted Schroeder. He turned professional a few months later and was decisively beaten by Jack Kramer. He had actually had only three summers of top amateur competition and was far from a finished tennis player.

His loss to Kramer put him out of the "big time" in professional tennis. He waited on the sidelines while Kramer annually played against the neophyte pro of the year. Gonzales was eager to get back on the pro tour. His annual competition was limited almost solely to Jack March's World Pro Championships in Cleveland, which he won with mo-

notorious regularity, and yet he did not receive a bid to tour with Kramer's boys. Eventually Pancho got his opportunity. Jake offered him $15,000—an all-time low for a feature player—to play against Tony Trabert, who was to receive $95,000. Gonzales reluctantly accepted, although the amount he received left him with bitter feelings towards his boss which have lasted to this day.

From here on Gonzales was the World Champion. He beat Trabert, Sedgman, Segura, Rosewall, Hoad and Olmedo. He barely edged past Hoad in 1957, losing in Ampol (tournament) points but winning out on day-by-day play. In a limited tour in 1960, he lost fewer matches than ever before in two-night tournament stands against Rosewall, Segura and Olmedo. In May 1960 he announced his retirement from professional competition, but has returned to thrill new audiences.

The Gonzales game has always been admired by every top player. He has no critics. He is universally recognized as a great stylist, a hungry competitor and a winner. It is a tennis aphorism that it is far easier to become a world champion than to stay at the top. Once a player has reached the pinnacle he can suffer from fear of losing or he can lose his hunger for winning. Pancho was always courageous and success never softened him. He is as hard today as he was while struggling for recognition thirteen years ago. He is as tough a competitor as the world has ever known. He gives no quarter, and the old venom that made him become a winner is still the most significant characteristic of his court personality. He is a tennis killer in the best sense of the word.

Gonzales has a great temperament for the game, albeit not in the grand manner of a Gottfried von Cramm or J. Donald Budge. Despite the fact that his attack seems to be motivated by sullen, cold fury or murderous determination, his inner turmoil has never caused him to lose a match. He can play badly and be beaten, or on a given day he can be trounced by a colossus such as Hoad, but his temperamental displays have never affected his own game. If he is licked by Hoad on a Monday, he is more than liable to reverse the score on Tuesday. Losing has the effect of stirring him up, and when he starts winning he is never headed.

At the beginning of a tour, after a four to six month lay-off, Gonzales has frequently been ten to fifteen pounds too heavy. Within a few weeks he is back to his regular playing weight, leaner and meaner than ever before. Although he has a friendly personality which will immediately make a stranger warm to him, he is basically a "loner"—a little withdrawn and aloof and living very much to himself. He can kid with Segura, josh with Olmedo and horse with Hoad, but mostly he will prefer to travel by himself. Among his close pals he still numbers many old friends from his Exposition Park days. His lack of desire to meet new faces or move in a different group is balanced by long-term friendships with loyal buddies such as Segura.

The Gonzales game has nothing but virtues. Every stroke is beautifully executed, he plays with consummate grace, and he never makes the wrong shot. He makes tennis look too easy. Gonzales has always been known as a great attacker, but he is equally as great in the role of defensive player. Everyone acknowledges the magnificence of his service, volleying and overheads, but he is just as strong in lobbing, running down balls and nailing placements on passing shots. Segura once said that Gonzales was the only big man who attacked who could also defend well. There is no hint of clumsiness in his game. He covers a prodigious amount of court with so little effort that few spectators realize how well he retrieves.

THE SERVE

The Gonzales service is a natural action that epitomizes grace, power, control and placement. The top players sigh when they see the smooth, easy action. There is no trace of a hitch and no extra furbelows. I have never seen a serve so beautifully executed. The toss is no higher than it has to be, and it is timed so that he is fully stretched when he hits it. The backswing is continuous, not as big as Trabert's nor as concise as Talbert's. The motion of the backswing blends into the hit and continues into the follow-through without a pause.

Pancho is not a heavy spin artist. His first serve is almost flat and the second has a modicum of slice or roll. Slice, as most players know, is produced by moving the racket face across the ball from right to left; American twist is given to the ball by moving the racket face from left to right with a pronounced wrist snap; the roll is halfway between the slice and twist and gives the ball forward spin rather than spin to the left or right. The slice or roll that Gonzales gives to the ball is just enough for control on second serve.

The strongest part of Gonzales' serve is his ability to put the first ball into play when the chips are down. At 0–40, 15–40 and 30–40, his batting average on first serves must be .950. It is incredible to have so high a percentage while still hitting hard and almost flat. The number of aces served on these important points is also astounding. No other player has so regularly been able to perform this feat, although Budge for two years was probably as tough on the serve. Vines could do it on a given day, but not day in and day out.

THE OVERHEAD

Pancho is not a leaper on the overhead and he does not have that wristy, flat snap that bounces them very high. He hits the ball with a little spin in a motion that is almost identical with his serve. He literally pole-axes the overhead just as he punishes the serve. Gonzales seems to have an infallible sense of where to hit the ball; more than any other player he catches his opponent going the wrong way. Bobby Riggs was deceptive, too, and so is Pancho Segura, but Gonzales has the edge of size.

by Julius D. Heldman / 277

THE VOLLEY

Pancho is a natural net player because of his anticipation and great coordination. He is not particularly a hard volleyer, except for high forehands which he tends to stroke as do so many of the top players. He has excellent control over sharp angle shots, which he hits rather than "dumps." Most players will use a very small action in "dumping" an angle shot, but Gonzales actually punches the ball to make his angle volley. He plays extremely close to net except, of course, when he is coming in behind service for the first volley. Standing this far in is dangerous but gives Gonzales an almost sure winner if he can touch the ball. He chooses mostly angle shots and only volleys deep on the first ball when he is caught behind the service line. Only a player with great height, reach and anticipation can use this type of tactics; the pros would lob a lesser man unmercifully.

Both the forehand and backhand volley are characterized by underspin. He holds the racket with fingers close in a "hammer grip" on the forehand side. Consistency in the volley is the mark of a top pro in today's game since the leading players literally camp on the net. Gonzales is consistent in his first volleys, which he plays deep, and in his angle volleys, which he hits sharp.

In the old days, the half-volley was a trick shot used by a player caught in "no man's land." Today it is standard equipment and is used regularly by the server in his approach to net. Gonzales on the forehand side will take a rather full swing on the half-volley. On the backhand he prefers to take a backward step so that the ball will rise off the ground. Then he uses heavy underspin, preferably crosscourt, and closes in on the net. He uses this technique so frequently that it is an integral part of his style.

THE FOREHAND

Pancho is one of the few great players who has been able to use the "hammer grip" successfully. The four fingers of the hand are held together rather than spread. Most players feel that the spread fingers give more feel and control, and yet Pancho has excellent touch and precision with the tight grip. His forehand is not grooved in a distinctive pattern: He will hit with closed or open stance, with a big backswing or none at all, and with a high or low follow-through. He would be the despair of a current teaching pro, but Bill Tilden would have loved him. Pancho uses many spins, although none are as pronounced as Tilden's. The latter used them consciously to affect his opponent's play, but Gonzales is simply doing what comes naturally.

Only when Pancho stays back does his forehand take on a grooved look. The backswing is lengthened and the follow-through definitely shows overspin. If you give him any short ball he is completely unpredictable. He may shove it from the hip down the line or leisurely come over it for the cross-court or snap his wrist to hit the desired spot on the court. He will block, chip or stroke on return of serve, hitting with all his might when he so desires. Mostly he will chip against the big serves since he is a "percentage" player and feels the odds are with the chip in keeping the ball in play. On passing shots he is not afraid to strike out very hard. He is flat and sharp and accurate. It is surprising since it comes in such contrast to his chip return of serve.

The forehand is a good one although not the greatest part of his game. It is certainly not as great a stroke as Segura's, and yet it is one of the better forehands in the pro game. It is not a vulnerable stroke, and it stands up well in the heat of a battle.

THE BACKHAND

Gonzales can hit the backhand in any of the three classical modes—with underspin, flat or with overspin. He prefers the underspin but will use one of the other two on passing shots. His flat backhand is extremely powerful, particularly when he is run out of court. The underspin is used on return of serve, which is usually a low crosscourt in the left court. This is his chosen gambit to slow down the game momentarily.

His control on the backhand is excellent. It is smooth as silk and well grooved. He generally slices when he comes in, but he will vary his backhands when he stays in the backcourt. Most people never appreciated the soundness of his ground game, but the early pro tour featuring the three-bounce rule permitted Pancho to demonstrate his all-around competence. He can handle Segura or Rosewall from the baseline!

For a decade players argued the relative merits of Tilden and Budge when discussing the never-ending question of the greatest player of all time. Budge himself now feels that "Gorgo" has earned the Number One spot. The players will never agree on an answer, but the general consensus among top players is a three-way split among Tilden, Budge and Gonzales. The present pros vote for Pancho because he has whipped them all with the net attack. He could not have beaten Don in a baseline duel, and whether he could have dominated Budge via the serve and volley is a question that unfortunately will never be answered.

FOUR   *Rod Laver*

1
___
IX

Rod Laver was eighteen years old when he first came to the United States to play our circuit. He looked very much then as he does now, although his red hair was usually hidden under a floppy hat, and he often had a handkerchief tied around his neck à la Rosewall. He was only of medium build, he looked fragile, and he hit the ball a ton. That year he won the U.S. National Junior title. Six years later he was to become the second man in history to win the Grand Slam —Australia, France, Wimbledon and Forest Hills. Within another two years he became the Number One professional, and today he is still acknowledged the Number One player in the world. He is the only man today who can go through the last rounds of a major international tournament without dropping a set, because he is the only player who can literally crush the opposition with his power. He is capable of being upset (he lost to Cliff Drysdale at the 1968 U.S. National Open and to Cliff Richey in the 1969 Madison Square Garden Open), but only he could win the 1968 Wimbledon Open and the 1969 South African Open so decisively over such strong opposition.

Rod swings at everything hard and fast. His timing, eye and wrist action are nothing short of miraculous. On either side, forehand or backhand, he takes a full roundhouse-loop crack at the ball, which comes back so hard it can knock the racket out of your hand. I saw Rod plug Osuna in the semifinals at Forest Hills in 1962. It was murder. In the last game, Rafe bravely served and ran for the net. Rod cracked a backhand back full speed, free swing, so hard that Rafe's racket wavered in his hand. Not so amazing, perhaps, but the same scene was repeated four points in a row. Rod literally knocked Osuna down with four successive returns of serve, and Osuna is one of the quickest and best racket-handlers who ever played.

On the backhand side, Laver often uses a heavy under-spin. Most players who come under the ball slow it up. Not so Rod; he is also moving in and hitting so hard that the shot is deep and attacking and has unusual pace. He often takes high backhands this way, but he is just as liable to come over the ball with a tremendous wallop, ending with wrist turning the racket head over and the ball going with incredible speed and accuracy.

From the ground, about the only shot that Rod does not clobber is a forehand underspin or chip. I don't recall his using the shot much or at all when he was younger, but as he matured he began occasionally to hold the ball on his racket with some underspin and place it carefully while he ran for the net. But the next time he would literally jump and throw his racket at the ball with all the force he could muster, wrist and arms snapping over at the hit. The shot is unreturnable. It always ends the point, one way or the other, and you can never predict when the lightning will strike, although you know it will happen often.

Volleying in top international tennis is more than technical proficiency. Rod is not a great low volleyer, but he is merciless when he gets half a chance. He is competent on low balls, handling them with underspin for control (more on the backhand than forehand, which he can net occasionally), but he will cream any ball at waist level or higher. As time goes on, Laver takes fewer unnecessary big swings at set-up high put-aways; he taps or punches them away. But if he needs to, he can and does hit high volleys with all his might as swinging drives or, on his backhand, sharp underspin angles as well. It is hard to believe a ball can be hit that hard and with that much angle, but Rod does it. No wonder he is the terror of all opponents.

There is not an Aussie net-rusher who does not have a great overhead to back his attack. Otherwise he would be lobbed to death. Rod has one of the best, quite flat, angled to his left sharply by preference but capable of being placed anywhere. While Rod is not tall, he is agile and leaps well and is hard to lob over. What is worse, if you do get a lob over him, he will run it down and, with his powerful stiff wrist, rifle a full loop past his helpless opponent. This happens so often that players have begun to say that they prefer to lob short to Rod, at least on his backhand. Actually, if Laver has a weakness, it is on his backhand overhead, on which he does err, but in a way that is silly: How are you going to get in position to play that shot to Rod often?

Some lefties make it primarily by virtue of their serve, John Doeg and Neale Fraser being good examples. Not so Rod. His first serve has always been hard and flat, and he makes his share of aces, but he never had a heavy, deep spin second ball. It was just adequate, at least in the context of world class. In the last year, Rod has made a conscious effort to harden up his second delivery. For a while, all his timing seemed to be affected—he had some eye trouble at the same time—but now he is serving better than ever.

Someone once told Chuck McKinley that he should just try to be steady because he was too small to hit the ball hard. He paid no attention and he won Wimbledon. A few well-meaning coaches advised Rod to temporize more on his shots if he wanted to win a big tournament. It went in one ear and out the other, and Rod rose to the greatest heights in the game. His shots are breathtaking, his talent is enormous and his drive to be the Number One has made him the most successful player in the world today.

FOUR   *Arthur Ashe, Jr.*

1 / x

Arthur Ashe is a natural player with all the strokes, which he hits with cool relaxation, but his apparent "looseness" has never disturbed his concentration, which is excellent.

Ashe uses all kinds of spins at will, and in this respect he is like Rod Laver or Manuel Santana. However, he does not put as much emphasis on spins as the latter. The key note to his game is variety. In Arthur's game one sees all kinds of shots—underspins, topspins, closed stance, open stance, touch and power. About the only shot he does not use is an extreme high-kick American twist serve to the backhand. Here he relies more on a "heavy" ball—a deep serve with less spin, either twist or slice.

I doubt that Arthur thinks about change of pace and strategy as consciously as Bill Tilden did, yet he practices the same kind of variations. The major difference is, of course, Arthur's continual attack. All top players today come in regularly behind serve except, perhaps, on slow clay.

Arthur has an Australian grip on the forehand, halfway between the Eastern and the Continental, and a backhand grip on everything else, as expected. He is known as a "wristy" player but in truth he keeps his wrist firm at the hit on most shots.

THE SERVE

Arthur's service is one continuous motion. He starts with his feet wide spread and his back bent over. He gives the ball one or two fast bounces before the action starts. Arthur has a characteristic sideways stance with the feet unusually close together after a half-step forward at the start of the motion. The right foot is next to and slightly to the right of the left (front) foot. The toss is over the right eye and slightly forward, perhaps one foot in the court. The toss is more forward on the second serve than on the cannonball first. On the wind-up Arthur bends both knees and arches his back. As he unleashes his serve, he straightens and stretches out so that there is almost a straight line from toes to the tip of the racket at the moment of the hit.

Arhur has a relatively fast motion with no pauses anywhere. He is very careful about foot-faults but he clearly jumps an inch or two at the hit. When you stretch out for maximum power, almost inevitably you will leave the ground slightly. This is more natural than "one foot on the ground" which was required until the foot-fault rule was changed about eight years ago.

Arthur's favorite serve is wide to the forehand, very hard but controlled with a little slice. If you cover too far, he will go to your backhand hard in the right court. Then, when you don't expect it, he will ace you on the forehand side again. This is what he did against both Graebner and Okker in the U.S. Open Championships.

Arthur rarely uses much American twist, although he knows this serve. His toss is too much to the right for the twist. He can come over the ball to serve to the backhand, but he serves with a minimum of spin. The whole delivery is based on a confident and secure approach. As Arthur's serve goes, so goes his game.

THE FOREHAND AND BACKHAND

No one becomes a champion without tremendous inner drive and fire, qualities which Arthur possesses. He is also calm, cool, unruffled, easy and relaxed. Outwardly his emotion never shows, and Arthur has complete control, even in the most provocative situations. Have you ever seen him in an argument on a line call? No one has, but it is interesting to speculate what would happen if he ever let loose.

Arthur's personal characteristics carry over into his game. His strokes are quite hard but never strained. This means his timing, balance and weight transference must be superb in order to hit the ball as hard as he does without excessive effort. Rod Laver hits with just as much pace but he takes a very full wallop at the ball; Arthur meets it squarely with a fast forward arm action and with all his weight moving forward without any jerking, and the ball whizzes back.

Fast action characterizes all of Arthur's strokes. The serve is one concerted motion, lightning fast. The drive wind-up starts rather late and is short and continuous, with no halt at the end of the backswing.

Arthur hits at his natural pace, which is extremely forceful. When still young he was erratic, which is inevitable with youngsters who beat the ball. Most Juniors learn to temporize for ball control, but Arthur learned his ball control by improving without softening his game. With this approach he is bound to lose matches when his timing is off, since he has no recourse to any softer, steadier game, but Ashe has had many fewer bad days in the last year than three years ago. Because he hits hard, Arthur is not considered to be a good player on slow clay, and yet he won our National Clay Court Championships. When he has his timing and his serve is working, he is as good on any surface. Perhaps his worst is indoors where he seems to see poorly and is handicapped by his glasses, yet he won the Madison Square Garden title last winter.

Arthur hits with topspin by preference on both forehand

and backhand. The loop is not as pronounced as Laver's nor as long a sweep as Santana's. It is more like Lew Hoad's but it is different in that it is a short, clean snap. On the forehand the racket face turns over and faces down just after the hit; on the backhand Arthur ordinarily ends up quite high. While topspin is his basic game, Arthur has underspin control as well and uses it naturally. He does not think about what ground stroke to use; he simply plays automatically. The thought processes are evident in lob and touch situations but not in ground stroke responses, where constant practice has made him react instinctively.

On return of serve, when Arthur "sees" the ball, he will take a full topspin swing on either forehand or backhand and the ball comes whistling back like a bullet. His backswing is quite short and the whole stroke is a forward motion. On the backhand where Arthur draws back the racket with the left hand on the throat, he either hits forward with astonishing speed, or from the same short backswing, he blocks the ball deftly back low over the net. He uses this return quite effectively against net-rushers.

Some players prepare for and execute their volleys very carefully, moving their feet and body into position properly, spreading their legs if possible, taking only a short backswing, then punching forward just a short distance with a firm wrist and with underspin for control. To the casual observer, Ashe doesn't match this description, and yet he carries out all these moves beautifully and precisely, with the possible exception that he never uses much underspin and sometimes none at all. Arthur has excellent volley techniques, but he appears so deceptively casual about his graceful, almost lazy movements about the court that people are often fooled into believing that his strokes are sloppy or slovenly. Nothing of the sort is true, of course, and his volleys are the most precise of all his shots.

Arthur's forehand volley is good from midcourt because

he hits deep, and he is good from close in because he angles sharply. He doesn't overhit but invariably tries for depth on his first volley coming into net—unless, of course, he has a kill, in which case he lashes out with a murderous forehand stroke-volley, usually crosscourt. Otherwise he places deep, but within minimum underspin, and advances closer. Whenever he is close to net, he angles or dump-volleys when he can, and his choice of shots is unassailable. Arthur has truly learned, so that now it is automatic, not to hit harder than he has to, and he has complete confidence in his ability to angle and drop-volley. Again, he does not execute the drop-volley like McKinley or Santana, with so much backspin that the ball dies or bounces back toward the net. Arthur depends on his soft shot to "die" without much spin. Don Budge was another great dump-shot artist who also had total wrist control and who used even less spin than Arthur, especially on ground strokes.

Arthur's backhand volley style is worth emulating: It is a model for beginners and advanced players alike. He has the body placement, balance and weight transference of all good players, but it is the left arm which is notable. He holds the racket throat in his left hand throughout the backswing, which is therefore necessarily short and also very precise. The forward motion is a short jab, now with a bit more underspin, and the short is wonderfully accurate. As far as I know, Arthur's backhand volley never deserts him. And again, it is depth on the first or low volleys, sharp angles or dumps from close in.

If a volleyer is to blanket the net, he must have a powerful smash, good leaping ability and confidence in his mastery of the overhead. Arthur qualifies on all counts. His smash is as good as his serve; he simply clobbers any ball he can reach. Here, however, is one place where his glasses can bother him (although he doesn't say so). Looking up high into the sun at a ball with glasses is no fun. Clark Graebner, before he changed to contacts, was clearly handicapped by them on the sunny side when he was lobbed, and I think Arthur is also, although perhaps less. This shows up in their running back to take high lobs after they bounce on the north side, where as on the south side of the court they will leap up for a deep lob like McKinley or, two generations ago, Ted Schroeder.

FIVE

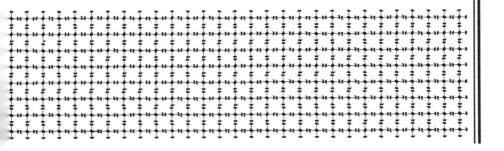

Tennis' Ten Most Historic Games
The Battle of the Bills — A Serial

The personal rivalry between Big Bill Tilden and Little Bill Johnston produced so many titanic court battles that historians are unable to agree which was the greatest.

Johnston partisans undoubtedly would choose the 1919 final of the National Championships. That year the frail, little man with the potent Western forehand cut Tilden down in straight sets 6–4, 6–4, 6–3. It was a humiliating setback for Big Bill, whose vulnerable backhand collapsed under Johnston's pounding, and he went into hiding the following winter to reconstruct his game.

Tilden favors the 1920 and 1922 finals for the championship, both of which he won. We'll touch upon the 1920 thriller, but since Big Bill insists, we must call the 1922 battle his greatest.

In 1920 Tilden was ready for his "revenge match" against Johnston. He had spent months working in secret on his backhand. He had also won Wimbledon, emblem of the world championship, the first American to do so.

The day was cold and cloudy. The match stood at one set each and Tilden was leading 2–1 in the third when the gallery of 5,000 was distracted by the sputtering motor of a small plane flying overhead.

Suddenly the motor coughed and died, and the plane plunged toward the ground, crashing only a few hundred yards from the court. The crowd gasped. A wave of near hysteria swept through the stands.

Tilden and Johnston paused momentarily, as if frozen to the court. "Let's play," the umpire barked. The match was resumed. Less than 100 spectators left the stands.

years later Miss Wills played at Wimbledon, and this time it was an attack of jaundice that forced Suzanne to default after the fourth round. Helen gained the final where, jittery, she lost to England's Kathleen McKane, and the next year she failed to go abroad.

Meanwhile, Suzanne went into seclusion at her family's villa in southern France. But she couldn't escape the growing cry for a showdown between her and the young American and some accused her of being afraid.

In January 1926 Helen Wills took time off from her studies and headed for southern France to participate in invitation tournaments. American newspapers trumpeted that she was making the trip for one purpose—a clash with Suzanne.

"This girl must be mad," Miss Lenglen told a close friend. "Does she think she can come and beat me on my home courts?" Nevertheless, she acknowledged she was nervous.

Weeks passed. Suspense mounted. The Lenglen villa was besieged by reporters seeking to know Suzanne's plans. At last the issue was joined as both women entered a tournament at the Carlton Club in Cannes.

Fans throughout Europe flocked to the scene. It was one of the major sports events of the day. Extra stands were erected by workmen who toiled night and day to complete the job. Thousands of francs were paid for privileged vantage points in the attic windows of the villas overlooking the courts.

Rumors were rife. There were reports that Miss Wills had received an exorbitant fee to play in the Riviera for the purpose of boosting tourist trade. Another rumor, later proved unfounded, was that a movie company had paid $100,000 for film rights to the match.

The event presented a study in contrasts. Suzanne was flamboyant, high-strung and hot-tempered. She appeared on court in calf-length skirts and low-cut blouses, sometimes in one-piece dresses under which she wore no petticoats. To the prim Twenties this was scandalous. She had a regal bearing, often making her entrance in ermine wraps. Miss Wills was quiet and reserved, almost expressionless on court. If Suzanne over-dressed, Helen under-dressed. She looked like a schoolgirl in her white middie blouse, pleated skirt and green eyeshade.

Tension mounted when rain delayed the tournament three days. Suzanne and her parents drove to the courts daily from Nice. She grew impatient and began to cough, a nervous symptom that had bothered her at Forest Hills. Nevertheless she was relieved to discover that the crowd was with her, despite the criticism to which she had been subjected. The restricted gallery was largely European and Suzanne was their girl.

She played almost flawless tennis in the first set, winning it 6–3. Gliding over the court like a fawn, she hit smooth sweeping strokes that seemed to obey her every touch. Helen, obviously nervous, played well but the Frenchwoman was too overpowering.

In the second set, Helen lost some of her early uncertainty and began hitting the ball with more confidence. She battled for every point and largely through tenacity broke Suzanne's rhythm. She began chasing Suzanne from one side of the court to the other. Mlle. Lenglen suffered coughing spells but her friend, Sophie Wavertree, was always there to give her a glass of champagne.

Helen gained a 5–4 lead and had set point. If she could win the second set she believed she could take the third, if on nothing more than stamina.

At set point, Helen hit a hard drive down the line to Suzanne's forehand. It caught the Frenchwoman flat-footed. The ball struck near the chalk. While the crowd and both players waited breathlessly, the lineman called "out."

It was the American's last chance. Suzanne collected herself, saved the game and finally took the match 6–3, 8–6.

Miss Wills left the court quietly and Miss Lenglen plopped down in a chair and began to sob uncontrollably.

"Bon Dieu que tu as mal joué! (Good God, how badly you played)," chided her mother and she received a scowl from Suzanne.

Miss Wills took the defeat graciously. "She is terrific," she said later of her conqueror. "I think it was one of my greatest matches."

<table>
<tr><td>FIVE</td><td rowspan="3">

The Old Man Finally Made It, and Everybody Cried
</td></tr>
<tr><td>1</td></tr>
<tr><td>III</td></tr>
</table>

It was the day Wimbledon cried.

Jaroslav Drobny had been a favorite of galleries in the All-England Tennis Tournament since he made his first appearance sixteen years before as a pink-cheeked, 16-year-old ball boy from Prague.

Since his first tournament in 1938, he had played in eleven Wimbledons. Six times he had battled his way to the semifinals. Three times he had gained the final. Always he had been beaten back.

Now he was in the last round again and, though his admirers were enthusiastic, practically no one gave him a chance.

The years had not treated him too kindly. To escape the Communists, who moved into his homeland after World War II, he had been forced to flee Czechoslovakia and become a citizen of the world, taking the nationality of any country that would have him—first Egypt, then England, finally just any court where tennis was played.

He was less than a month away from his thirty-third birthday. He had gained a noticeable paunch. His hair was thinning. He wore spectacles. His step was slowed, but he still was one of the master craftsmen of the sport.

It didn't hearten his supporters any that his opponent on this Friday, July 2, 1954, was a slender, dark-haired Australian named Ken Rosewall with a backhand that he could whip cross-court or send down the line with deadly accuracy.

It was a match between an aging tactician with the all-court game and a subtle young genius who handled a racket as if it had been attached to his arm at birth.

Drobny started shakily. Two rapier-like backhands down the line gave Rosewall a break and he led 2–0. But Rosewall was stiff and tense. Drobny, cross-courting beautifully, made it 2–2, then 4–2, with a second service break. He led 5–4 on service but Rosewall came alive with two great forehand passing shots to make it 5–5.

Drobny broke again for 7–6 but Rosewall broke right back, attacking his opponent's backhand. The spectators cheered the action wildly. King Gustav of Sweden stood in his box and applauded enthusiastically after spirited rallies. Princess Margaret and the Duchess of Kent found it difficult to retain their royal composure.

At 11–10, Rosewall had set point but Drobny saved it with a lunging smash return that hit the baseline. Then the former ballboy began pecking away at Rosewall's vaunted backhand and reeled off three straight games to pull out the set 13–11.

In the second, however, Drobny appeared to tire and lose concentration. He missed a volley and flubbed a drop shot as Rosewall broke him for 5–3 and although he saved two set points, the Aussie's fine volleying won the set 6–4.

Drobny changed tactics for the third. Instead of remaining in the back court, as he had done for the first two sets, he started moving into the forecourt, cutting off Rosewall's returns and putting the ball away in the corners. Rosewall tried to counter with a lobbing attack but it was no use. Drobny took the set 6–2 and went into the fourth set leading two sets to one.

Every spectator remained in his seat as the two finalists— the old man of the circuit and Harry Hopman's new protégé —began the final sets.

The set followed service through the first six games as tension mounted. In the seventh game, two searing forehands gave the Czech the advantage and a point for a break. Three times he had the advantage before Ken stumbled and hit a volley beyond the base line. A vital break. The score was 4–3. Drobny held to make it 5–3 and then Rosewall served powerfully to hold. It was 5–4.

Still Drobny was within a game of victory. There was hardly a sound as the veteran went to the baseline to serve. He won the first point, 15–0. On the next, Rosewall hit a shot that clipped the net and fell on the other side. Two whistling backhands down the line and an overhead smash by the Australian brought a rebreak. The score was 5–5.

Even Drobny's closest friends feared that this might be the end, and that the old Czech was doomed never to win at Wimbledon. But fighting desperately, Drobny again gained the advantage on Rosewall's service in the fifteenth game. There was a lively rally, ending when Drobny hit a shot that struck the top of the net and hung there a moment tantalizingly. The ball fell on Rosewall's side and failed to bounce. Once more Drobny needed only to hold service for the triumph.

He got the opening point, 15–0. Then Rosewall, a slim tiger, drilled a backhand down the sideline, scored on a crosscourt forehand and forced the Czech into a volleying error. Now Drobny was behind 15–40.

He brought the score to deuce with two good first services followed by winning volleys. He served an ace. Now it was match point. There was a long rally. Drobny hit a smash at Rosewall's feet. The Australian netted. The match was over. Drobny was winner, 13–11, 4–6, 6–2, 9–7.

For a full ten minutes the spectators stood and applauded the valiant but rubbery-legged Czech, a Wimbledon champion at last. Handkerchiefs were brought to the faces of hundreds to wipe away sentimental tears.

"I was holding my thumbs for you," the Duchess of Kent told Drobny afterward. "It was the finest tennis I have ever seen."

FIVE *Pancho's Greatest Hour at Forest Hills*

They said you could always tell when Pancho Gonzales was mad. The scar on his cheek—the mark left by an accident in his youth—caught fire. It sent an angry flame across his face.

The scar was a slash of red on this hazy September afternoon in 1949. Pancho, a twenty-one-year-old Mexican-American from Los Angeles who had come up the hard way, found himself face-to-face with an old adversary, Ted Schroeder, in the men's singles final of the U.S. Tennis Championships.

That in itself was not enough to set Gonzales' Latin blood boiling. Pancho was the defending champion, having won the year before when Schroeder did not compete. Yet he was seeded Number Two while Schroeder was Number One and Pancho considered this an affront.

More than that, every time he picked up a paper, Gonzales saw himself referred to as a "cheese champion" by some cynical sports writer. Also there was talk that promoter Bobby Riggs had his check book poised, ready to give Schroeder a $75,000 professional contract. This was a contract Pancho wanted, needed and he felt, deserved.

The strong sentiment for Schroeder was understandable. Ted had won the Queen's Club tournament and followed it up with a victory at Wimbledon, the unofficial world championship. Pancho, meanwhile, had had a rough year. In the spring, he had been brushed off the court in Houston by Sam Match in twenty-eight minutes. He had been trounced by Budge Patty at Paris and by Geoff Brown at Wimbledon. On the grass court circuit he had lost to Bill Talbert twice.

The old concrete horseshoe in Forest Hills was jammed right up to its eagles with tennis fans who were asking out loud:

"Does this Mexican kid have a chance against Schroeder?"

"Not much," was the inevitable reply.

All Gonzales had to do was keep his ears open to hear such discouraging remarks. This must have made the flame on his cheek burn hotter.

Schroeder didn't do much to cool the fire. He was a cocky, bulldog of a player who strode around the court with a swagger. He moved like a bowlegged cowboy. His shoulders were always hunched. There was an air about him that nettled the swarthy Mexican-American.

Pancho recalled afterward that Schroeder had a way of "psyching" him before a big match. They often changed clothes in the same dressing room.

Schroeder, an outgoing, talkative personality, would walk over to Pancho and say:

"Hello, Pancho."

"Hi, Ted," Gonzales, then a quiet, introverted type, responded.

"Good day for tennis."

"Yeah."

"You know I'm going to beat you again, Pancho . . ."

There went that scar catching fire again.

As the two players warmed up for their championship match, Schroeder was the picture of confidence. He clowned, laughed and wise-cracked. Occasionally he would wave to someone in the stands. Gonzales was grim, quiet—and so nervous he wanted to jump out of his skin.

The match started tensely.

Schroeder, the laughing boy, suddenly became deadly serious. He smacked the ball with vengeance off both sides, lunged to the net behind his high-bounding service and appeared well in control of the situation. Nervous as he was, Gonzales served well.

Game after game went with service: 1–1, 2–2, up to 5–5, 6–6, then 8–8, 10–10.

The sellout crowd of 13,000 got into the spirit of the occasion. There were howls when one player got within a point of a break, groans mixed with cheers when the crucial point was beaten off with a great service or a remarkable recovery shot.

At last, with the score 17–16 in favor of Schroeder, Gonzales fell behind 0–40 on service. Schroeder now had three chances for the set as a result of two slashing returns of service which caught Pancho flat-footed and a backhand crosscourt.

Pancho, fighting, pulled the game to deuce. Schroeder got a fourth set point with a ball that hit the net cord and fell limply—unreturnably—on the other side.

On the next point, Pancho punched a volley down the line. The crowd cheered. Gonzales saw chalk fly and thought he had made another save.

"Out!" bellowed the linesman. It was Schroeder's set after 73 minutes. Gonzales' broad shoulders slumped in despair.

At the start of the second set, Schroeder got permission to don spiked shoes. It was near late afternoon and the grass was becoming slippery. Gonzales had the same privilege but no spikes. Schroeder won the set in 24 minutes 6–2 and now had an imposing two set lead.

The picture looked bleak for Pancho. "Nobody gives this guy two sets and beats him," he reasoned to himself. He decided his only chance was to go for broke. He started hitting all out.

The strategy worked. The savagery of Gonzales' attack seemed to stun Schroeder, who was also experiencing a natural letdown. Pancho won four games in a row and took the set 6–1.

In the dressing room during intermission, Gonzales was consoled by his friend, Frank Shields, later a Davis Cup captain.

"That was a tough first set to lose," Shields said.

"I'll get him," Gonzales vowed determinedly.

"That's the spirit," said Shields, slapping Gonzales on the shoulder as he returned to the center court.

Pancho got an early break in the fourth set and went into a 3–1 lead. His service was murderous and Schroeder never came close to cracking it. Gonzales won the set 6–2. Now the match was level.

Going into the fifth and decisive set, Gonzales was aware that the scrappy Schroeder was the best fifth-set player in the world. But he realized, too, that his own confidence was booming.

The fifth set went with service through the first eight games and then Pancho gained the first break in the ninth game with two magnificent backhand returns of service. He led 5–4.

Serving, Gonzales fell behind 15–30 with a nervous double-fault but brought the score to 30–30 by forcing Ted into a volleying error. As excitement skyrocketed, Pancho fell behind again 30–40, deuced the score a second time and moved to match point with a perfect placement.

On the next point, the two engaged in a long rally before Schroeder hit a scorcher down the line. There was a moment that seemed like hours to Pancho.

Then the lineman yelled, "Out!" It was Pancho's match —perhaps the one he remembers most in a long and illustrious career.

FIVE

1

v

The Day Black Lightning Struck at Forest Hills

As twice winner of the U.S. National ladies' championship and two-time victor at Wimbledon, Althea Gibson, the plucky Negro girl from Harlem, figured in many great matches. But none was so dramatic or significant as one she lost in two nervous, hectic days at Forest Hills in 1950.

Tennis, a snobbish sport, was one of the last bastions of lily white competition.

For several years Negroes had sought to gain entrance to the famed outdoor championships. But the Eastern grass court clubs, West Side Tennis Club of Forest Hills included, had managed to restrict them by a subtle gentlemen's agreement. The answer to unwanted entries was always the same: "Refused. Insufficient information."

However, by the summer of 1950 outside pressure became so intense, particularly from a former champion, Alice Marble, that U. S. Lawn Tennis Association officials were unable to keep Miss Gibson at bay.

She was 21, a student at Florida A&M, a big, strong girl who had shown capabilities in Negro tournaments and in the National Indoor, a rather obscure meet held in a barn-like structure where she had played her first matches against white opponents.

In August, she was advised that she was one of fifty-two women whose entries had been accepted for the National Championship. She was the first of her race to swing a racket in the grass court event.

Althea had never seen Forest Hills. She asked a friend, Sarah Palfrey Cooke, a former champion, to show her around and obtain permission for her to hit a few practice balls. During the tournament, she stayed in Harlem.

Althea's first round match was with Barbara Knapp of England. The event was assigned to one of the field courts, Number 14, while Ginger Rogers, the Hollywood star, played a mixed doubles match on the club house court. In virtual privacy Althea defeated Miss Knapp 6–2, 6–2. This qualified her to face Louise Brough, a tall California blonde who earlier in the year had won her third straight Wimbledon title.

Now Althea had her big chance. Because of Miss Brough's stature, the match was held in the stadium. Althea was so tense she couldn't eat any lunch. A friend came up to her and commented, "Relax, Althea, you look scared to death."

If Miss Gibson was nervous before the match started, she was a candidate for a strait jacket once the first ball was hit. Her timing was badly off and she moved awkwardly. Miss Brough raced through the first set 6–1 and appeared headed for an easy victory.

Althea gritted her teeth and started hitting all out. She raked the sidelines with her big forehand shots. She soon had her favored opponent on the run.

"Knock her out of there!" a spectator yelled to Miss Brough.

This only increased Althea's determination. She won the second set 6–3 to tie the match. Word spread and fans gathered to watch the drama. About this time, however, a storm cloud appeared overhead.

Miss Brough won the first three games of the final set but Althea, fighting hard, slashed back with three service breaks to take a 7–6 lead.

She was within four points—one game—of scoring one of the biggest upsets of the generation. Then the bottom seemed to drop out of the heavens. Lightning flashed, thunder rumbled and rain fell in buckets.

The drenched players ran for the locker rooms. The fans scurried to shelter underneath the stands.

A bolt of lightning toppled one of the giant concrete eagles above the stadium but luckily no one was beneath as it crashed to the ground. Not that the storm didn't bear consequences. Although the skies cleared, the match was postponed until the following day.

"The delay was the worst thing that could have happened to me," Althea said later in her autobiography. "It gave me a whole evening—and the next morning, too, for that matter to think about the match. By the time I got through reading the morning papers I was a nervous wreck."

When play was resumed, she noted that Miss Brough was tense, too. But "the pressure on me was worse," Althea said.

Before a large gallery, with an unusually heavy turnout of newsmen, Miss Brough serving got to 40–0 in a hurry. Althea won the next two points with good passing shots but at 40–30 Louise scored on a half-volley for the game, tying the score 7–7.

In the next game, Althea fell behind 15–40, giving Miss Brough a setup at the net, serving a double-fault and banging a volley over the base line. She fought back to deuce it with a sizzling service ace and an overhead smash, then gained the advantage with another good service. Miss Brough, poised and machine-like, got back to deuce and won the game with two excellent service returns. She now led 8–7.

With service, Miss Brough raced to a 40–15 lead, with two match points, in the sixteenth game. Althea saved one match point with a good lob which Louise hit out of court. But on the next point, Althea hit a backhand out of court.

In eleven minutes, Louise Brough, the three-time Wimbledon queen, had escaped defeat at the hands of a nervous Negro girl from Harlem. The score was 6–1, 3–6, 9–7.

But it was a historic moment for Forest Hills, and the gallery knew it would hear more of the big girl who had finally cracked the racial barrier.

Of the match, David Eisenberg, writing in the New York *Journal-American*, said:

"I have sat in on many dramatic moments in sports, but few were more thrilling than Miss Gibson's performance against Miss Brough. Not because great tennis was played. It wasn't. But because of the great try by this lonely, and nervous, colored girl, and because of the manner in which the elements robbed her of her great triumph."

FIVE
1
VI

He Threw in the Towel — And Still Won

In sports jargon tossing in the towel is usually an expression of surrender. It proved to mean just the opposite on a chilly, rainy December day in Melbourne, Australia, in 1953.

The United States was attempting to wrest the Davis

Cup from the Aussies, who under captain Harry Hopman, had seized it in 1950 and refused to let go. Now, however, Australia's grip seemed to be loosening.

The Yanks, under freshman captain William F. Talbert, had forged into a 2–1 lead with a doubles victory by Vic Seixas and Tony Trabert. They needed only to win one of the two remaining singles to achieve the triumph, and everything seemed to be in their favor.

The Australians had lost their top Davis Cup aces, Frank Sedgman and Ken McGregor, to professional ranks and were trying to turn back the challenge with a pair of nineteen-year-olds making their first appearance in cup competition, Lew Hoad and Ken Rosewall.

Hoad was sent against Trabert in the fourth match. If Trabert won, what happened to Seixas and Rosewall wouldn't matter.

It was a gray day and rain began falling shortly after the first ball was struck in the well-known Kooyong Stadium. Nevertheless, the stands were filled to capacity and some fifty newsmen, sitting out in the open at one end of the horseshoe, continued to peck out their reports on soaked sheets of paper.

From the beginning it was obvious that a stupendous match was in prospect.

Trabert was a big, strong boy from Cincinnati with powerful legs and the arms and shoulders of a halfback, although his game in college was basketball. He was a heavyweight hitter. His drive off both forehand and backhand were like cannon shots. Every time he hit the ball he gave the appearance of trying to knock his opponent down.

Hoad also was a powerhouse, a stocky youngster with a blacksmith's build and murderer's heart whose game featured blockbuster serves and smoking volleys. At nineteen, he was four years Trabert's junior.

The first set was a knockdown, drag-out affair that hinted

at what was to come. The two players served with such blinding force that there wasn't a break for twenty-two games. Then Hoad, with a series of slashing returns, forced Trabert into errors, achieved a breakthrough and took the marathon after an hour and a half 13–11. Discouraged, the American let the second set get away 6–3.

On the sidelines, Talbert in rain gear put an arm around Tony's shoulders and spoke to him at length. The captain was also a native of Cincinnati, a close friend as well as a longtime teacher and adviser of his Davis Cup charge. The pep talk had its effect. Playing brilliantly, hitting out on almost every shot and taking the initiative completely away from his adversary, Trabert won the next two sets, 6–2, 6–3.

Although rain was falling steadily by this time and both players had donned spikes, not a spectator abandoned his seat. Hopman for the first time showed concern. Hoad looked damp, disheveled and disheartened.

When the final set began, most of the Australians in the stands believed their "bloke" had had it. Trabert was stronger and fresher. He moved with a quick pace as if anxious to finish the kill. Hoad became slow and sluggish.

Yet for all his loss of confidence, the Aussie had one big weapon left—his service. He still could deliver his cannonball at 110 miles an hour, and under the wet conditions it was hard to handle.

The last set began going with service, 1–1, 2–2, 3–3, 4–4. Observers noted that Hoad was having trouble holding service, frequently getting down as much as 0–30 and twice having break point against him. Trabert, on the other hand, was serving confidently and powerfully, winning most of his games at love or with loss of no more than a single point. It appeared only a matter of time before Hoad would crumble.

The end seemed near in the eleventh game. The score

was 5–5, Hoad serving. Lew lost the first point. On the second, they engaged in a long rally before the American hit a sharply angled volley near the net. Hoad lunged for it, falling face first on the wet grass and almost overturning Hopman's chair.

There was a gasp from the crowd and Hopman sprang up, wearing a grim look. Hoad lay on the ground a moment, then got to his feet laboriously, his white attire smeared with mud. Laughing, the Aussie captain flung a towel in his player's face and shaking off his bewilderment, Hoad broke into a big grin. Laughter echoed through the stands as the tension relaxed.

Down 0–30, Hoad rallied to save his service and then went to work on Trabert's delivery. He had been given a reprieve and now was a new man, hitting, moving, playing every shot aggressively. Two spectacular returns enabled him to bring the score to deuce. Trabert, upset and unsteady, sent two services into the net. Double-fault. The crowd cheered. The Australians were within a single point of preventing a loss of the Davis Cup. Trabert served again, Hoad belted it back at Trabert's feet and Tony hit a half-volley into the net.

That was it. Hoad was the winner 13–11, 6–3, 2–6, 3–6, 7–5 and Rosewall went on to beat Seixas in the decisive match the next day.

There were tears in Trabert's eyes when Ted Schroeder brought him into the television booth after the match. He was disappointed and bitter. "I don't know why they had to cheer when I served a double-fault," he said of the Australian crowd. "They're a pack of animals." Later he was sorry and apologized.

In time Hoad became one of the world's outstanding players and signed a $125,000 contract with Jack Kramer, while Hopman went on to mastermind thirteen Davis Cup victories in the next fifteen years and ensure his legend as a tactical genius.

The Davis Cup is the symbol of world tennis supremacy and, as such, attracts the attention of presidents and kings. Richard M. Nixon was Vice President when he visited and spoke to the U.S. Junior Davis Cup team at Forest Hills (upper left). President Calvin Coolidge made the draw on the White House lawn in Washington, D. C., in 1924 before diplomats (upper right). The cup serves as a backdrop as Big Bill Tilden congratulates his Australian victim, Hawkes, after a 1923 match at Forest Hills (lower left). The U.S. 1968 Davis Cup team fondles the enlarged trophy after recapturing it from the Australians in 1968. Stan Smith, Clark Graebner, Arthur Ashe and Bobby Lutz were the heroes (lower right).

The greatest rivalries for the Davis Cup have involved teams from Australia and the United States. At the top left, John Bromwich and Adrian Quist of Australia, U.S. Captain Walter Pate and American stars Joel Hunt and Jack Kramer (left to right) gather around the big trophy after the 1939 Challenge Round. Three captains gathered around the cup after it was returned from Australia in 1954 (left). They are Walter Pate, Alrick Man and William F. Talbert. The largest crowd ever to witness a Davis Cup series — more than 26,000 — saw the Americans beat the Australians at White City Club in Sydney, Australia, in 1954. An aerial view of the crowd is shown below.

USLTA

European

Members of the U.S. tennis team hold
the Wightman Cup which they
won at Wimbledon June 16, 1962,
with a 4-2 victory over the British.
They are, left to right, Karen
Hantze Susman, Margaret Varner,
Mrs. Margaret duPont (captain),
Darlene Hard and Nancy Richey.

Edwin Levick   Wide World Photos   Marvin M. Greene

Tennis is one of the most stylized of games, yet each of the great champions has had an individual specialty that set him apart. Alice Marble (shown in the sequence at the left) had a tremendously effective service for a woman, with good pace and topspin. Big Bill Tilden (upper left) was a master of all shots but possessed a picture forehand. Note its similarity with that of Arthur Ashe, Jr. (top center).

Pancho Gonzales (upper right) hit his high forehand with tremendous power. Donald Budge's backhand (lower left) was one of the most feared shots in tennis. But it was no more deadly than that of Rod Laver, shown hitting a backhand (lower center). Arthur Ashe prepares to unleash a service which had been officially clocked at 112 miles per hour (lower right).

Wide World Photos   Wide World Photos   World Tennis Magazine

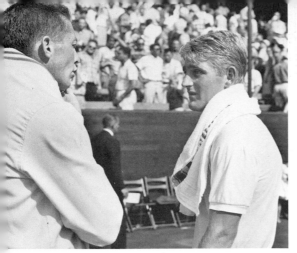

Wide World Photos

Wide World Photos

Australians consider Jack Crawford one of the greatest in a long and continuing line of tennis stars. His style was classic, his temperament impeccable. Crawford is shown (left) hitting one of his brilliant back-hands. Tony Trabert of the U.S. and Lew Hoad of Australia (upper center) in one of the most historic Davis Cup matches at Melbourne, Australia, in 1953. No less dramatic was the victory of 32-year-old Jaroslav Drobny, left (upper right photo), over Australia's Ken Rosewall, with whom he is shown shaking hands after the 1954 Wimbledon final. Billie Jean King (lower left) and Nancy Richey (lower right) engaged in many hard-fought matches, but none to compare with their great indoor duel at Madison Square Garden in New York in 1969.

Edwin Levick

Wide World Photos

Thelner Hoover

USLTA

Prim in stiff celluloid collar, black tie and mustache, H. W. Slocum, Jr., (upper left) president of the U.S. Lawn Tennis Association from 1892 through 1894, seemed to represent the inflexible rigidity of the game. Perry T. Jones (lower left) ruled the Southern California section and was a power in the national structure for years, developing many of the game's outstanding stars. Robert Malaga of Cleveland (lower right), a live wire promoter, served as a departure when he was named executive secretary of the U. S. Lawn Tennis Association in the mid-1960's.

However, tennis was moving away from the amateur associations into the hands of the pros. Promoter Jack Kramer introduced two of his latest pro signees, Earl Buchholz (left) and Barry MacKay (right) at a New York luncheon (upper right photo).

The pro tour was dirty canvas under lights and bright sunshine sifting through palm trees. The pros were laughing it up in this scene (above) in Nassau, The Bahamas, with Pancho Gonzales, Jack Kramer, Wendell Niles, Ellsworth Vines and Don Budge (left to right).

Margaret Court of Australia, the
world's Number One woman player
entering the 1970's, shunned lace
panties and frilly attire. The
statuesque Australian girl (left) wore
a simple white blouse and skirt as
she swept past all opponents with a

devastating attack. In 1949, Gertrude
"Gorgeous Gussy" Moran (above)
shocked and thrilled the Wimbledon
audiences with her sexy lace attire,
which ultimately became standard
for the girls on the circuit.

As tennis moved into the 1970's, the United States looked to a rangy, hard-hitting Californian, Stan Smith (left), as the player most likely to break Rod Laver's stranglehold on world honors, but Smith's career was interrupted by a call to armed service. The last American to win at Wimbledon, Chuck McKinley (center), retired and went into the stock brokerage business in New York. He is shown at the right when he was at the top of his game.

Nancy Richey, a little school marm from San Angelo, Texas, fought her way to the top of U.S. women's rankings in 1970 and then abandoned her throne by joining in a women's rebellion. John Newcombe of Australia (right, close up and in action) was viewed as one of the logical successors to Rod Laver's throne, when and if the little red-head elected to relinquish it.

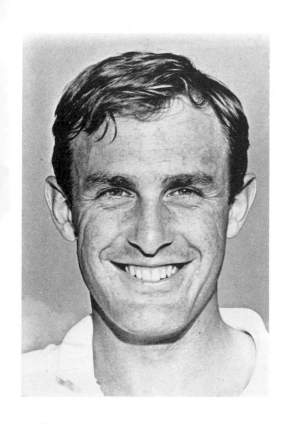

Max P. Haas

Dick Savitt (left) destined to win Wimbledon, and Herbie Flam, slated to become U.S. Open king, probably never dreamed they would reach such heights when they posed for this picture as promising juniors.

"Old Hoppy's towel did it," the Aussies chortled. "If it hadn't been for that towel, we would have been a cooked goose."

FIVE
1
VII
The Greatest Wimbledon of All

To the hardy Wimbledon faithful who saw Ellsworth Vines demolish E. (Booby) Maier of Spain, Jack Crawford of Australia and Bunny Austin of England in the final three rounds of the 1932 tournament, there seemed little doubt about the outcome of the 1933 men's title match.

The gaunt, tousle-haired Californian was back with his blazing cannonball service, his killing smashes and thunderbolt drives that left no margin for error. His opponent was Jack Crawford, a big, good-looking Australian and the best player to come from the bottom of the world since Gerald Patterson in the early 1920's. But to most observers he was a lamb being prepared for slaughter.

Crawford, however, was of another mind. In a poised, tactical masterpiece the Aussie pulled an upset in a match that has been acclaimed the greatest men's singles final to ever occur on Wimbledon's hallowed center court.

The score stood at 2–2 in the fifth set and Vines was a point away from a break. The packed gallery had sat tensely through more than two hours of brilliant tennis. Vines had won the first set 6–4 after leading 5–2. The second set followed service for nineteen games. In the twentieth Vines began making errors—"great risks make errors necessary"—and Crawford won 11–9. The third set was all Crawford, the fourth all Vines and now the match had reached a critical phase. A single point and Crawford's tremendous effort would apparently go down the drain. The fans overwhelmingly favored the underdog. He was, after all, the first British Commonwealth citizen since Patterson to gain the men's final.

Crawford served. Vines, returning sharply off his backhand, moved to the forecourt. The Aussie returned to the Yank's forehand. It was a low shot but it should have been put away easily. However, Vines charged the line boldly and missed by two inches. There was a momentary hush and then the stadium roared with approval.

Crawford held service and so did Vines as the score went to 3–3. The Australian held again and in the eighth game Vines hit a forehand two inches over the line. The linesman failed to call it. The crowd hooted. Crawford, displaying superb sportsmanship, raised his racket and signalled the fans to be quiet.

The score went to 4–4 as Vines whipped across three clean aces on service.

Jumping up and down, spectators tossed hats in the air. Newsmen reported that several women fainted, including Crawford's wife.

One commentator observed: "It was such a tremendous match, with so great an effort on the part of both men, that it would have been the fairest thing to stop it with the score 4–4 in the fifth."

But that was not the name of the game, and the battle continued.

Crawford fought to hold service in the ninth game and then, rising to the occasion, grabbed the initiative in the tenth. Instead of standing back and trying to block Vines' blistering cannonball service, the Australian moved three to five feet inside the baseline and met the delivery on the rise.

Vines' service had been clocked at 128 miles per hour, faster than Pancho Gonzales' biggest gun at its best. Once during the match a Vines service hit a ballboy on the chest and sent the lad spinning head over heels. His power was frightening.

With the score two sets each and Crawford leading 5–4 on service, Vines went to the baseline. Crawford returned a screamer and Vines netted. Score: 0–15. Another big service, another sharp return, another Vines volley into the net—0–30. The crowd was going wild.

On the next service, Crawford sent the ball down the line for a passing shot. Vines was down 0–40 and the Australian had three tries for the match. He needed only one.

A discouraged Vines hit a third volley into the net. He was broken at love. The match was over. Crawford was the king of Wimbledon.

Almost everyone—even Vines himself, a gentleman to the end—said he deserved it. Both players produced excellent tennis. Crawford proved a tactical genius in handling Vines' superior power.

None of the British Royal Family witnessed the titanic duel but former King Alfonso of Spain was among the gallery. He congratulated both players afterward.

Veteran observers compared the match with the memorable battle between R. N. Williams and Little Bill Johnston in the 1916 U.S. final, won by Williams in five sets. It combined brilliant tennis, drama, sportsmanship and a popular victory.

Normally blasé Wimbledon was left limp as a dish rag.

FIVE
1
VIII

Was Helen Really Sick? Or Just a Quitter?

It stands to reason that in the fifteen years between 1923 and 1938, when Helen Wills Moody won seven U.S. National titles and eight Wimbledons, the girl in the green eyeshade played scores of matches marked by brilliance and high drama. Ironically the two the world most remembers and talks about are two she lost.

One was the historic meeting with France's Suzanne Lenglen. The other was her stunning walkout on Helen Jacobs in the final of the 1933 U.S. Championships at Forest Hills.

Tennis buffs who witnessed the incident disagreed over the reasons behind the uncharacteristic move. Was Mrs.

Moody really in pain or merely seeking an "alibi" for an inevitable defeat?

Subsequent events indicated she was probably very ill and four years later she wrote in her autobiography that she had been on the verge of collapse.

The two Helens—Wills, tall, dark-haired and coldly methodical, and Jacobs, stocky, blonde and outgoing—were natural rivals. They both came from the San Francisco bay area. Both had the same teacher, Pop Fuller. Both had the same ambition: to be the best woman player in the world.

Helen Wills was the older and had two years of big time experience behind her when she crushed the younger Helen in their first meeting 6–0, 6–0. It was a practice match in Berkeley arranged by Fuller. Miss Wills' domination continued as the two women followed the circuit from Los Angeles to Wimbledon, Forest Hills to Paris, but the dogged Miss Jacobs kept cutting the margin. At last in 1932 she broke through to win her first U.S. women's crown, but there was little satisfaction. The older Helen, now Mrs. Moody, did not compete.

The situation was different in 1933. Mrs. Moody came back in full style. Miss Jacobs was being hailed as the principal threat to Queen Helen's throne. They stormed their way to the final at Forest Hills.

There wasn't a great deal of excitement over the match. The weather had been atrocious and the event had been postponed several times. Mrs. Moody was favored to win comfortably as in the past. The West Side Stadium was less than half full.

Miss Jacobs soon made it clear she had no intention of being a pushover. Covering the court well, chopping and chipping away at Mrs. Moody's stronger shots, she captured the first set 8–6. The reporters lounging in the marquee suddenly became awake. It was only the third set Mrs. Moody had lost since 1926.

The older Helen regained her poise, and pounding away with powerful drives from the backcourt, she levelled the match by taking the second set 6–3.

Starting the third set, Mrs. Moody dropped her service as Miss Jacobs sliced back sharp returns and followed the shots to the net. The younger Helen held and then gaining confidence broke the older's service a second time with an aggressive forecourt attack.

The score was 3–0, Jacobs.

At this point, Mrs. Moody strode to the umpire's chair and put on her sweater.

"I am sorry, my back pains me, I cannot go on," she said tersely.

That was all she said. Wearing a long coat, her familiar eyeshade pulled low, she strode to the dressing room. She declined an interview.

The fans were stunned. The press representatives recovered quickly enough from their shock to give the former court queen a thorough lambasting, accusing her of being a poor sport, a quitter and ungracious.

"At least, Mrs. Moody could have gone through the motions of playing the last three games, even if in pain, just to give Miss Jacobs the victory she deserved," said one critic. "She has denied Miss Jacobs the hour in the sun for which she has fought for so many years." Others echoed the sentiment.

Mrs. Moody added fuel to the criticism by agreeing to play a women's doubles match scheduled later in the day. This led detractors to say that the injury could not have been as severe as she pretended.

However, Queen Helen went back to the Pacific Coast after the match, underwent a back operation and played no competitive tennis for several months.

In 1937, writing her autobiography, Mrs. Moody for the first time gave a full explanation:

"I knew it was the end when the stadium began to swim

around in the air, and I saw Miss Jacobs and the court on a slant. I managed to get up to the umpire's stand and said, 'can't go on.'

"If I had fainted on the court, it would have been thought a more conclusive finish to the match in the eyes of many of the onlookers, for then they would have been convinced that I could not continue. However, the choice was instinctive rather than premeditated. Had I been able to think clearly, I might have chosen to remain. Animals, and often humans, however, prefer to suffer in a quiet, dark place.

"It was unfortunate that Miss Jacobs could not have a complete victory, as it would have been had I been able to remain a little longer on the court."

FIVE

1

IX

Hitler Called but Budge Didn't Hear

Back in the mid-1930's when Adolf Hitler made a telephone call, governments trembled and sometimes nations fell.

There was no such cataclysmic result when the feared Fuehrer rang the club house at Wimbledon in the summer of 1937 and asked to speak to his subject, Baron Gottfried von Cramm.

Von Cramm, Germany's top tennis ace, was pale and obviously shaken when he emerged from the club house after the conversation with his leader. History never recorded exactly what was said but no one, not even the baron himself, ever denied that the gist of it was a stern order from the Fuehrer:

"Win for the Fatherland."

The entire sports world had its eyes on Wimbledon's center court that tense, steamy day. The top tennis players of the United States and Germany had battled their way into the Davis Cup Inter-Zone final and now were face-to-face to see which country would challenge cup-holding Britain for the international trophy.

The event had even greater significance. Britain's brilliant Fred Perry had turned professional and there appeared little doubt that the winner of the Inter-Zone would go on to become Davis Cup champion. Perry's departure had also opened up competition for the world's Number One amateur title and Budge and Von Cramm were leading candidates.

In Germany Hitler was displaying his might with airplanes, tanks and goose-stepping troops and was proclaiming the superiority of the Aryan race. As in the Berlin Olympics the year before, he was continually exhorting German athletes to prove it.

Tension in the Inter-Zone final mounted when the United States and Germany split the first four matches and the decision rested on the final match—a best-of-five set duel—between the classy, royal-born Von Cramm, one of Europe's best, and Budge, the hard-hitting redhead from California.

The result was what many observers rate as the greatest match ever played in Davis Cup competition.

Budge and Von Cramm split the first four sets and the German shot to the front 4–1 in the fifth. America's hopes hung by a fragile thread.

"I realized I would lose the match unless I took drastic measures," Budge recalled. "I made up my mind that if Von Cramm missed his first service I would attack his second service and go to the net behind it."

The strategy worked. Budge held service and proceeded to break Von Cramm at love. Then he held again to knot the score 4–4. The match started following service. It went 5–5 and 6–6.

Finally in the eleventh game, Budge attacking furiously pulled off another break and led 7–6, needing only to hold his delivery to win the match and the series. But it wasn't that easy. The German battled like a tiger.

Budge described it this way:

"Five times I had match point and five times I couldn't

make it. Then came the sixth match point and the nervous strain was something fantastic. The crowd was so quiet I am sure they could hear us breathing. My frustration at failing to clinch my many opportunities was mounting.

"Finally, on that sixth match point, we had a long rally in the forecourt. Von Cramm lobbed over my head. I ran back and returned the ball. He hit a forehand cross-court wide to the forehand and came to the net. I tore after the ball. I was afraid I'd never reach it. I stretched and finally took a desperate swipe at it. As I swung I lost my footing and hit the ground on all fours.

"As I lay on the grass, I realized the ball felt pretty good on the racket. I looked up in time to see Von Cramm try to reach it on his right-hand side and miss it. It was the most beautiful fall of my life."

Budge won 6–8, 5–7, 6–4, 6–2, 8–6.

A detailed chart kept by an English reporter, Wallace Myers, showed that Budge had 115 placements and 19 aces in the match and only 55 errors. Von Cramm's box score showed 105 placements, 17 aces and 65 errors. Most top players consider it a good day if they can score on 40 percent of their placements.

The match didn't end until 8:30. Budge recalled that an hour and a half later, after he had rested and showered, he found hundreds of spectators still milling around the courts, discussing the dramatic duel.

They said Hitler never called back.

FIVE
————
1
————
x

Nancy Richey's Unbelievable Comeback

There was a stir of excitement among the 7,300 tennis buffs gathered in the new Madison Square Garden that chill March 29 evening, 1968 for the semifinals of the Garden Challenge Trophy Tournament. They anticipated that a small fragment of tennis history might be made, and they were not disappointed.

The great players of the amateur world were on hand—
Roy Emerson of Australia, Tom Okker of the Netherlands,
Arthur Ashe and Clarke Graebner of the United States—but
all the attention was focused on a pair of ladies—Billie Jean
King, the Wimbledon champion recognized as the best
woman player in the world, and Nancy Richey, a pert, baseline scrapper from Texas, who were scheduled to clash in
the semifinals.

Although they had been competing for Number One ranking among U.S. women players, they had not been on the
same court together for three and a half years. Those close to
the situation said the explanation was quite simple: They
did not like each other and thus avoided a confrontation.

Nothing stimulates tennis interest like a good, old-
fashioned feud, particularly between ladies. This particular
one, like the intense rivalry back in the 1930's between Helen
Wills Moody and Helen Jacobs, had some foundation in fact
but it wasn't nearly as serious as it was made out to be by
clubhouse gossips. The two girls weren't apt to start scratching at each other's eyes.

Nancy had been top-ranked nationally in 1964 but in
1965 there was such an argument on the floor of the U.S.
Lawn Tennis Association convention that delegates compro-
mised by naming Nancy and Billie Jean both Number One.
This infuriated Billie Jean, who felt her performance in
the major tournaments had earned her the position. Nancy
wasn't so happy, either.

The styles of the two girls were about as opposite as they
could be. Nancy, coached by her professional father, preferred clay. She became almost unbeatable on the slow surface, dominating the National Clay Court Championships.
She was a baseline player, depending on accuracy and
steadiness to wear down her opponents. Billie Jean was at
her best on grass or hard courts. She attacked relentlessly,
rushing to the net, volleying and smashing for winners.
Usually while Billie Jean was pursuing her career on the

grass court circuit, Nancy was playing the clay tournaments.

Now they were together, eyeball-to-eyeball, and few in the big, brightly-lighted arena felt that little Nancy had much of a chance against the hard-hitting Californian. Yet in the last match between the two—in the Nationals at Forest Hills in September 1964—Nancy had beaten Billie Jean in the quarter-finals 6–4, 6–4. More than that, she had come out ahead in five of their previous six matches.

"Nancy has the jinx on Billie Jean," a handful of observers said that evening at Madison Square Garden. "She has Billie Jean psyched."

"No, it's different now," countered Billie Jean's supporters. "Billie Jean's game has matured since the days she was losing to Nancy."

The match started as a majority of the crowd had expected. Billie Jean's service was crackling. She banged the ball into court, stormed to the net and put away volley after volley. It was a neutral surface—a stretched green rubber court, faster than clay but not as fast as grass. The bounce was consistent.

Billie Jean won the first set, appearing to be playing well within herself, and she built up a commanding 5–1 lead in the second.

"See, I told you," chortled her army of admirers. Even Miss Richey's most faithful backers despaired.

Nevertheless, Nancy, her freckled face a mask of grimness, managed to break Billie Jean for the first time in the seventh game of the second set and then hold her own service to make the score 5–3.

The cause still seemed hopeless for the Texan who, completely without emotion, stuck to the base line and continued to rifle shots down the lines. Billie Jean served well in the ninth game, although Nancy was more stubborn. The score went to deuce, then advantage—match point for Mrs. King.

At this stage, there was a spirited rally. Billie Jean went to the net behind one of Miss Richey's short returns and parked there for the kill. Nancy sent up a shallow lob that drifted only as far back as the service line. Billie Jean leaped for the overhead smash. This should have been the end of the match. Instead, she caught the ball a bit late and it hit just beyond the back line.

Now it was deuce again, and you could hear the crowd squirming. Given a new lease on life, Nancy hit a tremendous forehand down the line for the advantage and then forced Billie Jean into a volleying error. The score was now 5–4 with Nancy serving. She was back in the match.

The little Texan, her confidence buoyed, became a siege gun. Seldom did a shot get past her racket as she ran from side to side, playing the ball deep into the corners, hitting wicked angles and forcing her rival into errors. Billie Jean's powerful game collapsed. The harder she struggled to reverse the trend, the more frustrated and helpless she became.

Finally, Nancy scored on a cross-court backhand. The match was over, Miss Richey winning 4–6, 7–5, 6–0. Nancy tossed her racket high in the air. Billie Jean, crestfallen but never showing her misery, walked to the net and gently tapped Nancy on the head with her steel racket.

It was an astounding, unbelievable match, the last one played by Billie Jean as an amateur. Shortly afterward, she signed a contract with George MacCall's professional troupe and began a new career as a performer.

No champion in tennis history, at the prime of his or her career as was Billie Jean, ever suffered such an overwhelming defeat. From the match point which she smashed over the line, a total of 51 points were played to the match's conclusion and Billie Jean won only 12 of them. Trailing 4–6, 1–5, Miss Richey reeled off the last 12 games in a row, in effect—throwing out the games played before—beating the world's top woman player 6–0, 6–0.

"I blew it, I lost my confidence, I let it get away," Billie Jean said afterward. "This was my most satisfying win," declared Nancy.

The Unchanging Principles of Play

Unlike golf and football, which down through the years have often altered their rules, tennis has clung tenaciously to the standards established in those formative years when a plethora of varying equipment and rules created confusion.

For the last three quarters of a century the court has been rectangular and of consistent size, the net three feet high at the center and three and a half feet at the posts, players have served from behind the base line into a square service area, and the scoring has been the same used by monks in the Middle Ages.

In recent years, however, there has been pressure for change, mostly from those who desire a simplified scoring system and from those who would like to take some of the sting out of the big serve and volley game.

France's Jean Borotra, one of the famed Musketeers of the late 1920's and early 1930's, was one of the most militant advocates of changing the service. The cannonball power and finality of the modern delivery reduces the number of rallies and deprives the game of excitement, he insisted.

A war against the scoring system was waged by James H. Van Alen, master of the Newport Casino and originator of the Van Alen Simplified Scoring System knowns as VASSS. The VASSS system was similar to that of badminton or racquets, and its chief attribute was its elimination of prolonged deuced games and sets.

The pros preferred the system because it enabled them to schedule matches within an alotted time. However, though many tournaments experimented with simplified scoring, no general permanent changes have as yet occurred.

The first lawn tennis regulations were devised by Major Walter C. Wingfield, the originator of the sport. When the major went about commercializing his invention, he included a list of rules along with each set of equipment.

The regulations called for an hourglass-shaped court, narrower at the net than at the base lines. At first the court was 21 feet wide at the net, 30 feet at the base line and 30 feet deep. Later, the major altered these specifications to 39 feet wide at the base line and 42 feet deep on each side. The net was 4 feet, 8 inches high.

Players were required to serve from a small crease in the middle of each court, hitting the ball beyond instead of inside, the service line into the back half of the court. The receiver could return it on the first bounce or with a volley before it touched the ground. The rackets were similar to those used in court tennis and the balls were hard rubber without a covering.

The major favored the scoring system used in racquets. Fifteen points constituted a game.

As the popularity of tennis grew throughout England, it was necessary to decide upon uniform standards. Players met at Lord's and on May 24, 1875, a set of rules was made public by the Marylebone Cricket Club.

Each court was to be 30 feet wide at the baseline, 24 feet at the net—thus retaining the hourglass figure—with a depth of 39 feet. The net was raised to 5 feet at the posts and 4 feet in the middle. The center line ran from base line to base line. The service lines were 26 feet from the net. The player had to serve from the back line instead of the crease at the service line and the service could no longer be volleyed. In doubles, a ball served into the wrong court could be played by the partner. Scoring was on the racquets system.

Meanwhile in America, players in different parts of the East used varying rules. Some courts were hourglass-shaped, others rectangular. Nets differed as much as a foot in height. Balls were of various sizes and weights. Some used court tennis scoring, others the racquets system.

Controversies arising from matches between clubs adhering to different standards compelled the United States Lawn Tennis Association to meet in New York on May 21, 1881, for the purpose of determining uniform rules. It was guided in its deliberations by the actions of the All-England Croquet and Lawn Tennis Club at Wimbledon which had decided upon a new set of regulations for its first championship in 1877.

Under these the court was rectangular, 78 feet from end to end and 27 feet wide. The net was lowered to 3 feet, 3 inches in the middle but was left at 5 feet at the posts. The service line remained 26 feet from the net. The server could straddle the base line. Court tennis scoring was adopted and never changed.

For its own first National Championship the USLTA adopted a rectangular court but changed the height of the net to 3 feet in the center and 4 feet at the posts. The barrier was lowered shortly afterward to 3½ feet at the posts. The ancient court tennis scoring was made official.

Changes since then have been minimal, most of them pertaining to such trivial points as whether a server might throw his leg over the base line or have both feet off the ground when his racket touches the ball.

The sport's fathers, often criticized for being too conservative, did make one very important change. They approved open tournaments.

But it took them ninety-five years to do it.

FIVE   *The U.S. Lawn Tennis Association —*
––––
3   *Stuffed Shirts?*

Perhaps no ruling body in sports has been subjected to as much public abuse as the U.S. Lawn Tennis Association.

Directors of the USLTA have been called "stuffed shirts," "old fogeys," men with "coach-and-corset" philosophies trying to move forward in the jet age. For half a century they were berated for banning open competition. They have been chided for closing their eyes to the evils of "shamateurism"; for demanding nineteenth century decorum of spectators; for clinging to an outmoded scoring system and forbidding players to wear anything but bridal white.

Yet these men behind the scenes, serving wholly from a love of the game, have weathered a succession of storms and managed somehow to preserve a sport topped only by soccer in international appeal.

For all their faults and frailties they have tried to give the game some sort of standardization and sanity in an age when it is relatively easy—figuratively and literally—to go sailing off to the moon.

It was for such a reason that the United States Lawn Tennis Association was formed in 1881.

Only seven years before, Mary Ewing Outerbridge had introduced the game at the Staten Island Cricket and Baseball Club. And almost at the same time—so close that historians still debate who hit the first tennis ball on American soil—a group of New Englanders were trying the new game out at a resort near Boston and soon lawn tennis was being played at Newport, Rhode Island; Plainfield, New Jersey; Philadelphia and even as far south as New Orleans.

There was only one trouble. Most people were playing under entirely different conditions. In one city the net might be three feet high in the middle while in another it was four feet. Some played with frail, long-handled rackets weighing only 13 ounces, others with war clubs weighing a pound or more. The balls varied in size. Some rules came in sets of tennis equipment from England, others were made up on the spot.

These discrepancies came to light when players from throughout the East were invited to participate in a tournament at the Staten Island Club beginning September 1, 1880. Among the guests were Dr. James Dwight and R. D. Sears from Boston, who claimed to have played the first lawn tennis in the United States at Nahant, a resort not far from Boston.

Arriving at the scene, Dwight and Sears were astonished. The balls were about two-thirds the size of those they were used to. The net, 3 feet in the middle and 3½ feet at the posts, was 6 inches lower at the sides than their own version. Some players were accustomed to the racquets style of scoring, with fifteen points making a game, while others scored in "fifteens," the court tennis system which later became the popular method.

Dwight and Sears were outraged. They refused to play in the singles tournament. They were persuaded to compete in the doubles, however, and proceeded to lose rather one-sidedly to W.M. Wood and A.F.H. Manning of Morristown, New Jersey—only adding to their chagrin.

Subsequent informal events and inter-club matches showed that everybody had local rules. This concerned a group of leaders from New York, Philadelphia and Boston who got together and decided that some standardization was imperative. E.H. Outerbridge of Staten Island was delegated to contact every tennis club known to be in operation and to invite them to send a representative to an organization meeting.

The following invitation was sent out the first week in May, 1881:

It is proposed to hold a lawn tennis convention in New York about the middle of May, for the purpose of adopting a code of rules and designating a standard ball, to govern and be used in all lawn tennis matches of tournaments throughout the United States, with a view of enabling all clubs or individual players to meet under equal advantages.

A permanent organization will be formed under the name of the United States Lawn Tennis Association in which name the rules adopted at the convention will be issued. All regularly organized tennis clubs, or other clubs which number tennis among their games, are invited to send representatives to the convention. Clubs may send from one to three representatives, but no club shall have more than three, and each club shall be entitled to one vote only. Representatives must bring credentials signed by the secretary of the club which they represent. The undersigned clubs have organized this movement at the urgent request of the most prominent players in their respective districts, and the necessity of such action will be appreciated by all who take an interest in inter-club, inter-state and international matches.

It is hoped, therefore, that all clubs will come forward and co-operate in this movement, so that it may be as universal as possible, and insure the adoption of one code of rules and one ball to govern the game of tennis throughout the whole of the United States. Clubs wishing to co-operate and be represented at the convention will please notify the representatives of either of the three organizing clubs, whose addresses are given below, and regular forms of application, together with further particulars, will be forwarded to them.

(Signed) All-Philadelphia Lawn Tennis Committee:
Clarence M. Clark, Chairman,
Germantown, Pa.
Staten Island Cricket and Base-Ball Club:
E. H. Outerbridge, Secretary,
No. 23 South Street, New York
Beacon Park Athletic Association:
James Dwight, Representative,
Boston, Mass.

The meeting was held in Room F at the Fifth Avenue Hotel in New York City, May 21, 1881. Nineteen clubs were represented with delegates and fifteen others with proxies. A constitution, prepared by E. H. Outerbridge, was adopted in fifteen minutes. A panel of officers was elected, consisting of Gen. R.S. Oliver of the Albany Tennis Club, president; Samuel Campbell of the Orange Tennis Club, vice-president; Clarence M. Clark, of the Young America Cricket Club, secretary and treasurer. Dwight was included on the Executive Committee.

The first convention adopted no official ball but ruled

that it should be from 2½ to 2%₁₆ inches in diameter and from 1⅞ to 2 ounces in weight. The height of the net was to be three feet in the center and four feet at each side. The service line was fixed at 21 instead of 22 feet from the net. It was held that all scoring should be in "fifteens."

Some of the other specifications were interesting. The decision of the umpire was to be final. The server was to stand with one foot beyond the base line and the other within or upon the base line. The net or the post could not be touched. A let service was counted a fault. The ball was not to be volleyed before it passed the net. Upon appeal, the umpire could direct players to change sides after every game in the deciding set.

The first national championship was awarded to Newport. The entrance fee was $5 for each club which was permitted to enter four singles players and two doubles teams. At the next annual meeting, it was reported that the total receipts for the tournament amounted to $250. Expenses were $245.68, leaving a profit of $4.32.

Meanwhile new clubs were admitted and new tournaments approved at such places as Beacon Park, the University of Pennsylvania, Orange Lawn Tennis Club, St. George's Cricket Club in Hoboken and the Young American Cricket Club in Philadelphia.

In the early conventions, the greatest controversy centered around the ball, which was still an uncovered, hollow sphere. The Ayres ball made in England drew criticism. The USLTA Executive Committee, however, could find no suitable substitute, and so made the ball official until an American version could be developed. This occurred in 1883 when a covered ball, a combination of examples presented by the New York Rubber Company, Peck and Snyder and Wright and Ditson, was accepted.

The question of amateurism was settled early by the following stipulation: None but amateurs shall be allowed to enter for any match played by this association." It was a rule that persevered against constant attack for seventy-five years.

The national championship was limited to members of associations belonging to the USLTA. Foreigners were not allowed to compete. In 1884 the USLTA voted down a move to admit Canadians. The treasurer's report showed a balance of $19.01, a profit resulting from the sale of used balls.

In the decade that followed, the presidency was passed from hand to hand but in 1894 Dr. James Dwight was elected for the fourth time and continued in office for the next seventeen years. Growth was rapid. A women's national championship was inaugurated. Invitation tournaments mushroomed. The National Indoor made its debut at the Seventh Regiment Armory, an arrangement that lasted more than fifty years. There was a constant modification of rules.

Originally concentrated in the East, the game moved across the country to the Midwest and the Pacific Coast. The Pacific Coast Association and the Southern California Association battled for territorial rights.

Southern California became a hot-bed of tennis talent, producing such stars as Ellsworth Vines, Jack Kramer, Ted Schroeder and Pancho Gonzales, and on the distaff side, Maureen (Little Mo) Connolly and Billie Jean Moffitt King. A key figure in this surge was a slick-haired, round-faced man named Perry T. Jones, director of the Los Angeles Tennis Club and longtime president of the Pacific Southwest Tennis Association.

Outside of his own little domain, where he was regarded as a czar, Perry Jones was a mysterious figure. He seldom came East for the National Championships. He was quiet and reserved, not given to public statements. Stories emanated from the West about his white flannels and dapper straw sailor hat, his stern discipline with juniors and his iron-fisted organization.

For decades, Jones wielded a powerful influence in the workings of the USLTA but the strength of the Eastern vote bloc always was sufficient to keep the East in power. That was the case until 1957 when a combination of Pacific Coast, Midwest and Southern delegates pulled a coup in the convention and for the first time seized the reins.

Victor Denny of Seattle, Washington was elected president. Changes were swift and surprising. Without so much as a phone call's notice, Denny came to New York and announced that Perry Jones would be the new Davis Cup captain, succeeding William F. Talbert, who had served the previous five years. The action stirred a tempest of protest. Talbert, twice a runner-up in the National singles and winner of numerous doubles titles with Gardnar Mulloy, had been very successful, taking the American team into the Challenge Round five times and winning the cup in 1954 against overpowering odds.

Denny also set up committees to explore the open tennis controversy, a work carried on by his successors, George Barnes of Chicago; Edward Turville of St. Petersburg, Florida; Martin Tressel of Pittsburg and Robert Kelleher of Los Angeles.

Whether professionals should be allowed to compete against amateurs became a much discussed issue in the early 1930's, but conservative factions both in the United States and abroad managed to kill off any serious move in that direction.

In 1960 the U.S. Lawn Tennis Association joined with Britain, France and Australia in a campaign to push through open competition and to grant autonomy to the individual countries. The Soviet Union block with the support of the smaller nations managed to defeat the move by a narrow margin.

Kelleher, a tall Los Angeles attorney who had led the United States to a Davis Cup victory over Australia in 1963, took over the drive when he succeeded to the presidency in 1967. By this time the All-England Club, sponsor of the famed Wimbledon tournament, had determined to open the doors to professionals with or without the approval of the International Federation.

The British had the backing of Kelleher and progressive forces in Australia and France.

"We know that charges of 'shamateurism'—often accurate —have hurt the game," Kelleher said in one of his reports. "We want the players to know exactly where they stand. We realize that they desire to be governed by fair, enforceable rules and we are working on such rules now. We intend them to be reasonable and we intend to enforce them."

Tennis and the USLTA had come a long way since that inaugural meeting in 1881.

FIVE
4
*The International Lawn Tennis Federation —
Big Voice and a Little Stick*

"Speak softly and carry a big stick," advised Teddy Roosevelt. The International Lawn Tennis Federation, guardian of the sport throughout the world, operates on a different rule. The ILTF bellows threateningly, then attempts to enforce its will with a straw.

This timid authority was never more graphically illustrated than in the historic 1968 battle for open competition. The ILTF repeatedly knocked back every effort to permit professionals to compete against amateurs. Finally Britain took the matter into its own hands and announced plans to promote the 1968 Wimbledon Championships as an open event.

The ILTF, faced with the withdrawal of other leading tennis nations and perhaps the dissolution of the entire Federation, discreetly pulled in its horns. Member countries not only were granted permission to stage open tournaments— an historic decision—but also were allowed to set up a player category that virtually meant the end of the amateur.

The major role of the ILTF, in the more than fifty years

of its existence, has been to try to set a uniform standard for amateurs. In this cause, it failed miserably. Players throughout the world flagrantly ignored the rules and demanded whatever fees the traffic would bear.

This brought a new word in the sports lexicon—"shamateurism," a contraction of sham amateurism. The ludicrous part of the whole situation was that purists whispered about "under the table payments" when the illegal payoffs were not subtle or secretive at all. They were out in the open for everyone to see.

It was ironical, too, that some of the worst abuses were perpetrated right under the nose of ILTF president, Giorgio Di Stefani of Italy. Promotors in the French Riviera and the resort cities of Italy paid the highest prices for talent. Players never tried to hide it.

Nicola Pietrangeli and Fausto Gardini, two world-rank Italian Davis Cup players of the 1950's and 1960's, frequently complained when their country advanced to the Inter-Zone finals or Challenge Round, forcing prolonged campaigns in the United States or Australia.

"I wish I were back in Italy," Pietrangeli once commented during a preliminary match in Australia. "I could be making $400 a week in tournaments in Europe. Here I get $20 a day." Gardini also spoke openly of profitable guarantees and expense accounts in amateur tournaments.

In 1960 Tony Trabert, then serving as business manager of the professional tour, called a press conference during the Olympic Games in Rome to announce that Pietrangeli was turning professional. Twenty-four hours after the announcement the Italian Davis Cup ace declared that he had had a change of heart and planned to remain amateur. It was an open secret that Italian patrons of the game had approached him with a better deal than the $50,000 pro offer.

Similar action by the Lawn Tennis Association of Australia delayed Frank Sedgman's entry into pro ranks after he had helped defend the Davis Cup in 1951. Sedgman wound up with a gasoline service station and a bundle of cash, obtained through a public solicitation of funds, as a result of postponing his pro decision for twelve months.

The ILTF was founded in 1913, thirteen years after Dwight Davis had put up the $700 silver bowl that became emblematic of world tennis supremacy. While the ILTF is supposed to control the competing nations, it has no power over the Davis Cup competition. This remains the jealously guarded prerogative of the Davis Cup nations.

Although the United States waited ten years before joining the ILTF, the Federation was actually the creation of an American, Duane Williams. Williams, whose son R. N. Williams won two national singles crowns and played on the Davis Cup team, had noted the rapid expansion of tennis and felt there should be some world-wide body to set and enforce uniform standards and generally administer the game.

Williams made the suggestion to the secretary of the Swiss Lawn Tennis Association, who in turn passed on the idea to Henry Wallet, president of the French Federation. Representatives of twelve nations met in Paris and formed the ILTF.

The United States had a representative at the organizational meeting but declined to join for several reasons. As father of the Davis Cup, it tended to resent any movement that might detract from the great international spectacle. The Americans also took exception to the by-laws.

They did not agree with the amateur code, which was much stricter than the USLTA's. They bitterly objected to the ILTF move to set up a World Championship Tournament, to be played annually at Wimbledon. The Americans felt their own championship should be equal to that of the British.

Efforts to draw the United States into the Federation were to no avail as long as the ILTF persisted in labeling Wimbledon the World Championship. Watson Washburn, chairman of the USLTA constitution committee, advised the British: "The USLTA does not want the World's Championship in any one country because we believe it is not conducive to the best interests of the sport." In 1914, the USLTA adopted a resolution declaring that the Davis Cup shall be "the sole international team contest of the world."

In 1923 the ILTF adopted a set of international rules amenable to the United States and withdrew its recognition of the World Championship, sanctioning instead four national championships—All-England, France, United States and Australia—which were to become the "Big Four." The United States joined and thus became a member of the international family.

Each national association was allowed to remain virtually autonomous in the regulation of its tournaments and players but regarding amateurism it was supposed to adhere to the ILTF code. In principle a tennis nation might have stricter amateur rules than the Federation, but not looser ones. However, this was a policy the ILTF discovered it could not enforce.

There were no problems at first. Most players were so-called "gentlemen" or "ladies" who competed for the love of the game. They paid their travel expenses to tournament sites and were responsible for room and board, although many of them were housed and fed by patrons or friends of the sport.

As tennis expanded and stretched to all areas of the world, the expense problem became more acute. Few competitors were able to pay for a voyage across the Atlantic Ocean and maintain themselves while competing for a month or more on the continent. It was compulsory that they receive aid, either from their home association or from the tournament sponsors.

The emergence of tennis as a big time spectator sport in the late 1920's and 1930's made abuses inevitable. Top players refused to go to tournaments unless they were promised full expenses. These expenses usually ran well over the amount needed to cover travel, room and board, providing a cozy bonus.

ILTF members became alarmed at the wide increase of such practices and in 1933 set up a special committee to probe into the problem and bring its findings to the Federation for a possible solution.

The committee presented an exhaustive report to the general convention of the ILTF in July 1934. Walter M. Hall and Dwight Davis represented the United States. Delegates were shocked. They proceeded to implement the amateur rules which specified that a player be limited to travel expenses and a specified amount for room and board.

The latter allowance ranged from $15 to $20 a day, depending on the site, a figure that grew to $28 in the late 1960's.

In attempting to enforce a rigid code of amateurism, the ILTF found itself in an untenable position. It could determine rules but was powerless to make them stick. Thus abuses escalated.

Top players could clear as much as $400 a week. Lew Hoad, the Australian who received a $125,000 pro contract from promoter Jack Kramer, once said it was possible for a good player to make as much as $10,000 a year, exclusive of other sources of income. Kramer and others were equally frank about loop-holes in the system.

Generally the player set a figure and stood on it. The sponsor could take it or leave it. If the best players did not compete, the tournament proved a bust. The promotor had no alternative except to meet the demanded figure.

The ILTF made gestures toward correcting the situation, but they were futile. Most of the associations—the USLTA was one of the strictest—either condoned the abuses or looked the other way.

The Federation gave the individual associations almost complete autonomy in 1946 for regulating player expenses.

It was just a way of saying: "We can't do anything about it, now you try." Few tried, or even cared to try.

The ILTF discarded its amateur committee in 1947 and replaced it with a sub-committee in 1950. Another special committee on amateurism was appointed in July 1962, but by this time officials had recognized that mushrooming tournaments and improved air travel made it virtually impossible to control the runaway giant.

The amateur committee made these confessions:

1. It is impossible to devise a code of rules which will be accepted by a majority of the associations.

2. The ILTF is not equipped to police and enforce the rules.

3. It is useless to draw up any new rules. They would be defied just as were the old ones.

4. In many countries amateurism is not a sacred moral code and tends to mean less and less.

It was a complete surrender.

The United States still sought to get adoption and enforcement of a uniform code, but its efforts fell on deaf ears.

George Barnes of Chicago, serving as president of the USLTA at the time, charged, "Every time we go into international competition, we are meeting professionals." An Englishman, D.J. Erlebach, told his home association: "The leading amateur players of the world are not amateurs at all. The bigger the drawing power of the player, the greater his expenses."

The USLTA fought to hold the line but in the end had to succumb to the popular tide, agreeing in 1969 to permit players to play for prize money without becoming professionals.

The ILTF had to give in on the point of open competition, after holding out for decades.

Membership in the Federation swelled from its original dozen members in 1913 to a total of eighty-two, but it was a giant without power, a figurehead meeting once a year to put a rubber stamp on the actions of its members.

FIVE
5

The Amateur Tour — Great While It Lasted

A pundit once remarked that the ideal life was that of a touring amateur tennis player. "You travel the world at someone else's expense," he said, "and you travel with a harem."

Our sidewalk philosopher was not far off the truth. For decades, the amateur tennis player, early tagged with the title of "tennis bum," lived an exciting, glamorous existence. With the advent of open competition in 1968, there was question whether the tennis world, saddled now with the responsibility of getting up rich purses for the pros and the semi-professional registered players, would be able to pay the bill.

It was the financial looseness of amateur tournament promoters that resulted after a long and arduous battle in permission for the professionals to compete against non-professionals in the big time venues—Wimbledon, Forest Hills, Stade Roland Garros and Kooyong.

Promoters were accused of paying star players lavish bonuses under the table in defiance of the rules of the ineffectual International Lawn Tennis Federation and the various national associations.

Charges of "sham amateurism" were made for years, but the game's fathers discreetly looked the other way. A move to crack down on the violators, they apparently realized, might mean the destruction of tennis as a major competitive and spectator sport.

Jack Kramer, an amateur champion who later became czar

of the pros, confessed in a magazine article after he had left amateur ranks that he accepted money from organizers seeking his appearance as a gate attraction at various tournaments. "I was a paid amateur," Kramer said, charging that most other top-line players were equally guilty.

Nicola Pietrangeli of Italy, who ranked among the world's Top Ten during the 1950's and 1960's, repeatedly spurned professional offers. "I can make more money as an amateur," he said. "It is a good, easy life and I get as much as $400 a week."

Pietrangeli, Orlando Sirola and other Italians pouted when they were successful enough to make the Davis Cup Inter-Zone Final and Challenge Round. This involved weeks of training and sometimes a long trip to Australia where they had to spend the Christmas Holidays while other tournaments, with rich lures, thrived on the Riviera.

The amateur circuit followed the sun and lasted from January through December. While the U.S. Lawn Tennis Association was more rigid than most other national bodies, limiting the period that American players might compete overseas and keeping a sharp eye out for expense irregularities, Italy, France, England and for a while Australia gave their players carte blanche.

The tour opened in January with the Caribbean courting players from North and South America while the Riviera wooed those from Europe. Australians, who usually left home right after their National Championships in January and played the entire year, divided their talents between both areas, whichever offered the greater lure.

Invitation tournaments dotted the European map, from the Scandinavian countries to the Mediterranean and from the Iron Curtain to the English Channel and beyond. While the pecuniary incentive was not always as great or the fringe benefits of pleasure as attractive, the United States had its share of tournaments on both the clay and grass court circuits for which sponsors paid dearly for talent.

The arrangement was a simple one, strictly business. A city or summer resort staging a big time tournament would find itself in need of leading stars. Invitations would be sent and the players, accepting, would specify travel and other expenses.

Travel; accommodations and food for a Wimbledon or U.S. champion inevitably cost more, much more, than for a performer of moderate rank. Usually he could name his own price and get it. If the tournament were big and rich enough, the fee might run to $1,000. The going rate was around $400.

Players were able to pad accounts by calculating expenses from their original point of departure at the beginning of a tour. Hence an Aussie ace who entered events in Brussels, Hamburg and Bournemouth, England, might demand from each of these competitions fare for a round-trip airplane ticket from Sydney—or say about $1,400 each.

Lew Hoad, the Australian Wimbledon champion who signed a $100,000-plus contract with promotor Jack Kramer in 1957, explained these devious devices. He spoke of them unashamedly because he knew the practice was widespread with the onus of guilt not on the players but on the game's administrators who permitted the situation to exist.

"But it is vastly overrated," Lew Hoad said. "When I was at my peak I don't think I ever made more than $10,000. And I spent a lot of that taking my wife, Jennie, around with me."

In 1961 the Australian Association almost precipitated a strike among its top players, including Davis Cup aces, by imposing a restriction on when they might leave the country for overseas competition. The date was set at April 1. This would have kept them from some of the most lucrative and enjoyable events of the season, including those in the Riviera and the Caribbean.

The players balked. Some even took up nationality elsewhere. Bob Mark, a rugged, beetle-browed youth who made an international tour at eighteen with Rod Laver, went to

Johannesburg. Marty Mulligan moved to Rome and later became a member of the Italian Davis Cup squad. Ken Fletcher fled to Hong Kong. Owen Davidson emigrated to London and later became professional at Wimbledon.

Alarmed Australian directors quickly pulled in their fangs and modified their stand. But the hypocrisy of amateur tennis left a sour taste in the mouths of most players.

Barry MacKay and Earl (Butch) Buchholz described it best upon turning pro after their ill-fated Davis Cup campaign with the United States team in Australia in 1961.

Announcing their plans in an interview arranged by Jack Kramer, they said:

"I feel clean for the first time. I don't have to take dirty money any more."

FIVE
——
6

The Pro Tour — Theater on a Canvas Court

In the Golden Twenties, when money was loose and Americans were on a spiral of high-living, there was an enterprising promoter in New York named Charles C. (Cash and Carry) Pyle who operated on the same theory as circus magnate P. T. Barnum: "A sucker is born every minute."

Pyle recognized that pockets jangled with restless dollars and people were thirsty for amusement—any sort of amusement. He found ways of satisfying this thirst while gently extricating the dollars. He would promote anything: six-day bicycle races, dance marathons, flagpole sitters or anything that happened to meet the popular fancy.

When newspaper headlines began blaring the exploits of Suzanne Lenglen, the famed French tennis champion, Pyle became intrigued.

"We will have to get this French chick over here," he told intimates.

rolls as were a couple of women, Jane Sharp and Mrs. Ethel Burkhardt Arnold. The project lost around $22,000.

When Tilden and O'Brien decided to get out of the promoting business, Big Bill's old doubles partner, Francis T. Hunter, now a successful businessman, joined with S. Howard Voshell in taking over the enterprise. The first thing they did was to persuade Fred Perry, the great English star who had won three straight Wimbledon titles as well as the Davis Cup for Britain, to turn professional.

Perry, a handsome, dark-haired man with classic strokes, was thrown against Vines at Madison Square Garden in the opening match of their tour on the evening of January 6, 1937. The Englishman was in top form and Vines was erratic. A crowd of 17,630 paid $58,120—a record for the tour—to see Perry draw first blood.

The flashy Briton, with his devastating forehand, won the first six matches but Vines finished strong, winning 32 matches to 29. The tour grossed $412,181. Under his guarantee, Perry received the biggest slice, $91,335, while Vines had to settle for $34,195.

They repeated as co-stars and co-promoters in 1938 with Vines winning 48 matches, Perry 35. The tour brought in only $175,000 and the two split $34,000.

Forever in need of a fresh face, the pro game found it in 1939 in the florid, freckled countenance of Don Budge. The California redhead with the murderous backhand had the previous year achieved the first Grand Slam, winning the Australian, French, Wimbledon and American titles in a single year. He had gone through two seasons without a single defeat. He was indisputably the world's Number One player.

If the pros themselves had any doubts, they were quickly convinced. Budge made his bow at the Garden before a crowd of 16,725 who paid $47,120, and crushed Vines 6–3, 6–4, 6–2. Later he made a second Garden appearance against Perry, smothering the Englishman 6–1, 6–3, 6–0. On

They were horrified. Tennis was a stuffy sport which at its best drew minimal sports crowds. Besides, what did Cash and Carry know about tennis? He couldn't even keep score. His advisors cautioned against it.

Pyle's mind was made up. In 1925, after Suzanne had won her sixth Wimbledon ladies' title, the American promoter deposited $50,000 in a Paris bank. Miss Lenglen could have it all if she would agree to a professional tennis tour.

Cash and Carry's friends thought he was out of his mind. There was no way for the project to succeed. They became more alarmed when Suzanne, to the surprise of the tennis world, accepted.

The tour was set for 1926. To oppose Miss Lenglen, Pyle obtained Mary K. Browne, a leading American player who had won three U.S. Championships before World War I. As props, he signed four men players, Vinnie Richards, Harvey Snodgrass and Howard C. Kinsey, all Americans, and a Frenchman, Paul Peret.

The troupe made its debut at Madison Square Garden in New York. The gate grossed $40,000. Pyle took his show on the road, playing to near-capacity houses everywhere. The tour was such a success that Miss Lenglen was paid a $25,000 bonus over her $50,000 guarantee. Richards received $35,000, Miss Browne $25,000, Kinsey $20,000, Snodgrass $12,000 and Peret $10,000. Pyle himself pocketed $80,000.

The promoter had proved that sports fans would pay theater prices to see top tennis played indoors. Thus the pro tour was born.

After his successful opening venture, Pyle characteristically became restless and moved on to what he thought were more inviting fields. Richards, who as tennis' onetime "Boy Wonder" had teamed with Big Bill Tilden in winning doubles championships, picked up the discarded opportunity on a half-volley.

He decided to inject an international flavor. In Europe,

fans were acclaiming Karel Kozeluh, a Czech, as the greatest player in the world, pro or amateur. Kozeluh was a tremendous athlete, a former soccer player, who had taken to tennis naturally. He had faultless ground strokes and a safe-cracker's touch at the net.

The rugged Czech star was brought to the United States in 1928 for a head-to-head professional duel with Richards who doubled as promoter. Kozeluh proved superior on clay and hardwood, winning a majority of the matches on the tour, but he lost to Richards on grass in the match billed as the Professional Championship of the World.

Kozeluh practiced diligently on grass for the next several months, returned to the United States in 1929 and whipped Richards for the pro championship.

When Big Bill Tilden turned professional in 1931, having no more amateur worlds to conquer, Kozeluh was the natural opponent. The Czech was by far the best of a crop of top European professionals, including Roman Najuch of Germany, Albert Thomas and Edward Burke of France and Major Rendell of England.

Tilden, who had assumed the promotional reins in partnership with entrepreneur William O'Brien, and Kozeluh opened their tour at Madison Square Garden on February 18, 1931. The nation was in the throes of a dreadful depression. Banks had closed. Business had gone bankrupt. Hungry people were queuing up for apples on Manhattan streets. Yet the match drew a crowd of 13,600 and a gate of $36,000.

The Tilden-Kozeluh troupe, with Francis T. Hunter, Robert Seller and Emmett Pare playing subordinate roles, crossed the country to San Francisco's Cow Palace, played for big galleries at almost every stop and grossed $238,000.

It was obvious the tour was a going concern. Players flocked to the pro ranks—Hans Nusslein of Germany, Henri Cochet of France, Bruce Barnes, Berkeley Bell and George Lott, Jr. Richards spearheaded the formation of the United States Professional Tennis Association, which br peans as well as Americans under its umbrella.

Tilden, although aging, continued to be the gate attraction and dominated the tour throu thirties. His court antics still were pure thea feating Kozeluh in 1931, Big Bill took on Vinn 1932, grossing $86,000, and Hans Nusslein i receipts dropped to $62,000.

The tour obviously needed some new blc with the emergence in 1934 of H. Ellswor dynamic player and an electrifying personal the U.S. Amateur Championship in 1931 and tured Wimbledon in 1932, thus establishing world's best amateur player. A poweful hitte erratic, given to double-faults and periods on his best day no one, pro or amateur, cou

Vines' interest in the amateur game cool 1933 and O'Brien and Tilden pounced on fanfare, the hard-hitting Californian made Tilden in the Garden in the winter of 1 14,637 paying $30,125 was on hand.

Big Bill now was forty-one years old. I mendous player for his age and a great match for the younger ace. In their cross-c overwhelmed Tilden, winning 47 matche doubles, however, the two Americans ha Frenchmen Henri Cochet and Martin P $243,000, of which Vines received $5 O'Brien halved the profits.

The tour was repeated in 1935, with C Lester Stoefen, the world's amateur doul ing the cast, but interest sagged and $188,000.

Tilden and O'Brien sought to keep two separate tours in 1936. Bruce Barr

the tour, Budge won over Vines 21–18, and over Perry 18–11. He collected his guarantee of $75,000 from the $204,503 gross. Vines got $23,000, then deserted tennis for a successful golf career.

In 1941 Hitler was casting an ominous shadow over Europe. Goose-stepping Nazi legions and exploding mortar shells drowned out the sound of tennis balls against a catgut racket. But the show went on. Tilden, forty-seven years old, came out of semi-retirement to face Budge. They played in the Garden on January 6 with two outstanding women players, Alice Marble and England's Mary Hardwick, performing the preliminaries. Opening night drew only $25,614 and the tour was a relative bust, Budge winning 51 of the 58 matches.

The following year little Bobby Riggs got into the act, playing Budge in the Garden with Perry and Frankie Kovacs as the supporting cast. The troupe played 71 cities and drew a total of only 101,915 fans. It was decided that the pros should lower their curtains until the end of World War II.

There was one break in the suspension. On March 14, 1944, a match was staged in the Garden for the benefit of the Red Cross. It pitted Lt. Donald Budge, the pro champion, against a young Coast Guard cadet named Jack Kramer, an amateur permitted by the U.S. Lawn Tennis Association to compete against a pro for this one occasion. Portending things to come, Kramer surprisingly won 6–3, 6–2.

Budge came out of the service considerably bigger around the middle and a half-step slower. The long layoff had affected him more than the bouncy, relentlessly retrieving Riggs, who won the 1946 tour 23–21. By this time, the promotional reins had been taken over by a Los Angeles matchmaker, Jack Harris, with backing later from a Philadelphia sportsman, Lex Thompson.

Budge dropped from the picture and in jumped Jack Kramer who in 1947 won Wimbledon and his second U.S. crown and also helped defend the Davis Cup at Forest Hills against Australia.

Kramer signed a contract with Harris for no bonus at all, in contrast to Budge, who had been guaranteed $75,000 or 30 percent of the total receipts.

"My opinion was that if I couldn't draw, I had no right being in the business," Kramer said later. He asked for 35 percent of the gate, and got it. Riggs settled for 17½ percent.

The Kramer-Riggs tour was launched on December 26, 1947, the night of one of New York's most violent blizzards. The wind howled up to 50 miles an hour. Snow was hip deep. City transportation was virtually paralyzed.

"I felt like an explorer, walking from my hotel to the Garden," Kramer recalled.

Yet a crowd of 15,114 battled its way to the Garden to witness the match, won by the wily Riggs 6–2, 10–8, 4–6, 6–4. It was a brief moment of glory for the little tactician who had dethroned Budge. Kramer won the cross-country series impressively, 69–20; the gross was $248,000.

Riggs broke with promoter Harris late in 1948 and took over the tour. It was Bobby's hope to turn Ted Schroeder pro and pit him against Kramer. But after Schroeder won the 1949 Wimbledon title he decided to remain amateur. This forced Riggs to turn to Richard (Pancho) Gonzales, winner of the U.S. Amateur crown in 1948 and 1949.

Kramer and Gonzales, who later were to engage in a bitter and long-running contract feud that carried into the courts, came face-to-face as pros in the winter of 1949. Big Jake had too much know-how for the raw rookie from California's Mexican settlement and he trampled Gonzales on the tour, 96–27.

In 1951 Riggs discarded Gonzales, hired the colorful Francisco (Pancho) Segura, a native of Ecuador, as Kramer's foe, and signed a pair of good-looking girls for sex appeal—gorgeous Gussy Moran and Pauline Betz.

Miss Moran had shocked Wimbledon galleries by appearing on the center court in provocative lace panties and had become the most publicized woman player in the game. Miss Betz, 1946 national champion, was a tall, leggy blonde who didn't need lace to get attention.

The tour, opening at the Garden before a disappointingly small crowd, fell short of success. Segura proved no match for Kramer who clobbered the bow-legged Latin in their cross-country campaign 64–28. Miss Betz sought to upstage the glamorous Gussy by wearing leopard-skin shorts, peek-a-boo blouses and other eye-catching apparel. Adding insult to injury, Pauline also beat Gussy on the tennis court.

That was enough for the ladies, and after a year's suspension during which a move to land Australia's Frank Sedgman failed, it also was enough for promoter Riggs. This opened the door for Kramer, who didn't hesitate to stick his foot in it.

Big Jake's first move as a promoter was to lure Sedgman from the Australian amateur authorities, who the year before had persuaded him to remain amateur through a sizeable slush fund, raised by public donations. Sedgman and his teammate, Ken McGregor, both turned professional in an atmosphere of secrecy following their successful defense of the Davis Cup against America at Adelaide, Australia, in December 1952. Sedgman received a $75,000 guarantee or 35 percent of the gate.

However, despite his popularity in Europe and his home country, the Australian failed to capture the fancy of American fans. Kramer, though suffering from a chronic back ailment, won the 1953 series, 54 matches to 41, and began looking around for new talent.

It was right under his nose. Since losing to Kramer in the 1949–1950 series, Gonzales had virtually dropped from sight. He had fought himself back into top shape and become perhaps the world's best tennis player with no place to go.

In 1954 Pancho established his claim to a top spot in the pro echelon by defeating both Segura and Sedgman in a round robin.

In 1955 Tony Trabert, a thick-legged slugger from Cincinnati who had teamed with Vic Seixas the year before to recapture the Davis Cup, won both the Wimbledon and American singles titles and became the hottest commodity in amateur ranks. It was natural that Kramer should eye the former University of Cincinnati basketball player with interest. But who was his likeliest opponent? Gonzales, of course.

Kramer signed Trabert for $50,000 or 30 percent of the gate. He entered into a seven-year contract with Gonzales that gave the Mexican-American a 20 percent slice, an agreement later regretted by Pancho who sought to have it cancelled.

On the 1955–56 tour Trabert proved no opponent for the vastly improved Gonzales, who ran away with the series, 74–27. Ken Rosewall, the frail-looking Australian with the siege-gun backhand, was next to be lured into Kramer's web and he put up little better resistance. Pancho smashed him down 50–26.

Lew Hoad, the other half of Australia's Davis Cup "twins," followed Rosewall. Holder of the Australian, French, Italian and Wimbledon titles, the blond bomber from Sydney was the most potent force in the amateur game. In need of someone to spice up the pro tour, Kramer made him an offer that was highly enticing—a $100,000 guarantee plus a $25,000 bonus should he win again at Wimbledon.

While Big Jake chewed his fingernails on the sidelines, Hoad hammered his way through the Wimbledon field, defeating countryman Ashley Cooper in the final. He immediately accepted Kramer's deal.

The Australian ace was sent against the seemingly unshakeable Gonzales. Their 1958 tour touched eighty-seven cities in the United States, Australia and Europe. At the end there stood Pancho, still king of professional tennis by a margin of 51–36.

But he was a disgruntled king, stuck with a contract that netted him only 20 percent of the receipts. He was drawing paychecks one-half and often one-third as large as those being grabbed by the men he was battering into the ground.

He demanded redress. Kramer was burdened with commitments to other players and it was impossible for him to give Pancho better terms. When the dispute went to court, he prevailed and for a time afterwards the promoter and his star refused to speak to each other.

In the 1958 Davis Cup matches in Brisbane, Australia, Kramer found himself in an uncomfortable position. He had been tapped by his longtime friend and benefactor, Perry Jones, to assist with the U.S. team of which Jones had been named captain. As a tennis promoter, he had negotiated with Australia's two top aces, Ashley Cooper and Malcolm Anderson, to join the tour the following season.

Kramer's patriotism got the better of his business sense. Doing his coaching job well for Captain Jones and Uncle Sam, he helped prepare Alex Olmedo for a near single-handed American victory. Thus he took much of the lustre from his latest pro recruits, Cooper and Anderson.

Again Pancho Gonzales proved unconquerable as he swept through a 1959 round robin that included Hoad, Cooper and Anderson. Pancho found little comfort in the fact that he collected $29,150. Hoad had received $28,250, Cooper $18,700 and Anderson $16,900.

By this time the tour had undergone change. The head-to-head duels, originating with Suzanne Lenglen and Mary K. Browne and including historic battles involving Tilden, Vines, Budge and Perry, were being put aside. The new formula was the round robin, several players competing for purses determined by the number of victories and defeats.

Olmedo, a Peruvian who became an American citizen after attending college in California, entered the scene in

1960, competing with Gonzales, Segura and Rosewall. Again Gonzales was the overall victor.

That same year Kramer voluntarily relinquished his role of promoter, turning the tour over to the players who were to run it as an association with a member of their ranks serving as advance man, publicist and director. The job was bestowed upon Tony Trabert, who established an office in Paris.

"I felt that my presence in the movement might be detrimental to the pro game," Kramer said. "It was necessary that the pros work in harmony with the amateur associations. I didn't want to be a stumbling block."

Without Kramer the pros operated rather loosely. Growing in numbers, they barnstormed around the country, staging tournaments instead of exhibitions. As in the case of the golf pros, they competed for staggered purses. Yet they failed to sell their product.

The average fan never ceased to regard pro matches as anything but a show. He paid to see talent on display. When he wanted competition, he went to amateur championships. This was the stigma the pros had to fight. They possessed the talent but the amateur associations possessed the big stadiums and the prestige tournaments.

The pro title passed from Gonzales, who nearing 40 went into semi-retirement, to Ken Rosewall and then to Australia's redoubtable Grand Slammer, Rod Laver.

They were the greatest shotmakers of their day but they performed in virtual obscurity until the long, hard fight for open tennis was won in 1968.

With the doors of Wimbledon, Forest Hills, White City and Roland Garros finally open to the pros, the game acquired a fresh look. But the move did not bring an end to the touring pro.

George MacCall of Los Angeles, an insurance executive who served as unsuccessful captain of the U.S. Davis Cup team from 1965 through 1967, formed a syndicate which bought up the contracts of such established pros as Laver, Rosewall, Gonzales and Andres Gimeno of Spain and added a distaff branch which included three-time Wimbledon winner Billie Jean King, Ann Haydon Jones, Rosemary Casals and Francoise Durr. The group was known as the National Tennis League.

Meanwhile, a Dallas millionaire, Lamar Hunt, put up money for a second professional troupe which operated under the name of World Championship Tennis, Inc. At first directed by a New Orleans promoter, Dave Dixon, later by Al Hill, Jr., Hunt's nephew, and eventually by Bob Briner, from the American Football League, the second group advertised itself as "The Handsome Eight," although its ranks grew to ten, then twelve and beyond. It comprised the new breed of pro tennis—Australia's John Newcombe and Tony Roche; America's Dennis Ralston and Marty Riessen; Nicola Pilic of Yugoslavia and Cliff Drysdale, among others.

Both groups lost money during their first year 1968, but found business on the upgrade as they swept into the 1969 season with new concessions from the national amateur bodies.

Briner purchased and Hunt underwrote tennis contracts so avidly that one French tennis official remarked:

"The next thing I expect is that Lamar Hunt will buy Wimbledon and Forest Hills and stage his own private tournaments."

According to a story told in football locker rooms, Hunt dropped $1 million during his first year's venture in the American Football League with a Dallas franchise that later was moved to Kansas City.

Apprised of this loss by curious newsmen, Hunt's father is reported to have stroked his chin and said: "That's too bad. At that rate, Lamar will be broke in 100 years."

The two pro groups, keen rivals at first, joined forces to draw concessions from the associations.

Negotiations were carried out in a historic meeting in

London in late February 1969. MacCall and Briner met with leaders from the Big Four tennis-playing nations—Britain, United States, France and Australia—to hammer out a blueprint for future cooperation.

Under the agreement, the associations agreed to pay the groups travel and expense allowances in return for pro participation in the major open events.

One of the chief advisors at the London meeting: Jack Kramer. There were recurring reports that the pros some day would tap him for the role of tennis czar.

FIVE	*The Open War—*
7	*Britain's Stubbornness Wins Out*

On March 30, 1968 at the Place de la Concorde in Paris the eighty-two nations of the International Lawn Tennis Federation voted without dissent to sanction a limited number of open tournaments.

The stalemate was broken. The uphill battle to permit amateur players to compete against professionals was finally won. The real victor was Britain's renowned bulldog stubbornness. In the face of widespread opposition and threat of ostracism, old John Bull rammed the issue through while other tennis-playing countries vacillated.

For decades, the conservative fathers of the sport had successfully resisted all effort to lower the barrier between the amateur and professional. They remained unheedful as tennis dropped to secondary status as a spectator sport and was increasingly branded with the stigma of sham amateurism.

Golf permitted open competition as far back as 1895. Top professional football teams staged annual contests against all-star collegiate elevens. New York major league baseball teams thought nothing of travelling up the Hudson River for exhibitions against the Army forces at West Point.

But to the men controlling tennis such events were to be avoided like the plague.

In the game's early years there was no need for concern. Tennis was played at exclusive clubs and on private estates where the notion of professionalism would have been unthinkable. As late as 1910 there were no teaching pros in America and by 1921, when Big Bill Tilden was emerging, there were no more than twenty-five, according to Joanna Davenport from the department of physical education at Ohio State University.

America's—and perhaps the world's—first real awareness of professionals came in 1926 when a New York promoter named Charles C. (Cash and Carry) Pyle paid France's Suzanne Lenglen $50,000, plus a $25,000 bonus, for a tour with Mary K. Browne, former U.S. Champion.

In 1927 under the leadership of Vincent Richards and Howard O. Kinsey, the United States Professional Lawn Tennis Association was formed. The group elected officers, framed a constitution and fixed a $10 initiation fee "for all tennis professionals of accepted standards."

The U.S. Lawn Tennis Association recognized the new body, half-heartedly proffered its support but viewed the project with suspicion.

The USLTA slapped the wrist of the Palm Beach (Florida) Tennis Club for allowing its facilities to be used for a professional tournament, and it rejected a request from the Longwood Cricket Club in Brookline, Massachusetts to permit a pro-amateur exhibition during the National Championships.

"If we let the pros have exhibitions at amateur tournaments," George Wightman told a USLTA meeting, "we take away from the fundamental purpose for which all tournaments are run—namely, to develop tennis. Our Association is formed to develop amateur tennis players. That is our job, and the minute we sidle in pros with amateurs we take away the prestige of the Association."

In 1930, with Tilden preparing to launch his pro career, his home club, the Germantown Cricket Club outside Philadelphia, made an application to stage an open tournament in order to fatten its depleted treasury. The USLTA granted permission, dependent on approval from the International Lawn Tennis Federation.

The USLTA went before the ILTF with a proposed amendment to the Federation's Rule 23, the amateur rule, which would permit pro-amateur matches when approved by a national association. The request was soundly beaten.

Thus rebuffed, the USLTA adopted a resolution that no further move be made in that direction until the ILTF relaxed its attitude. Directors warned that open competition would turn the game over to the pros and kill amateur tennis.

Yet in 1933 the Germantown Cricket Club repeated its request and the Association president, Louis J. Carruthers, decided again to take the matter to the international body. Carruthers, a lawyer, felt Rule 23 had loop holes which would allow such competition.

However, the USLTA failed to send a properly delegated official to the ILTF meeting in London, letting a subordinate embassy representative plead its case, and again the move was beaten. The ILTF used the occasion to reaffirm Rule 23, declaring that there was no place in the constitution permitting such a tournament.

The Americans were persistent. They reopened the issue the next year with Carruthers personally arguing the case at the meeting in Paris. He urged that national associations be granted autonomy on the question of open competition. The USLTA president was so persuasive that the ILTF appointed a special committee to study the problem and report later in the year. The result was the same: Open play was disallowed.

The ILTF adopted a new and clearer law which remained in effect until 1968. The law prohibited amateurs from participating in a tournament with players other than amateurs but left the door open for exhibitions between amateurs and professionals, subject to consent of the ILTF on application made by the national association.

In 1937 the fashionable Greenbrier Golf and Tennis Club staged what it called the "First U.S. Open Tennis Championship." The sponsors, taking the bull by the horns, decided to go ahead with the project without seeking permission. The event was held. Six amateurs competed in the field of professionals. The USLTA cancelled the membership of the Greenbrier Club and suspended the six amateur players.

In 1938 India led a drive for open competition by proposing that each country be allowed to hold one such event. The USLTA tacked on its pct autonomy clause but hedged by saying it wasn't interested in holding an open tournament. The measure was beaten, 118–51.

During World War II the rules were relaxed to permit exhibitions between amateurs and professionals for the Red Cross and similar causes. On March 14, 1944, Jack Kramer, a Coast Guard cadet who was Number Two in the national rankings, played Don Budge, the reigning pro champion, in a Red Cross benefit match at Madison Square Garden. Kramer won 6–3, 6–2. Pancho Segura, a pro, and Sidney Wood, 1931 Wimbledon winner, were on the same bill.

The open issue lay dormant for close to two decades, only to be revived in 1957 by USLTA president Renville McMann.

In the interim, the game had undergone changes. Kramer, an enterprising and imaginative promoter, had taken control of the touring pros. Flashing a big checkbook and tossing out guarantees of $50,000 to $125,000, he was grabbing off amateur talent as quickly as it rolled off the associations' assembly lines.

He snatched up Australia's Frank Sedgman and Ken McGregor after they won the Davis Cup in 1952. He signed

Pancho Gonzales to a seven-year contract. He added Tony Trabert, 1955 winner of the Wimbledon and U.S. Championships. He plucked Australia's Ken Rosewall and Lew Hoad in their prime, giving the latter an unprecedented $125,000 contract. He was cornering the tennis market.

Amateur tennis suffered noticeably from these raids. Attendance at the major tournaments, all except Wimbledon which apparently thrived on tradition, hit a sharp decline. Personalities were being pirated before they could make a name for themselves. Tennis was degenerating into a secondary spectator sport, greeted with a polite yawn by the news media and obscured by booms in big time pro golf, football and basketball.

On top of this, the sport was getting a world-wide reputation for dishonesty.

Kramer staggered the complacency of the tennis world when he confessed in an article written in a Sunday supplement: "I was a paid amateur." Kramer acknowledged that as an amateur he toured the world at another's expense, padded expense accounts and took under-the-table payments from promoters. "Everybody does it," Jack said. "It's the only way an amateur can make the tour."

Lew Hoad admitted that he often cleared as much as $10,000 a year as an amateur. As we know, Nicola Pietrangeli, the Italian ace, said he disliked to be bogged down with Davis Cup competition because he could make $400 a week playing tournaments in Europe. Nicola never turned pro. After signing pro contracts, U.S. Davis Cup players Barry MacKay and Earl (Butch) Buchholz said they felt clean for the first time. "I am tired of taking dirty money," MacKay said.

It was with this situation in mind that McMann went before the USLTA and asked that a special committee be formed to study the pros and cons of open tennis.

"The time has come when we must take a good look-see

on this question," the USLTA president said. "I don't feel if we have one [an open tournament], we'll lose control of the game. But if we don't give it thought, we may lose control.

"Let's call a spade a spade, particularly with the under-cover payments and hypocrisy that exists in some quarters of the globe in our game. But there are dangers connected with an Open. What would happen to the Davis Cup?"

He named a high-powered committee, headed by Perry Jones, longtime czar of tennis in Southern California, and including not only highly-regarded tennis officials but businessmen and newspaper personalities as well. The group assembled a mass of data and came up with the recommendation that open competition be tried on an experimental basis. The proposal was rejected by the Executive Committee of the USLTA, twenty to eight.

Meanwhile, rumblings were being heard from other nations particularly England, Australia and France. These were, with the United States, the major tennis-playing countries. All of them recognized that the game needed a stimulant. The pros had all the good players but lacked the organization, the venues and the public acceptance of their authenticity. They were still viewed as actors and exhibitionists. The national associations had the organization and the stadiums but lacked the talent. The amateur crop, constantly being bled by pro raids, was dull and unexciting.

Jean Borotra, one of France's famed "Four Musketeers" and a commanding voice in his country's tennis administration, came up with a revolutionary proposal.

Why not create a new class of player, Borotra suggested. Instead of professional or amateur he would be an "authorized" or "registered" player. This category would fit a large majority of the world's tournament competitors. They would be allowed to compete for prize money—just as contract pros—merely by signifying their intention to play for the purses. If they preferred, they might ask for expenses instead. This arrangement, Borotra insisted, would eliminate the hypocrisy of the amateur game. Furthermore, it would keep many top players under the umbrella of the national associations.

This proposal was presented by a special ILTF committee set up to study the problem. A second recommendation was that the ILTF approve a limited number of open tournaments on an experimental basis.

USLTA delegates went to the ILTF meeting in Paris in July 1960 committed to vote for the experimental opens but strongly opposed to the idea of "registered players." American officials had caucused privately with representatives of France, Britain and Australia and had gained enough support to push through the former recommendation.

Then came the vote. The "authorized player" question ran into so much opposition it was never brought to the floor. When the matter of open tournaments was raised, one delegate with a block of twelve votes in favor of the proposition happened to be in the men's room when his name was called. The proposal was defeated by a margin of five votes.

"It was a strange quirk of fate," Jack Kramer lamented afterward. "That one unthinking blunder may have cost us the chance of an open tournament in our lifetime." Jack was overly pessimistic.

The matter was pursued further in 1961 at the ILTF meeting in Stockholm, Sweden. The United States again submitted an amendment which would permit each individual association to stage an open tournament without jeopardizing the amateur status of its players. The British Lawn Tennis Association asked permission to make Wimbledon an open event in 1962.

Federation delegates ducked the issue, deciding to postpone a vote until the next year. At the same time members were asked to consider three proposals dealing with the question.

They were:

1. Abolish any reference to "amateurs" and "professionals," leaving to the national associations autonomy to make rules.

2. Retain the present rules and organize a central ILTF control to insure compliance throughout the world.

3. Retain the present rules but give each national association the right to define allowable expenses and to enforce its laws.

Before the ILTF convention in Paris in July 1962 there was a definite shifting of the American position. The USLTA presidency had passed into the hands of George Barnes of Chicago, a conservative, who expressed alarm over the growing support for the establishment of a single category of player.

In a talk before the USLTA Executive Committee, Barnes warned that such a move could result in a players' union.

"To save and strengthen the amateur game," he insisted, "we must continue to recognize two classes of players—amateurs and professionals—those who wish to play for mere expenses or pleasure of the game and those who wish to make it their livelihood."

Federation delegates defeated the proposals to establish a general player category and to give each association autonomy in the designation and enforcement of its amateur code. As for setting up a uniform control of the rules within the ILTF, the matter was laid aside for further study.

The move to permit open tournaments on an experimental basis failed to get the necessary two-thirds majority, although there were 120 votes for it and 100 against. The

United States, Britain and France led the pro-open fight. Australia, Germany, Italy, Russia and the Iron Curtain countries were against.

Among the 82 tennis nations in the ILTF, the Big Four —Britain, France, Australia and the United States—have greater voting strength. But the smaller nations opposed open tennis because they feared they would be unable financially to compete for talent. The Soviet Union and its satellites were categorically against the move. As Communist nations, they contend they have no professionals since their athletes are subsidized by the government.

Tennis progressives who battled through the years for the elimination of the archaic barriers separating pros and amateurs were shaken in 1963 when the USLTA, once a champion of change, suddenly reverted to an opposite course. Led by the Texas and Middle States Associations, delegates adopted the following resolution:

Resolved, that the USLTA declare of record its opposition to the principle of Open Tennis and instruct its officers and delegates to the ILTF to oppose any change in the rules of the ILTF which would permit the holding of open events, and be it . . .

Further resolved, that such officers and delegates are hereby instructed to oppose any action by the ILTF through committees or otherwise to act in furtherance of such open tennis until otherwise instructed.

The British Lawn Tennis Association refused to be discouraged by the loss of a former ally, and its chairman Ted Avory announced that he was in favor of breaking away from the ILTF, if necessary, to hold an Open Wimbledon.

Wimbledon was the one major amateur championship which had not suffered from the drain of star players to pro ranks. Rich in tradition, a sort of British festival, an event loved and respected by the players themselves, the tournament always drew top-notch fields and record crowds.

The British Association's determination to throw the tournament open to the pros was an artistic rather than a mercenary one. The Wimbledon fathers wanted their tournament to be the best in the world. They realized this was not possible under a system which barred most of the game's great players, who had gravitated to the pros.

Britain went to the 1964 ILTF meeting with two proposals: 1.) That member associations have autonomy to decide whether or not to hold open events, a move long pushed by the United States; 2.) That the ILTF permit an experimental Wimbledon Open in 1965 and 1966. Both proposals were beaten, with the U. S. delegates forced by the 1963 resolution to vote against them.

The stubborn British decided to carry the banner alone. On October 5, 1967, the Council of the British Lawn Tennis Association voted to recommend that Wimbledon be conducted as an open event. This was a declaration of war to the ILTF, which had rejected every previous move in this direction, over-riding the last attempt by a vote of 139 to 83. The Federation warned that it would be forced to suspend the British Association if it sought to go through with its plan.

Britain's obstinacy shook the tennis world. This was the country where lawn tennis was born. This was the home of Wimbledon, the greatest of all tournaments. If the Federation reacted with an expulsion, it would mean that every player competing at Wimbledon would be declared ineligible for other events. What of the Davis Cup? What of the Wightman and Federation Cups?

Questions were numerous. Was Britain pulling a bluff? Observers thought not. Would she defy the Federation? Yes, most tennis authorities agreed. The situation was tense.

On December 14, 1967, the British put an end to speculation by voting 295–5 to conduct the 1968 Wimbledon tournament as an open championship. In another drastic action, the country's tennis directors decided to abolish all distinction between amateurs and professionals in favor of a general player category.

The effective date was fixed for April 22, 1968, the opening date of the British Hard Court Championships at Bournemouth, England. This would be the world's first open.

The reaction of the ILTF was swift. From Rome, on January 8, 1968, Giorgio Di Stefani of Italy, the ILTF president, declared that unless it altered its collision course the British Lawn Tennis Association would be suspended, effective April 22.

The British refused to budge. But there was alarmed fidgeting in other quarters. In Australia, where sentiments for open tournaments had run the gauntlet from hot to ice cold, there were second thoughts and C.A. ("Big Bill") Edwards of Brisbane, president of the Lawn Tennis Association of Australia, made a blustery speech in favor of open competition.

Most people turned their eyes to the United States, which had always exerted a powerful influence on the game.

The USLTA presidency was in the hands of Robert J. Kelleher of Los Angeles, an attorney, one of the most astute and liberal personalities in the sport. Kelleher long had favored giving open tennis at least a trial run. However, he strongly opposed the "registered player" concept.

The USLTA convened for its eighty-seventh annual session at Coronado, California on February 3. Lining up behind the British, the body took a strong position in favor of open tennis but voted unanimously to maintain the distinction between amateur and professional.

In a historic resolution, proposed by the New England Association and seconded by Henry Benisch of the Eastern Association, the USLTA posted the threat of resigning from the ILTF if the international body did not sanction open competition. There was only one dissenting voice—from the Middle States Association.

The American action, coming on the heels of Britain's

bold gesture, appeared to break the logjam. The Australians, strongly against open tennis in 1962, endorsed both the open game and the single player classification. Sweden, fearing disintegration of the ILTF, joined with Kelleher in calling for an extraordinary session of the ILTF in Paris March 30 to re-study the situation.

There was considerable trans-continental lobbying before members of the ILTF gathered at the Place de la Concorde in Paris on March 30 for deliberations that would affect the game for decades to come.

The Federation, without dissent, agreed to sanction a limited number of open tournaments. The ceiling was placed at twelve for 1968. The number was raised to thirty-one for 1969. The battle had been won—almost.

The Federation refused to end the distinction between amateur and professional, voting for "retention of the notion of amateurism in the rules of the ILTF, as its removal would indisputably weaken the ideal which the ILTF has the duty to protect and develop."

However, this was largely rhetoric. Despite strong protest from Kelleher, the international delegates did make it possible for any country so desiring to set up a class of registered player who might accept prize money in open events. Later even the United States had to come around to this type of revolutionary thinking, although in its 1969 meeting it did establish a player category while preserving the terms "amateur" and "professional."

The pros moved arrogantly into Bournemouth for the world's first open tournament in mid-April 1968. There were the established veterans from George MacCall's stable— Rod Laver, Ken Rosewall, Pancho Gonzales and Andres Gimeno, among others. Absent were the hungry young Turks of the World Championship Tennis, Inc., with Lamar Hunt's millions behind them. They included the formidable Tony Roche, John Newcombe, Dennis Ralston, Cliff Drysdale, Nicola Pilic and others of the "Handsome Dozen."

The amateurs must have felt nervous and uncomfortable when play started. This was the pros' game. They were supposed to take it over.

One of these fidgety amateurs was Mark Cox, a British Davis Cup player with a shock of curly blond hair and a fighting heart as big as the court itself. The odds were heavily against the British amateur when he walked onto the salmon-colored clay court at the West Hants Lawn Tennis Club to face the great Pancho Gonzales.

Thousands came out to see the return of the dark-haired Mexican-American, who for so long had been acclaimed the greatest shotmaker of them all. Cox stunned the gallery by polishing off the great Pancho in five sets. Then he crushed Australia's Roy Emerson, winner of every major title, 6–1, 6–0, 7–5. The amateurs had proved they could walk onto the same court with the celebrated pros. The tension was broken. It was immaterial that the tournament was won by one of the established pros, Ken Rosewall.

At Wimbledon, two American amateurs, Arthur Ashe, Jr., and Clark Graebner, swept into the semifinals of the first Wimbledon Open and Australian Rod Laver fittingly won the championship. In the inaugural U.S. Open at Forest Hills, amateurs proved even more troublesome for the pros. Two of them, Ashe and Holland's Tom Okker, stormed into the final over broken mercenary bodies where Ashe, as the pure amateur, collected a loving cup and $28-a-day expenses for winning and Okker, as a registered player, banked the $14,000 top prize money for being the runner-up.

It was one of the incongruous features of the new game. As tennis swept into the 1970's, officials were debating how and when the Davis Cup might be thrown open to the pros, and the pros were making complaints that formerly had been characteristic of the amateurs.

"When," they asked, "are the tennis authorities going to quit treating us like second-class citizens and give us equal status with the players?"

The Boom of the 1960's —

Tennis Snaps at Golf's Financial Empire

On July 8, 1968, *The Wall Street Journal* made a surprising announcement: Tennis was big business.

"Everyone's for tennis," wrote Thomas B. Carter, a *Journal* staffer, in a front page article. "What happened to golf a generation ago and to skiing a few winters ago now is happening to tennis. Suddenly the courts are full."

Tennis, for decades overshadowed by such big time sports as golf, football and baseball, was definitely on a spiral. It was the "Boom of the Sixties."

Men who formerly relied on weekend golf matches were suddenly turning to tennis. They got their exercise in an hour and a half instead of six hours, counting an hour's break for lunch after nine holes and two hours of drinking with the boys in the locker room after a round of golf.

The number of active tennis players in the United States alone increased to nine million, soaring a full million over the number of golfers. There were 100,000 tennis courts in the country and new ones being built at the rate of 7,000 a year. Sporting goods companies reported they could not keep up with the demand for steel and aluminum rackets, selling at between $45 and $60 each. The number of tennis balls sold in 1968 was 15.8 million, 50 percent more than in 1962.

A company in which former doubles champions William F. Talbert and Gardnar Mulloy had an interest was doing a landslide business constructing balloon-type court coverings for winter play. Inflated with air, the coverings were suitable for clay and even grass courts under normal conditions. They cost $25,000 each. One of them—offering a bizarre sight to Long Island Railroad commuters—was acquired by the sedate West Side Tennis Club in Forest Hills,

New York, site of the National Championships. Members were charged an extra fee for its use.

Indoor courts mushroomed. Businessmen formed tennis clubs, playing once a week in some dank armory or in a new, well-heated, well-lighted complex which, like bowling alleys, offered restaurant facilities, sauna and steam baths.

The late Senator Robert Kennedy was one of a host of congressmen, judges and ambassadors in the nation's capital who relaxed with two fast sets on an indoor or outdoor court. It was tennis that brought Kennedy into contact with Donald Dell, ex-Davis Cupper, Yale University star and Davis Cup captain, who became the Senator's advance man in his ill-starred 1968 presidential campaign.

Kennedy's brother-in-law, Sargent Shriver, former head of the Peace Corps and U. S. Ambassador to France, played in the Wimbledon Senior Championships as a partner of Robert Kelleher, President of the U.S. Lawn Tennis Association. Senator Jacob Javits, although bald and middle-aged, was an avid devotee. President Richard Nixon, bemoaning his inability to play golf as well as Dwight D. Eisenhower, acknowledged that his game was really tennis and hinted—perhaps in jest—that he might tear up Ike's putting green on the West lawn and replace it with a turf court.

The Wall Street Journal reported a large number of golfers defecting to tennis.

"Golf just isn't active enough," the paper quoted Kenneth Hansen, a thirty-five-year-old veterinarian from San Francisco. Stephen Steinberg, a twenty-eight-year-old graduate student from the University of California, admitted he made the shift because tennis "was not as time consuming."

The sudden burst of popularity was due to some extent to the nation's growing obsession with exercise and conditioning. Before his death President John F. Kennedy urged Americans to take long walks, and later jogging became a craze. But these were found to be lonely, uninteresting means of fighting middle-age bulge. Tennis, on the other hand, provided the same results and was more fun.

James H. Van Alen, the Newport, Rhode Island socialite who ruled the Newport Casino and the Tennis Hall of Fame, dedicated himself to promoting tennis, as opposed to golf, as the ideal sport for exercise and recreation.

"I must laugh when I hear a television broadcaster speak of a golfer as burning up the course," Van Alen said. "If you look at the screen you see a player such as Jack Nicklaus, 210 pounds, his paunch hanging over his belt-line waddling up the fairway at the rate of about one mile an hour.

"Golfers are not athletes. They hire young boys to carry their clubs. It takes them four hours and sometimes five to play eighteen holes, walking the equivalent of about five miles. During that period, they will take anywhere from 65 to 75 swings, 100 and more for the non-tournament golfers. Now you take tennis . . ."

Still, tennis proved no match for golf in luring equipment and the entertainment dollars. In 1968 tennis players spent an estimated $24 million compared with the $279 million paid out by golfers. Golf, better organized and with a big head start, had a considerable edge in spectator and television appeal.

Tennis players insisted their sport would close the gap now that open competition had been approved, permitting the pros to compete against amateurs.

This was borne out by the financial reports from Wimbledon and the U.S. Open Championships at Forest Hills, thrown open to the pros for the first time in 1968. Wimbledon reported the highest interest since World War II. Forest Hills, accustomed to vacant seats in its concrete stands, said receipts were almost double those of the year before, reaching close to $500,000. The first Open in Paris produced crowds of 12,000 and above for the first time since the days of Rene Lacoste and Henri Cochet.

Prize money still fell well below that being offered the

golfing pros. While Arnold Palmer, Billy Casper and other top golfers were playing for $100,000 to $200,000 purses weekly, with an overall tour value of $6 million, Rod Laver, Pancho Gonzales and the tennis pros had to be content with cutting up money pies of $20,000 and $30,000.

Yet Laver, the leading tennis professional, earned more than $80,000 in official winnings during 1968 and lesser pros, such as John Newcombe, Ken Rosewall, Tony Roche, Earl Buchholz and Dennis Ralston, were in the $50,000 bracket. It was recalled that pro golf languished in the financial doldrums for years before its stock began to soar. Ben Hogan was golf's leading money winner one year with only $10,656.

The progressive tennis element bolstered the game's financial structure by employing some of the methods used in golf. They tapped organizations and sponsors with promotional know-how. Both the USLTA and the pro promoters signed contracts with Madison Square Garden in New York, an arena with a long history of successful promotions.

The Garden joined the USLTA in helping promote the 1968 Open Championships at Forest Hills, lending its wide experience in public relations and ticketing. The tournament was the most successful financially in history. The Garden also joined forces with the pros in promoting open tournaments at the Garden with original prize money reaching $30,000.

The pros went into the ghettos of big cities such as New York, Los Angeles and Boston, giving free clinics to stimulate interest. Companies such as Clark Gum Company of Richmond, Virginia, Atlantic-Richfield Company of Philadelphia and Philip Morris, Inc., of New York were persuaded to buy thousands of tickets for free distribution.

One gold mine that tennis was slow to crack was that of network television, which poured millions into other sports. The reason was not that tennis lacked TV appeal. It was one of the best for television purposes because it was fast-paced and could cram all its action onto a 21-inch screen.

Sponsors and television directors hesitated to enter into tennis contracts because the game's scoring system made reliable scheduling impossible. With so many players possessing the big serve, many top matches could be expected to last two and three hours, and there was always the danger of overlapping into prime time.

As the game moved into the 1970's, its less conservative architects were seeking a means of living with and prospering through the TV tube.

The future of tennis as a big time spectator sport hinged on their finding the correct formula.

FIVE
9
Where Do We Go From Here?

On the evening of May 17, 1969, in an all-Australian final at New York's Madison Square Garden, Rod Laver cracked a smash that almost bounced to the ceiling and then jogged to the net to shake hands with his victim, Roy Emerson, and collect a $15,000 check.

The check was the largest ever won by a professional tennis player in a single tournament, and to emphasize this fact, directors presented the redhaired Aussie with a trophy measuring about five feet by three feet.

This was big time, modern day tennis on the move. The question was: Where was it going? How fast? And when?

It took the golf tour approximately thirty years after the establishment of the Professional Golfers Association circuit to produce a first prize of such magnitude. For decades pro golfers played for peanuts and until the boom that followed the rise of Arnold Palmer a $5,000 first prize for a weekend tournament was regarded as luxurious.

Moving out of the controversial 1960's into the question-mark 1970's, the court sport faced a promising future. Indications were that with promotion and enterprise tennis might rise to challenge golf, baseball and pro football for a healthy share of the entertainment dollar.

"I read after the Masters golf tournament that the tour was beginning to get tired and jaded," said Owen Williams of South Africa, upon being summoned from Johannesburg to conduct the 1969 U.S. Open Tennis Championships at Forest Hills. "I think the time is ripe for tennis to move and lay claim to world-wide interest.

"It is my aim to make the American Nationals one of the outstanding sport spectacles anywhere, regardless of the sport. I see the day at Forest Hills that we will have half a million spectators with players competing for a $500,-000 purse."

The signs were good. The International Lawn Tennis Federation, prodded by Britain, the United States, France and Australia, had lowered the outmoded barriers forbidding professionals to compete with amateurs. Associations, including Wimbledon as well as Forest Hills, were bringing high pressure Madison Avenue techniques into their operations. People were beginning to watch tennis again.

There were some drawbacks. Professional promoters, who put up small fortunes to finance touring road shows, resented the move by amateur associations setting up categories that made competitors professionals in everything except name.

These special players were permitted to take prize money, and they could also compete in Davis Cup matches, a privilege denied the contract touring pro. The only difference in the two groups was that the touring pros were under contract to a private promoter while the registered players were under contract, in effect, to their national associations.

The contract pros charged that this was discrimination.

They threatened to boycott the big tournaments. Their unhappiness was alleviated somewhat when the associations agreed to put up special bonuses for the pro promoters at major championships. Some associations called such demands "blackmail."

It seemed the associations would ultimately take control of all players—professionals and amateurs alike—and the role of independent promoter would be reduced to that of a personal manager. All tournament players then would be under one umbrella and there would be two designations instead of three—the tournament competitor and the amateur, the latter being a college or club player unable to accept money of any kind.

To compete with golf, tennis still had to make it big in television by presenting a package attractive to millions of pro-oriented fans.

The sport had the ingredients. It was a fast, exciting game played by well-conditioned, attractive athletes in an area small enough to fit into a camera's eye. There was no necessity for shifting—as in golf—from one hole to another or waiting for long periods while a player trod the hundreds of yards between shots.

Scoring presented a problem. Under the traditional court tennis system in which a player must have a two-point margin for a game and a two-game margin for a set, a match could last interminably, and frequently did. This proved poison for networks with sponsors paying as much as $70,000 a minute of advertising time.

The answer appeared to be a simplified scoring system, an anathema to tradition-steeped administrators. The trend was in that direction, particularly for special invitation events.

Tennis' main need, it seemed, was for exposure, the emergence of personalities such as Big Bill Tilden, Helen Wills and Pancho Gonzales, and new, influential friends.

The game was getting the latter. The powerful Madison Square Garden made contracts with both the professional promoters and the U.S. Lawn Tennis Association—an apparent bet on the future. Large corporations were getting interested in the game's promotion.

In brief, the prescription for the sport's success appeared to be internal peace and time.

INDEX